FLORIDA PARKS

A Guide to Camping in Nature

By Gerald Grow

Long leaf
Publications

To my parents:

ELVA WHITE GROW
WILLIAM A. GROW, SR.

. . . oaks among the pines.

Florida Parks: A Guide to Camping in Nature
Fourth Edition
Copyright © 1981, 1983, 1987, 1989 by Gerald Owen Grow

ISBN 0-939638-54-1

Printed in the United States of America.
Typography by RapidoGraphics, Tallahassee.
Cover & Graphics by Randy Johnson.
Cover photo by Chuck Pittman.

The information contained in this book is believed to be correct at the time of publication, but the author and publisher assume no liability arising from the use of this material. Park policies, procedures, and facilities change from time to time. When something is important, double-check it.

Longleaf Publications
P. O. Box 4282
Tallahassee, FL 32315

1234567890

Here's what reviewers and readers are saying about
Florida Parks: A Guide to Camping in Nature

"Every visitor to Florida, and every resident of our state, should read *Florida Parks*. Buy, beg, borrow, or steal a copy of this book. Read it and use it. Your life will be greatly rewarded."—*Florida Audubon Magazine.*

"An excellent planning guide, and a testament bearing witness to the awesome power and silent consolation of vanishing natural Florida."—*Tallahassee Democrat.*

"A complete, up-to-date, practical guide to camping in Florida. Recommended."—*Herb Allen, Tampa Tribune.*

"Long needed for nature lovers in Florida."—*Miami Herald.*

"A book for anyone who has ever thought about camping in the state of Florida. Covers nearly every angle. The book is a gem. Worth your time and money."—*Dothan Eagle.*

"The real delight of the book is how well Grow details each site, what to do there, what to look forward to, and what to look for."—*Apalachee Audubon Journal.*

"Highly readable. Helpful. A valuable reference."—*TODAY.*

"Definitely a must. Grab this book, head for the woods."—*Florida Flambeau.*

"The 50-page introductory chapter is a masterpiece of practical information about Florida's ecosystems and sensible advice about getting out and exploring it. The remaining chapters give thorough reviews of where to go."—*Spectrum*

"Contains some of the most inspired recent nature writing in print. The most complete Florida natural area guide ever printed."—*ENFO*

"Sure to become the classic camping guide to which all others will be compared."—*Ney Landrum, Director, Florida State Parks.*

"Well done. Thoroughly detailed. Written with a fondness for nature that is rare in books today. Beautifully illustrated throughout."—*New Hampshire News.*

"Gives you enough information so you can decide in advance which parks you really want to visit and how long you will want to stay. Once you begin reading it, you will want to drop everything and go camping."—*Camp-O-Rama.*

...More reviews and comments at the end of the book.

Preface to the Fourth Edition

The biggest news for this edition is that, after years of cheap fees for camping, the Florida State Park System has raised its prices. Those prices are still changing as this edition goes to press, but the latest information I could obtain is reported in the Updates to the Introduction (pg. 51). You would do well to contact the park system for details if you need more exact prices.

The parks people are in a dilemma. They want to make parks available to everyone inexpensively, but they need more money to run them. Unless the parks find a new source of funding, the user—you—will pay a greater share of the costs.

This edition of *Florida Parks* adds a number of new parks that campers and nature lovers will want to know about and makes more than 100 updates and corrections to the previous edition.

At the end of each section—Introduction, NorthWest, North, Central, West and SouthEast—you will find updates giving the latest information on parks covered in that section. You will also find new parks described there.

So, after looking up a park, be sure to check at the end of that section to see if there have been any updates on it.

Thanks again to readers who wrote me with suggestions, corrections, and information on new parks. Your letters have helped keep this book up to date, your comments have meant a great deal to me, and your support has helped make *Florida Parks* a self-publishing success story. I am especially glad so many of you expressed appreciation for this book's emphasis on nature.

I wish you many happy days using this book. Now that this edition is finished, do you know what? — I'm going camping.

Preface

During a turning point in my life, I took a long camping trip through Florida to reconsider my plans. On that trip, a number of things went wrong. I got lost repeatedly in one of the large national forests. I went to parks shown on the maps and found them no longer there. I found roads open on the maps that were closed in reality. I arrived at some parks too late and found gates locked. I looked for solitary natural areas and found myself spending the night in noisy, crowded, outdoor suburbia. Some nights the only sounds I could hear were from the television sets of other campers. Another time, I found myself so remote from the nearest town that I had to drive ten miles an hour to the nearest station, eking out the last fumes in my gas tank.

Still, I found wonderful places to camp. Later, though, I found that I had missed other wonderful places, because I did not know about them when I was nearby. I missed some places I was looking for, because I could not get directions on how to find them. Most of the agencies that manage Florida's public parks had good information on the parks under their jurisdiction, but there was no simple way even to get the addresses of all the agencies in Florida that administer parks—and there are many. On this trip, I discovered how hard it was to get all the information you need to camp in Florida's public parks.

By the time I had gathered enough information to plan a good camping trip in Florida, I no longer had the time to go.

That settled it: I decided to write a book to help people plan a camping trip in Florida to places they have not been before.

Then the research started in earnest. I spent several months in Tallahassee, studying the files of the state parks, recreation areas, and historic sites. I frequented every state and federal agency that dealt with parks—the national forests, state forests, national wildlife refuges, state parks, and others. I took courses in Florida ecology, read extensively, studied the superb publications of the State Comprehensive Plan, reviewed materials in the state geology department, DOT aerial maps, Water Management District documents, Corps of Engineers reports, Department of Environmental Regulation studies, and began interviewing any knowledgeable person willing to talk to me about Florida parks—and there were many.

I set out to learn not only where the parks are, how to get there, and what you will find when you visit, but also how different parks are run, what management plans they have, what their problems are, what goals they pursue, and how they fit into the larger picture of Florida's natural systems, exploding population, and multiplying problems.

During this period, I was fortunate to obtain a three-month appointment with the Department of Natural Resources editing lengthy, detailed plans for nearly a hundred parks, preserves, historic sites, archaeological sites, botanical sites, and endangered lands under their jurisdiction. Here was a wealth of background material! During that time, I made acquaintance with the men and women who run most of Florida's parks and gained a profound respect for their dedication, hard work, and far-reaching goals.

As a native of south Georgia and north Florida, I had visited many Florida parks. But now I began to revisit them with new eyes. On a number of long trips around the state, I went to almost every one of the more than 200 parks or camping areas covered in this book. Whenever possible, I visited the same park again during a different season of the year. My wife and 2-year-old son camped with me in dozens of the places described in the book.

Throughout my travels in Florida parks, I interviewed rangers, park superintendents, law enforcement officers, biologists, ecologists, recreation directors, wildlife officers, campers, park naturalists, state officials, backpackers, retirees living in RVs, college kids on canoe trips, educators, loners hiking in search of their souls, environmental activists, foresters, phosphate miners, and families out swimming, camping, tubing, boating, fishing, or just having a picnic. I listened to people tell about the problems and pleasures of camping. I listened to celebrations of wonderful new parks. I heard detailed laments for disappearing parklands—shrinking as they are encroached upon by roads, airports, oil wells, strip mines, adjacent housing developments, and pollution. I learned how gravely many of Florida's natural systems have been threatened by draining, diking, dams, water use, overbuilding, exotic plants and animals, stormwater runoff, and pollution from cities, cars, industries, farmlands, and feedlots.

I talked to individuals and groups who are trying to protect natural Florida from just such threats—and from the ultimate threat of them all—too many people. I saw how Florida's natural habitats and historic sites were disappearing with alarming rapidity into housing developments, shopping centers, strip mines, freeways, farmlands, ranches, parking lots, and amusement parks. I saw famous fishing lakes now threatened, dying, or already dead. I saw more and more interest groups competing for less and less outdoor land. I saw huge areas of the state, once world-famous for their natural beauty, now covered with concrete, steel, cars, and condominiums. In some areas, there is hardly a native tree still to be found. I discovered that Florida contains some of the worst problems—and some of the finest natural beauty—on the East Coast. I saw that, most of the time, the problems and the natural areas are at odds with each other. And the problems are dangerously close to winning.

Writing this book opened my eyes to the hard decisions that have to be made if our grandchildren are going to have a chance to know natural Florida. While working on this book, I began writing for ENFO, the environmental publication of the Florida Conservation Foundation, and soon became editor. I joined the local chapter of the Sierra Club and became an officer. What started, then, as a camping guide, became for me an urgent appeal for people to care more for natural Florida—to visit it, see it, learn more about it, love it, and work to preserve more of the marvelous, diverse, beautiful range of natural areas in the state. While there is still time.

I have gathered the best available information on each public park or park-like area covered in this book—over 200 of them—and fleshed out this information with thousands of miles of travel, park visits, hikes, ranger-guided tours, and camping trips. There were a small number of places I simply could not get to. In some cases, I was unable to get the information before I had to leave the area. (A few counties were notoriously difficult to get answers from.) For most of the parks I did not visit, I studied their literature, looked up articles, telephoned people familiar with the places, and talked to park managers. Relevant sections of the manuscript were critiqued for accuracy and completeness by officials at almost every state and federal agency that manages parks in Florida.

I have tried to describe parks so you can imagine what they are like. Facilities are covered, but not dwelt on. After all, who spends much time looking at a faucet? I have put the greatest effort into helping you visualize and appreciate the natural setting of each park, because nature is the basis for all parks, and nature is what makes the visit worthwhile.

To keep the maps a convenient size, I have arbitrarily divided the state into five sections: Northwest, North, Central, West, and Southeast. Within each section, parks are listed alphabetically. Where a park is known by more than one name, or where a park has changed names (Fort Pickens State Park, for example, became Gulf Islands National Seashore), the multiple names are cross-referenced in the index.

On the maps and in the margins alongside each description, parks are identified in terms of the following symbols:

▲   Nature park with camping

△   Nature park without camping

▲   Park with camping

△   Park without camping.

These symbols are used in a slightly different way in the state and national forests, as indicated on the corresponding maps.

I commissioned professional cartographers to make the maps, so you would have a clear, uncluttered picture of the general location of each park. Detailed directions are included in the first paragraph of every park description. The maps are not meant to be complete. Always travel with a good road map

(Florida gives one away at the welcome stations), and if you are planning to wander very far from main roads and trails, first obtain detailed county maps and perhaps the relevant U.S. Geological Survey maps for each section. Many individual parks publish brochures with useful maps in them. You can usually obtain brochures at the parks, or you can write for them in advance (see Addresses).

For those who wonder how books get written, let me say that while many people gave generously of their knowledge, time, and encouragement, this book received no public money or foundation grant support. Parks charged me their regular fees.

The Introduction contains information useful for native Floridians and newcomers alike. Few natives will know all the natural habitats described there. Most newcomers to Florida learned about nature somewhere else, and they may need to adjust their concepts of nature to fit what Florida has to offer. All newcomers will want to pay special attention to the section on pests and problems. No short introduction can contain everything you will need to know, however, so consider this one a stepping-off point.

When you do step off, I wish you happy camping in the Florida parks you choose to visit, and happy travelling in those you visit only in your mind.

Acknowledgements

Many people provided information and inspiration for this book. My deepest debt is to the rangers, superintendents, naturalists, managers, custodians, and officials who run Florida's public parks. They provided me with guided tours, hikes, slide shows, photographs, contacts, literature, leads, and encouragement. Many of them gave generously of their time and knowledge, often during their days off, to teach me the special qualities of the places in their care.

For particular help and inspiration, I would like to thank Ney Landrum, James Cook, Pete Hartsfield, Jim Stevenson, George Apthorp, James Birch, and John Sommers of the head office of the Florida Division of Recreation and Parks; the District Naturalists of the state park system: Ken Alvarez, Richard Demmer, Charles DuToit, Tom Francis, Kevin O'Kane, Dick Roberts, Noel Warner, and Donald Younker; the photographers of the Florida News Bureau; Norm Heintz and Dave Parrish of National Parks in Florida; Al Simmons, Paul Wills, George Albritton, and the resident rangers of the State Forests in Florida; Brad Hartmann of the environmental office of the Florida Game and Freshwater Fish Commission, and Don Wood of their endangered species office; Andre

Clewell, formerly of Florida State University Botany Department; Bill and Joan Partington of the Florida Conservation Foundation; Bruce Means of Tall Timbers Research Station; Helen Hood of the Suwannee River Coalition; Archie and Marjorie Carr of Florida Defenders of the Environment; Chuck Carr of Florida Audubon; Jack Gestiehr of Palm Beach County Parks; Dick Workman of the Sanibel-Captiva Foundation; Audrey Dunham, Sev Sunseri, and Randy Johnson of the Department of Natural Resources Education and Information Office; Joe White of the St. Marks National Wildlife Refuge; the interpretive naturalists at Everglades National Park; Dick Tillis of the Environmental Education Office; Pete Heard of the Soil Conservation Service; Dale Allen of the Florida Chapter of the Sierra Club; Inez Frink of Florida Trails; author Betty Watts; poet and naturalist Tom Morrill; Jack Merriam, formerly of the House Natural Resources Committee; Pam McVety, Chuck Littlejohn, and Forrest Fields of the Department of Environmental Regulation; Curry Hutchinson, formerly with the Department of Community Affairs and author of some remarkable manuscripts on the history of natural Florida; and the many others who took the time to talk to me.

Relevant portions of the manuscript were critiqued by Jim Stevenson of the Division of Recreation and Parks, Norm Heintz of National Forests in Florida, George Albritton of the Florida Division of Forestry, Pat Tolle of Everglades National Park, and Dale Allen of the Sierra Club. For their many suggestions, additions, and corrections, much thanks.

Special thanks to my brothers, Bill and David, for loan of camping gear when mine was wearing thin. To my sister Sherrie for a week of much needed rest and recuperation. To Harriet Mitchnick, who spent a decade convincing me I could write. To Satti Khanna, whose twenty years of friendship reflect on every page.

My deepest gratitude goes to my parents, Elva and Bill Grow, who, along with many forms of encouragement and support, offered to pay the rent so I could complete the final chapters of the manuscript; to my wife Christl, who was willing to take the gamble; and to Ariel, who was too young to know anything but the parts that were sheer joy. My father died suddenly as this book was going to press. It is, in many ways, a memorial to his spirit.

Individual photo credits will be found at the end of the book. Most of the pictures were supplied by the Florida News Bureau, the Department of Natural Resources, National Forests in Florida, the Florida Division of Forestry, the Florida Game and Freshwater Fish Commission, and myself. Photographer Bob O'Lary gave generously of his darkroom expertise.

The maps were made by Peter Krafft, Jim Anderson, and Craig Remington.

Finally, thanks to the staff at RapidoGraphics, for their care and patience while typesetting the book, to Randy Johnson for the cover, graphics, and design, and to Chuck Pittman for taking the cover photograph.

General Location Map

Northwest

Pensacola

Tallahassee

Apalachicola Nat. Forest

North

Jacksonville

Daytona Beach

Ocala Nat. Forest

Orlando

Tampa

Central

West

Southeast

Miami

Everglades Nat. Park

Introduction

Northwest

North

Central

West

Southeast

Index

Introduction

Natural Florida

Wherever you go in Florida, you find something subtly humming in the background, something that quietly deepens every setting and gives a profuse vitality to every corner of the state. It is natural Florida: the still-healthy portions of the great Florida wilderness. Even though priceless portions of it have been obliterated, many parts of natural Florida are alive and well today, preserved in fine parks where you can visit them safely.

Although Florida is mainly known to the outside world for its beaches and tourist attractions, there is another world besides these. Deep cypress swamps stand in dark mirroring streams. High rolling hills wear a forest-crown of tall longleaf pines. Tropical "hammocks" crowd into a tangle of jungle-like trees. Empty expanses of bird-rich marsh stretch to the horizon; little wild creeks open just enough for a few canoes. Pine and palmetto modulate the harmonies of the lush flatwoods and the desert-like sand-pine scrub. There are remote island beaches and wind-tossed dunes, huge spreading rivers, and little savannahs carpeted with tiny insectivorous sundews. Native prairie spreads out around big central lakes, and, along the riverbanks of north Florida, forests of an Appalachian diversity flame into color on late autumn days. Behind many of the beaches, an extraordinary coastal forest of gnarled oaks and rising palms waits unadvertised, while in places limestone caves and sudden sinkholes surprise you with a glimpse of underground. Whole coastlines sit sealed in the mystery of impenetrable mangrove swamps. And, across the flat south Florida heartland, equally mysterious Everglades alternate through seasons of flood and fire. Lush steephead ravines slice through the dry pinewoods, and huge salt marshes ramify into twisting estuarine creeks. The South Florida sea parts to reveal a technicolor dream-world of coral reefs. Moonlit orchids bloom on the bark of sleeping oaks. A whole wandering river vanishes underground, to rise again downstream in a clear single spring.

And more. It is a living land, a vital, wild landscape, springing from a climate unlike any other in America. Even today, natural Florida supports a wealth of wildlife. There are still bald eagles nesting here, still panthers in the deep woods, black bear, sea turtles, manatees, and a host of rare and endangered species. Native animals, birds, and fish thrive in the still-natural parts of the state, and, in winter, thousands upon thousands of birds migrate here in flight from the killing cold. In places hawks concentrate in amazing numbers each spring and fall. Fish still abound in numerous lakes and rivers, and the mild

1

evenings sing with a symphony of insect song. Egrets, herons, spoonbills, and the cackling jungle-laugh of the limpkin fill the wide wetlands with a life that has—so far—been irrepressible.

To most of the outside world, Miami Beach is the essence of Florida. But this book is about parks where you can visit natural Florida, an unadvertised place of enormous richness and variety.

No matter what people come to Florida for—the castle kingdoms, diving mermaids, alligator zoos, carillons and palaces, resort beaches, cool summer-time springs, great fishing lakes, mild winters, abundant wildlife, outdoor sports, beach-front condominiums, or growing economy—natural Florida is what gives life to them all. In spite of incredible abuses, a landscape of great beauty, diversity, and integrity still supports and deepens all the other attractions of the state.

And now, for more and more people, natural Florida is becoming the state's main attraction.

If you want to find natural places worth experiencing, worth your time, attention, and patient exploration—places that will open before you, grow on you, multiply your senses, and surprise you with a shy richness—this book is for you. The parks of Florida still contain deposits of the natural treasures that make up the state's real wealth. And like unspoiled nature everywhere, Florida's great parks provide a special place for reconsidering who you are, where you came from, and what miraculous creatures have shared this earth's journey with our own prodigal species.

Yes, there is still an amazing amount of natural Florida left. But when you look more closely, you see that it is vanishing with a dizzying rapidity. As more and more people crowd into Florida, they increasingly destroy the very beauty that brings them here. Natural areas all over the state are being replaced by cities, industries, roads, developments, power lines, airports, strip-mines, tree plantations, farms, and ranches. Pollution is degrading many lakes, waterways, and estuaries. Water control projects are disrupting ancient natural cycles. Fish and wildlife are declining, and exotic (foreign) species crowd out more and more native habitats. Erosion, aggravated by man's activities, takes an awesome toll. People cause greater and greater strain on the environment as each individual uses more resources and creates more wastes. Technology vastly increases our power to change the environment, but does not give us the wisdom to build so that people and nature can, together, thrive. Only as natural areas disappear do we realize their monetary value by having to pay for the services—such as flood control and water purification—that nature once gave us free.

For millions of years, nature was the only home our species knew. Then, for millinnea, people lived on little islands of development, surrounded by a sea of nature. But we are changing this, perhaps irrevocably. Already in parts of Florida, a surging manmade landscape of concrete and steel has drowned everything except a few scattered "islands of nature" that remain in little parks.

The clouds move in like mountains over bird-rich Myakka River.

If we continue this way, soon only protected lands—such as parks—will still contain remnants of the natural world.

I hope this book will help you know, visit, and love the natural Florida that public parks—your parks—have preserved, and perhaps move you to help protect more of what is left.

The Range of Parks in Florida

How do you decide where to camp in Florida? With so many different agencies running so many different kinds of parks, you may feel overwhelmed at first, even if you have decided what parts of the state you want to visit. You may want a wilderness experience but unknowingly choose a busy, noisy urban park. Or you may just want a place to park the RV, watch television, and feed the pet ducks—and instead spend an unprepared night alone in a primitive area, miles from the conveniences you need. This guide will help you avoid mistakes like these and choose parks where you will find the kind of experience you are looking for.

It helps to think of Florida parks in terms of two things: *recreation* and *nature*. The balance between developed facilities and undeveloped natural area varies a great deal from one type of park to another. This balance can tell you a lot about what to expect and guide you in choosing where to visit. With this guide in mind, you can decide how much your main interest lies with active recreation—tennis, softball, swimming, beach activities, etc.—and how much it lies in a more contemplative experience of undisturbed wild nature—such as hiking, camping, scenic photography, birding, and nature study.

The chart gives an idealized picture of the balance between recreational facilities and undisturbed natural areas in each major type of park. At one extreme you find neighborhood playgrounds, softball fields, swimming pools and schoolyards—which require no "nature" at all, just enough open space to put a facility in. At the other extreme, there are the preserves and wilderness areas, places almost entirely for nature, with very limited human activity.

Between these extremes, over a dozen different types of Florida parks offer you many different kinds of activities and many different blends of recreation and nature.

Since this guide is concerned with camping, we will not deal with playgrounds, golf courses, country clubs, miniparks, or picnic stops. (Camping is not allowed in highway rest areas in Florida.) But we will include some *city parks* that have camping facilities—many of which include playgrounds, ball fields, swimming areas, golf courses, or other recreational facilities, often in a setting of lovely oaks or beautiful lakes. There will be more *county parks*, which offer extended recreational space and facilities—often several hundred acres of playing fields, tennis courts, running tracks, golf ranges, and swimming areas, with areas of mowed lawn, open forest, and wooded walks. Fort DeSoto, Wickham, and Crandon are good examples of county parks.

Regional parks are still rare in Florida. They offer more space for nature-oriented recreation—more room to hike or run outdoors, more bicycle paths, larger areas for wildlife and nature study. These may be the "green belts" around urban areas. Regional parks may include marshlands and other wildlife

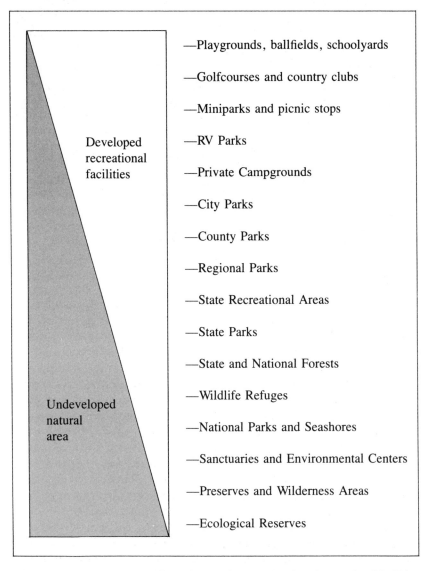

Developed recreational facilities

—Playgrounds, ballfields, schoolyards

—Golfcourses and country clubs

—Miniparks and picnic stops

—RV Parks

—Private Campgrounds

—City Parks

—County Parks

—Regional Parks

—State Recreational Areas

—State Parks

—State and National Forests

—Wildlife Refuges

—National Parks and Seashores

—Sanctuaries and Environmental Centers

—Preserves and Wilderness Areas

—Ecological Reserves

Undeveloped natural area

Each type of park contains a different balance between developed recreational facilities and undeveloped natural area.

With the help of the descriptions in this book, you can choose to immerse yourself in the busy, crowded activity of a convenient urban beach . . .

areas, and are sometimes located on land that must be kept natural to protect the local water supply. The Savannahs, Lower Hillsborough River, and Starkey Wilderness belong in this class.

In the middle of the scale, *State Recreation Areas* have roughly 50% of their area developed for active recreation and 50% left in the natural state. Anastasia State Recreation Area is a good example. Most of what you see is the fine stretch of beach, extensive picnic areas, a large campground, and good spots for fishing. But behind this highly-used portion of the park, there are quieter woods of rich coastal hammock, nature trails, and places kept just for the wildlife. The undeveloped natural areas help maintain a high-quality environment in the high-use recreational areas of the park. Without these natural areas, visitors would see much less wildlife and birdlife, and the "feel" of the beach would be subtly but devastatingly degraded. That "unused" 50% of the park is what gives depth and quality to the heavily-used half.

State Parks have still more natural area—usually 80% or more. The state parks in Florida serve to perpetuate samples of the original Florida landscape in its natural condition, often looking as it did when the first Europeans saw it hundreds of years ago. The most commonly visited areas in state parks frequently have rich wildlife and birdlife. Plant communities are large and

. . . Or seek out long stretches of solitary shores.

varied. State parks offer visitors good access to some of the finest, most authentic natural areas in Florida. The facilities and activities in state parks are all tuned to make possible a deep experience of nature. The campgrounds are excellent, but do not attempt to provide all the latest conveniences. There are few "active" recreational facilities (like ball fields), and, except for a few rustic rental cabins in a few parks, there are no lodges or hotels. Instead, a high-quality segment of the original Florida terrain provides the enduring attraction at Florida state parks.

While county parks and state recreation areas often have ranger-led activities, those in state parks are more extensive. State parks often contain museums and exhibits; many also have important historical sites (such as O'Leno and Fort Clinch). A state park may have remote areas that are hard to get to, or virtually impossible to penetrate—like the mangroves of Collier-Seminole. A few contain wilderness preserves.

State parks and state recreation areas usually permit fishing, but hunting, timbering, mining, collecting of plants, animals, rocks, and other "consumptive" uses are prohibited. If you think how thousands of such acts, over years, would progressively alter the natural environment and make it into a man-shaped environment, you can understand the rule. For the same reason, the feeding of wildlife is strictly prohibited; it makes them artifically dependent upon human food.

The State and National Forests, which I also cover in this book, are active, working forests containing many thousands of acres of woods, most of which are under cultivation for timber production. You may encounter timbering activities or signs of cutting and planting on your visit. Portions of these forests, and certain timbering operations, are planned and managed to promote deer, turkey, quail, and other game animals, or to protect certain endangered species. The state and national forests in Florida permit hunting in season, and allow some other uses, such as cattle grazing, oil wells, and mining.

Recreational areas in the public forests range from highly developed, popular campgrounds (like Juniper Springs and Silver Lake) to remote primitive sites with few or no facilities. These are described in appropriate chapters of this book. State and national forests offer naturalist programs, and certain campgrounds have regular ranger-led activities. More adventurous visitors can make their own campsites in remote areas of the national forests.

State and national forests offer easy access to large outdoor areas. By contrast, state and national parks (and preserves) offer more regulated access to more pristine natural environments.

Many parks have excellent programs. Here a ranger at Everglades National Park takes a group on a hike through one of the tropical "tree islands" in the river of grass.

National Wildlife Refuges exist still more for the benefit of nature, and less for "active" recreation by visitors. The natural setting is managed for wildlife preservation, with room for compatible outdoor recreation, such as hiking, nature study, photography, scenic appreciation, and the renewal that comes from being out in nature. Refuges are outstanding places to observe birds and wildlife. Most refuges permit some kind of hunting in season, and since this happens during the best time of the year for hiking, the two may conflict.

National Wildlife Refuges in Florida do not permit camping and often provide only minimal facilities for visitors. As outdoor space becomes more and more rare, refuges will become increasingly important to both wildlife and people. Although originally established to perpetuate ducks and other hunted waterfowl, refuges increasingly attempt to provide homes for birds and animals that are losing their habitat elsewhere in the state. They are also playing an increasing role in environmental education.

National parks and national seashores seek to perpetuate a major natural environment. In Florida, the vast and fragile Everglades and a string of islands in Biscayne Bay are the only national parks. A few sections of a national park, such as Flamingo in the Everglades, may be highly developed—even containing motels and restaurants—but the vast proportion of parkland is natural, and sizeable portions are pure wilderness. National parks and seashores are dedicated to preserving an outstanding natural area—a true natural "resource"—while encouraging compatible outdoor recreation. Like the Florida state parks, they preserve a viable portion of our natural heritage and protect it for us and our descendants to enjoy.

Florida's national parks have excellent exhibits, talks, trails, and naturalist-led interpretive programs.

Sanctuaries, though tiny compared to national parks, move a step further in the direction of preserving nature and offering very limited, high-quality visitor experiences. Corkscrew Swamp is a fine example, and one of the few sanctuaries in Florida. Sanctuaries do not have camping facilities and usually preserve some especially critical remnant of natural Florida—a vital rookery for the vanishing wood ibis, one of the last virgin cypress swamps, a very rare uncut pine flatwoods.

Smaller still, *Environmental Education Centers* earn a special place on this list. These are day-use facilities, many of which have nature trails, boardwalks, exhibits and classes. Such centers give residents and visitors alike a unique opportunity to learn about nature in Florida.

State Preserves are large areas, generally ten to thirty thousand acres, that have been set aside to maintain a living portion of Florida's original environment, free from major human disturbance. These are immensely valuable parks. In order for the diverse and fragile balance of nature to continue relatively undisturbed, preserves have to be large and undeveloped. Waccasassa Bay is a good example. It consists mainly of thousands of acres of water and salt

In addition to dozens of outstanding parks, Florida has many nature centers, museums, and environmental education centers. The Tallahassee Junior Museum contains an authentic 19th century farm, along with excellent exhibits on nature—including large outdoor habitats where native animals live.

marsh, prolific with life, with scattered tree-islands and a tangle of snake-tongued estuarine creeks. It is a place where you can still read the original expression on the face of nature. All the preserves are miracles of environment. They are among the few places in the East where you can see animals living entirely in their original natural setting, without significant interference by humans.

Preserves have few if any visitor facilities and are available only for limited, careful use. This may include hiking trails, boating access, and occasionally primitive camp sites. Preserves are places for nature and for visitors who want to go out of their way to study, appreciate, commune with, and protect nature. Since they contain relatively undisturbed ecosystems, preserves are frequently used for scientific study.

Wilderness areas—which are found in some state parks, preserves, national forests, and national parks—are closed to motorized vehicles and offer the very rare opportunity to hike or canoe into a region virtually untouched by human activities. Most wilderness areas in Florida permit primitive camping from canoe or backpack. To protect fragile areas and to offer a real wilderness experience, the number of visitors is often restricted.

Wilderness areas that permit camping are found at St. Josephs Peninsula State Park, Myakka River State Park, Collier-Seminole State Park, Gulf Islands National Seashore, and at Bradwell Bay in the Apalachicola National Forest. Wilderness areas without camping are found at St. Marks and Chassahowitzka National Wildlife Refuges, and Canaveral National Seashore. Other areas function like wilderness areas, such as the remote reaches of Everglades National Park and the state preserves.

A wilderness-like experience is available in several other parks that have backpack trails which lead to a primitive campsite. These include Jonathan Dickinson State Park, Torreya State Park, and portions of the statewide Florida Trail (see *Addresses*).

The final category of park is a very exciting one just being proposed for Florida: *ecological reserves*. Similar to the National Biosphere Reserves, these places would be for nature alone. Except for guided environmental classes in selected areas, visitors would not normally be allowed, and recreation is not part of the plan. Natural areas relatively free from human influence are rapidly

Each day, more of Florida's history and archaeological past are covered over forever. Parks help preserve that history. Here a ranger at Castillo de San Marcos in St. Augustine plays the part of the Spanish soldiers who manned the fort in 1696.

vanishing worldwide—and especially in Florida. Ecological reserves could preserve viable examples of what nature in Florida was like, so that in the future people can have some standard of comparison by which to judge their altered environment.

Ecological reserves could become one of our greatest gifts to future generations. Let's hope these are established while there is still time and nature left.

State historic sites, state archaeological sites, and ***national historic memorials*** do not fit on this scale, because they are not primarily concerned with recreation or nature, but with the preservation of important historical sites. Most of these offer some recreational opportunities, including visits to the historical site itself and other activities like fishing, picnicking, hiking, or nature study. Some historic sites have wonderful natural settings, like Koreshan and Bulow Plantation State Historic Sites. Several have intriguing "living history" reenactments, in which rangers wear period clothing and play the part of the people whose presence made the site memorable. Living history programs are found at Castillo de San Marcos National Historical Monument,

The survival of the roseate spoonbill in Florida—with its dawn-fresh wings and ancient eyes—depends almost entirely on decisions made by human beings. Many threatened and endangered species can survive only with the help of the space provided by parks and the water protected by politics. That's a hard spot to be in.

Marjorie Rawlings State Historic Site, Olustee Battlefield State Historic Site, in Fort Clinch and Kissimmee State Parks, and others.

The public parks in some states contain lodges, rental cabins, and amusement rides. Florida parks emphasize the setting. They are scenic, natural areas, many of which contain attractive but unlavish campgrounds.

The numerous *private campgrounds* (not covered in this book) offer a wide variety of settings and amenities. They range from crowded urban RV parks to fish camps on remote rivers. Facilities range from luxurious to ramshackle. Because they must pay all expenses out of fees, fees are generally somewhat higher in private campgrounds than in public parks. As part of your preparation for a camping trip to Florida, I highly recommend that you write (well in advance) and ask Tourist Information to send you the free "Camping Packet," which contains the official state map and a useful booklet describing many private campgrounds. (See *Addresses* at the end of this chapter.) If you have little interest in nature but primarily seek convenience, security, familiarity, and easy access to developed tourist attractions, you may do best to stay in a private campground, hotel, or motel, instead of a public park.

And if you want to go on jungle cruises, watch alligator wrestling, see ski shows, spend your afternoons on amusement rides, watch trained dolphins—there are private attractions throughout the state that provide this and much more. But not the public parks. With the exception of a few low-key tram and boat tours, public parks offer no amusement activities.

Public parks in Florida are about outdoor recreation. That's two things: a quality outdoor natural environment, and opportunities for recreation in that environment.

I hope the "scale of parks" described here will help you choose the right mix of nature and recreation for you.

With a few exceptions, this book is limited to those public parks that have camping facilities or that preserve some outstanding feature—natural or historic. Most of these fall on the scale between the larger city parks and the state preserves.

Essentials

Climate

On the average, Florida has wet summers and dry winters, hot humid summers and mild sunny winters. But not entirely—not everywhere in the state, and not every year. It can get quite cold—below freezing—even in south Florida. In north Florida, you can count on some very cold winter weeks, with temperatures in the 20s. One February, you may find snow in north Florida; another February, the ground may be covered with blossoms. In mild, dry years, north Florida winters are serenely autumnal, and south Florida basks in a warm sun.

Florida summers are hot and humid. Sticky. At that time, bugs and biting insects abound in parks. But if you don't mind sweating, or if you can find a good breeze and a beach, lake, river, sinkhole, or spring to swim in, summers can shower you with a luxuriance of vegetative wealth, mountains of luminous clouds, and a buzzing, twittering profusion. In parks, heavy summer nights may be blessed by fireflies and colorful moths.

Paradoxically, Florida is a very wet place threatened by serious water shortages. Although rainfall is high—averaging 54 inches a year—several factors complicate the state's weather. Rain is not spread evenly throughout the year. Storms and hurricanes can dump huge quantities of rain in a short period. Central and south Florida usually have a wet season in the summer and a long dry season in the winter. In north Florida, a second wet season often comes in the winter.

Rainfall varies widely from year to year, and from place to place in the state. Areas only a few miles apart can have very different weather patterns. I have seen a thunderstorm in which one side of the street was flooded, while the other remained dry.

Water is the heartline of Florida. It is the common solvent that connects all the state's attractions and problems. Since so much of the development in Florida has been made without regard for natural systems and water cycles, there is often too little water when people want it and too much when they don't. Learning to live in Florida means learning to live in a fragile near-desert terrain that borders on paradise only through the presence of a precarious water-cycle. It remains to be seen whether people will learn to build in Florida without undermining the natural systems that support the water, which in turn supports all of us.

Camping Facilities

Facilities vary somewhat from one park to another, but there is a general norm you can expect. Most public parks provide well-laid-out, "developed" campsites with tables, grills, and nearby restrooms. The restrooms in many parks have hot showers. There is usually a water faucet at each campsite or nearby. Larger parks often offer some sites with electricity and occasionally with sewer connections for those in Recreational Vehicles—but you can't always count on getting these sites. Most larger parks furnish some central sewage disposal station. Parks specializing in RV camping will have more of these conveniences than general camping parks. Except in primitive camps, camping is almost always restricted to designated sites. See the individual listings for details.

If you need electricity, be sure to inquire when you enter the park, or when you make reservations. It is not wise to depend entirely upon my description,

A typical park restroom: clean, sufficient, simple.

since electric lines can fail, and park policies do change. A park with electrical and sewer hookups one year may be a primitive camp after the next hurricane. Always ask.

The same holds true for washer-dryer facilities. I have not always mentioned them, because I have found them to be so unreliable. Washers and dryers break down. Drain lines clog. Coin-boxes get full. Vandals attack the machines. Even if there are washers and dryers, there is no guarantee they will be working. You should always be prepared to do your laundry in the nearest town.

Restroom facilities vary quite a bit. Most are neat, clean, and adequate. Most of the toilet stalls are enclosed and have doors, but a few sit open in the room. Camping requires some adaptability, especially in large, busy parks where personnel cannot clean up every hour.

Also, remember that park personnel do many things besides act as janitors. If you come in some morning and find the restroom a mess, do complain. But sometimes this happens because rangers had to be out all night fighting a wildfire or looking for lost hikers. Realize that in remote parks they can't just call a plumber when something breaks. Chances are, the toilet will be cleaned and repaired by the same rangers who registered you at the gate.

"Primitive camping" is a special category. Most primitive campsites consist of nothing but an open area and a water source. Some don't even have water. It's always wise to be prepared for primitive camping—since you never know when a park will have all its developed sites full.

Less-developed camping areas, especially those in the State and National Forests, usually provide only chemical toilets and hand pumps for water. In the toilets in less-developed camping areas, you should be mentally prepared for lots of unexpected company: a variety of harmless spiders, moths, lacewings, beetles, and other natives—most of whom mean you no harm. You'll be amazed how fast you get comfortable sitting a couple of yards from a tarantula-sized wolf-spider. After some primal shock, you may slowly realize that the spider is bracing itself not to attack, but to get away from you.

Most fee-areas (campgrounds that charge money) have gates that are locked at sundown for security. When you register for the night, you receive either a pass-key or the combination to the gate lock, in case you need to go out or come in after the gate has been locked.

Because most fee-areas (such as State Parks) lock their gates at sundown, you must arrive before that time in order to register. If you are delayed, it is important to phone ahead to arrange for late admission.

All parks described in this book are open by 8 A.M. and close no earlier than sundown. (That's sunset, not dark.)

Busy Seasons

North Florida parks are busiest in the summertime, while Central and South Florida parks are busiest from Christmas to Easter. At those times, you cannot count on finding a place to camp unless you have an advance reservation.

The un-busy and generally wonderful seasons are: for North Florida, any mild day in late fall, winter, or early spring. For Central and South Florida, late fall and late spring.

North Florida, in particular, is almost undiscovered in the wintertime, even though some of the year's most glorious days happen then. Watch out, though, for cold rain and a sudden freeze.

In the hot, humid summer months, wetland areas all over the state swarm with mosquitoes. Attendance at many inland south Florida parks drops off in the summer.

Fees

Prices are changing everywhere, so if I give prices in this book, they will probably be wrong by the time you read them. To get around this difficulty, I have grouped parks in three cost-ranges: *average, below average* and *above average cost.*

Camping fees are approximately as follows:

Average cost: $8 to $19 per night.

Below average: less than $8 per night.

Above average: $19, to as high as $30 per night.

Popular parks, like those in the Keys, cost the most. Most parks charge $1 to $2 extra for electricity and sewer hookups.

Some parks charge an entrance fee, which may or may not be included in the camping charge.

If you need to budget closely, it's a good idea to write ahead for full costs at the parks you plan to visit.

The Florida State Parks system has changed its fees twice in the past year, adopting a complicated pricing schedule, and the prices may not yet be settled. See the Update on page 51 for latest information.

The National Forests and State Forests also charge "average" fees at all of their "highly developed" sites—such as Juniper Springs in the Ocala National Forest.

National Parks and Seashores charge "average" to "below average fees."

City, county, and regional parks assess widely varying charges, as noted in the description of each.

If you visit primitive campsites in the state and national forests, you are likely to find toilet facilities of this type.

There may be additional charges for entrance to some museums and special exhibits—usually 50¢ to a dollar. Boat tours, tram tours, snorkel tours, and other special activities vary in price, but always cost extra. Current prices range from $2 up for rides and tours. Snorkeling tours on the coral reefs, though, are $15 and up.

You can buy an annual entrance permit for the state parks, state recreation areas, historic sites, and preserves. This permit covers only the entrance fee. The state park system no longer sells an annual camping permit; you have to pay the camping fee for each day you camp.

Florida residents who are 65 years or older may apply for permits allowing them to camp at reduced rates at most state parks during specific times of the year. National parks offer a similar discount.

For information on these annual permits, write the Department of Natural Resources (see *Addresses*), or inquire at state parks that have camping. National park information is available through Everglades National Park.

Note: Almost all parks restrict the number of persons and vehicles permitted to use a single campsite. If you are travelling with a group, find out in advance what these restrictions are.

Pets

You can bring pets to most parks if you keep them on a leash, but different parks have different policies on camping with pets. Pets are prohibited from many campgrounds because of problems with noise, sanitation, wildlife, damage to vegetation, and danger to other visitors. The *state parks*, *state recreation areas*, and *state historic sites* do **not** permit overnight camping with pets. Pets are also prohibited from the developed campgrounds in the *national forests*—though you can camp with pets in the less developed camping areas in the national forests. The *state forests* restrict camping with pets to two special areas—Horse Stable Camp in Withlacoochee State Forest, and Coldwater in Blackwater State Forest.

You can camp with your pets in certain campgrounds in the *national parks* and *national seashores*. Most *city* and *county parks* permit camping with pets, though this varies from park to park. Most *private campgrounds* permit pets.

For health reasons, dogs are prohibited from *public beaches* throughout the state.

If you are travelling with a pet, please plan ahead and choose parks where you can stay with your pet.

Road Numbers

There are several different conventions for labelling "state maintained roads" in Florida. The following names all refer to exactly the same road, and may be used interchangeably in various publications:

Florida 20
Fla. 20
State Road 20
S.R. 20

This book uses the form "Fla. 20" for state roads.

Please note that there are also federal, state, and county roads which have their own separate numbering systems. There is a US 19, a Fla. 19, and may well be a county road called C-19 nearby. These are all different roads.

"F" or "F.R." preceding a number indicates "Forest Road," a designation used only in the National Forests.

Before learning these distinctions thoroughly, I got lost a number of times in remote areas of the state. Perhaps this note will save you the trouble.

A tent, a campfire, the great outdoors, just you and your dog. This idyllic scene is possible only if you pick one of the many campgrounds that permit camping with pets.

Planning Your Trip

If you don't have any pressing reasons to choose one route over another, consider these suggestions:

—Visit each section of the state.

—Visit different kinds of parks: beach, spring, lake, forest, historical, river, marsh.

—Introduce yourself to each of the major habitats of Florida—as described in the section, "Florida Habitats."

—Consider travelling off the main roads. Isolated little towns contain some of Florida's finest people, history, and natural beauty.

Backpacking, Canoeing, and Day-Hikes

The following parks contain excellent trails or areas for backpacking (with primitive camping), canoeing (some with primitive camping), and day-hikes of at least several miles.

```
Key: B  = Backpacking
     C  = Canoeing
     CC = Canoe camping (in addition to day canoeing)
     D  = Day-hikes
     R  = Ranger-led
     P  = Planned
```

Apalachicola Nat. Forest	B	CC	D
Big Cypress Nat. Preserve	B		D
Blackwater River St. Park and St. Forest	B	CC	D
Blue Springs State Park		CC	
Bulow Ruins St. Hist. Site		C	
Canaveral National Seashore			D
Cape St. George State Preserve	BP		D
Chassahowitzka NWR		C	
Collier-Seminole St. Park		CC	
Ding Darling NWR		C	
Everglades Nat. Park		CC	D
Fakhatchee Strand St. Preserve	BP		D
Faver-Dykes State Park		C	
Fisheating Creek Wilderness		CC	D
Florida Caverns State Park		C	
Ft. Pierce/Jack Island			D
Gold Head Branch St. Pk.	B		D
Gulf Is. Nat. Seashore	B		D
Hillsborough River St. Pk.		C	
Hontoon Island St. Pk.		C	D

Ichetucknee Springs St. Pk.		C	D
Jonathan Dickinson St. Pk.	B	C	D
Koreshan St. Hist. Site		C	
Lake Kissimmee St. Pk.		CP	D
Lake Woodruff NWR		C	D
Loxahatchee NWR			D
Lower Hillsborough		C(CCP)	DP
Lower Wekiva River St. Pres.		C(CCP)	
Merritt Is. NWR			D
Myakka River St. Pk.	B	C	D
Ocala Nat. Forest	B	C	D
O'Leno St. Pk.	B	C	D
Osceola Nat. Forest	B		D
Pioneer Park		CC	
Prairie Lakes St. Pres.	B		D
Kelly Park (Rock Springs)		C	
St. George Is. St. Pk.	B		D
St. Joseph St. Pk.	B		D
St. Marks NWR			D
St. Vincent NWR			D
San Felasco Hammock St. Pres.			D
The Savannas		C	
Suwannee River St. Pk.		C	
Tomoka St. Pk.		C	
Torreya St. Pk.	B		D
Tosohatchee St. Pres.	B		D
Waccasassa Bay St. Pres.		CCR	
Wekiwa Springs St. Pk.	BR	C	D
Withlacoochee St. Forest	B	C	D

RULES	State Parks/ Rec. Areas	National Forests	State Forests
TIME LIMIT	14 days	See Note 1	14 days
PETS IN CAMPGROUND?	Prohibited	Prohibited from all developed campgrounds.	OK only in CW&I
CAMPING OFF DESIGNATED SITES?	No	OK except during hunting season	No
RESERVATIONS?	Yes, most parks	None	Only CW&HS
DRIVING OFF ROADS?	Prohibited	OK, except in restricted areas	OK *only* Buttgenb site
COLLECTING SPECIMENS?	Prohibited	Some OK	Some OI
FISHING	Yes	Yes	Yes
HUNTING	Prohibited	Yes, in season	Yes, in season
LOCKED GATES AT NIGHT?	In all campgrounds and most park entrances	In fee campgrounds	In fee campgrc

Note 1: One to two week limit in fee areas. In each non-fee area, you can stay up to 14 day
month. If you want to stay longer, you must move to another campsite at least one
away (Federal regulation).

Note 2: At Everglades National Park, time limits are: 30 days from April 30–Nov. 1; othe
14.
At Gulf Islands: 14 day limit from May 15 to Labor Day; otherwise 30.
At Biscayne National Park: 30 day limit.

*Coldwater and Horse Stable Camp.

Nat. Parks Nat. Seashores	Nat. Wildlife Refuges
See Note 2	No camping
OK in cert. areas	Day-use only; pets on leash
Only in wilderness areas	No camping
None.	Not Applicable
Prohibited	Prohibited
Prohibited	Prohibited
Yes	Yes but closed to freshwater fishing 10 / 15 to 3 / 15
Prohibited	Yes: season varies by refuge
Entrance stations staffed all night	State and county roads remain open but Refuge, facilities & grounds closed. Day-use only.

on Locked Gates: Most fee-charging camp-
ds lock their gates at sundown for security.
you register, you get a key or combination, to
you to leave or re-enter at night.

You cannot care about natural Florida without caring about what threatens it. In some parts of the state, progress has brought major alterations in the environment, sometimes threatening entire ecosystems.

Wildlife Alert!

You can help wildlife in Florida. If you see *any* problem involving wildlife—whether it is an injured hawk, an escaped boa constrictor, someone hunting at night or out of season, the killing of songbirds, the harassment of endangered species, suspicious hunting and fishing activities, trespassing on public lands, or abuse of wildlife kept as pets—call:

1-800-282-8002 (toll free, day or night).

You can remain anonymous if you wish. Get the most detailed information you can, including license plate numbers, descriptions of persons and vehicles. Write it down, then call.

The operator will relay your information to a wildlife officer in the field. You will not be obligated to testify or appear in court. There may even be a reward.

If you do not have this number handy, call the toll-free number listed in the inside cover of any Florida telephone directory, under Florida Game and Freshwater Fish Commission.

Your help does make a difference.

Crime in Parks

Until recently, you could leave anything out in a campground and nobody would bother it. Unfortunately, as more people come to parks, more crime comes too. Theft, vandalism, and violence are increasing. Take sensible precautions. In particular, conceal your valuables. People stay more honest the less they are tempted.

Weapons are forbidden in Florida's state and national parks. Guns are allowed, however, during hunting season in the wildlife management areas of the state and national forests.

Most of the parks listed in this book have resident rangers, and most of the major parks have law enforcement officers on duty.

In certain parts of the state, parks preserve the only remnants of the original natural setting.

What Park Rangers Do

The job of park ranger has moved in recent years from an easy-going outdoor-lover's dream, to a professional position with great public responsibility. Here are some of the things today's park rangers do:

1. *Resource management*: Fight fires, set controlled burns, clear springs of exotic waterweeds, control erosion, protect historical artifacts, restore dune vegetation, remove damaging exotics (such as Australian pine).

2. *Visitor services*: Everything connected with your visit, from admission to giving campfire programs. "Interpretive services" such as ranger-led walks are an increasingly popular and important aspect of a ranger's work.

3. *Protection*: Protect the park from wildfire, trespass, poaching, pollution and

other threats. Protect visitors from natural hazards. Protect visitors from each other. Law enforcement.

4. *Administration*: Tend to all that paper-work, planning, reporting, surveying, writing, and filling out of forms.

5. *Maintenance*: Keep up fences, bathrooms, bridges, lights, camping facilities, playground equipment, park automobiles, trucks, boats, tractors, and special equipment. Clean up. Pick up after careless visitors.

In some parks, each ranger does only one or two of these, but in many parks, every ranger does it all. In a remote park, rangers have to know how to do everything. Or it doesn't get done.

Parks Need People

Not all parks came about by high-level governmental decisions. Many parks throughout Florida owe their existence to the caring of individual people or small groups. Some were donated outright. Some were sold at greatly reduced rates to ensure their preservation. Some were saved by local civic groups. Many outstanding parks depended on people like you and me to see them, know them, love them, and work for their preservation.

Here is a list of some of the parks in Florida that owe much to individual people and groups for their existence:

Bulow Plantation: gift of Volusia Hammock State Park Association
Cedar Key State Museum: land donated by Cedar Key Shores, Inc.
Eden Mansion: gift of Lois Jean Maxon
Falling Waters: gift of Washington County
Faver-Dykes: gift of Hiram Faver
Highlands Hammock: gift of the Roebling Family, Highlands Hammock
  Inc., Florida Botanical Garden and Arboretum, Inc.
Hugh Taylor Birch: gift of Hugh Taylor Birch
Koreshan: gift of Koreshan Unity
Lake Talquin and Lake Rosseau Recreation Areas: gift of Florida Power
  Corporation
Maclay Gardens: gift of Mrs. Alfred Maclay
Natural Bridge and Gamble Plantation: gift of the United Daughters of the
  Confederacy
New Smyrna: gift of Florida State Historical Society
Oscar Scherer: gift of Elsa Scherer Burrows
Washington Oaks Gardens: gift of Louise P. Young

Everglades National Park owes something to many people, including the Florida Federation of Garden Clubs, who first purchased land for a park in this area in 1916.

Corkscrew Swamp Sanctuary was created through contributions from thousands of individuals, with a sizeable donation from the Tidewater Cypress Company.

In addition, dozens of parks have had vital acreage donated or made available cheaply. Many Florida parks owe their existence to such generosity and caring, or the long-term persistence of a few determined individuals—such as John Pennekamp and Bill Baggs.

Let's hope there will be many more.

Threats to Parks

Few people appreciate how important—and how threatened—public parks really are. There are recurring moves to use parklands for roads, interstate highways, power line easements, airports, drainage projects, reservoirs,

Although it is normally rich in rainfall and groundwater, most of Florida is vulnerable to drought.

pipelines, logging, grazing, radar installations, strip mining, college campuses, prison sites, water towers, and other structures. Parks are threatened by pollution, sewage outflow, runoff from cities and farms, litter, dumping, arson, and vandalism. There are recurring attempts to convert rare nature parks into hunting preserves or commercial forests. In the near future, you may well see attempts to use public parks in Florida for hazardous waste dumps, tree farms, biomass production, or power plant sites.

Relatively undisturbed natural areas are getting rare everywhere in the world. There is increasing competition for the use of these remaining wild lands, especially among state and federal agencies. Lovers of parks cannot depend entirely on the legislature and state agencies to protect the parks. Indeed, some of the major threats to parks each year come from these sources.

To survive intact, Florida's public parks need to be recognized as the valuable community institutions they are. They need strong local support. Those parks that have had strong local groups to back them have survived best over the decades.

Get to know your parks and support them. Their future may well depend on you.

The state forests, national forests, and national wildlife refuges described in this book contain some of the most popular hunting areas in Florida.

Carrying Capacity

Every system has a "carrying capacity." Ten acres of pasture, for example, can graze only a certain number of cows. Double that number and the pasture will be overgrazed, damaged, and possibly destroyed.

The number of people inside a park has to be limited to protect the limited facilities, and to preserve the immensely valuable natural setting.

Many parks already fill up and have to close their doors on pleasant weekends and holidays. Many central and south Florida parks are booked full of campers every night from Christmas to Easter. Many north Florida parks are beginning to fill on hot summer weekends.

If you get turned away, please understand. Perhaps some day there will be enough parks for everyone—though the present trend is toward more crowded parks.

In the descriptions, I have tried to indicate each park's busy season (if it has one). Those are the times to make reservations and arrive early, to be sure you don't get closed out.

Pests and Problems

There are a number of pests and problems you should be prepared for when camping in Florida. Everyone will have a different list and different remedies, so the following is only offered as a helpful sketch.

The fertile climate of Florida produces a wealth of insects and animals. Most of these are harmless to humans, but a few are worth knowing about and preparing for.

Chiggers ("redbugs") are microscopic mites that burrow under the skin and cause an itchy local swelling for a few days. After that, they drop off. If you scratch it, the itch can last for weeks.

Chiggers are found primarily in wooded, brushy areas, but in hot weather, they seem to be ubiquitous. All trampers in the Florida woods need to go prepared. A little forethought can save many a night of itchy insomnia.

Prevention: Chiggers need a few hours to burrow into your skin. A hot, scrubbing bath after a hike gets rid of a lot of them. Spray the openings of your clothes (especially cuffs and sleeves and waist) with repellant, or use powdered sulfur from the drugstore.

Remedies: Don't scratch! There are several drugstore remedies. Some people dab on a drop of clear fingernail polish atop each itchy red spot (the chigger is in there). You can try soothing lotions to relieve the itch. Patience, however, is the ultimate cure. After a few days, the chiggers leave on their own.

Fire ants can be identified by two characteristics. They usually build much larger mounds than other Florida ants—often prominent foot-high mounds standing in open fields—and, when disturbed, they move with alarming rapidity and attack ferociously in large numbers. When disturbed, most ants scatter in some confusion. Fire ants focus and attack with amazing speed.

29

The sting of fire ants is a significant nuisance, leaving pustules that can itch badly and last for weeks. Watch out!

The nests can be easily hidden in vegetation and grass, so pay attention to where you sit and stand out of doors. They probably won't bother you unless you bother them.

Remedies: There is at least one commercial remedy for fire ant stings available at drugstores. People have reported having success dabbing on diluted household ammonia immediately after the sting. Also papain-containing meat tenderizer and baking soda have been recommended, as well as general soothing lotions.

Now protected by state and federal laws, the alligator has made an amazing comeback from near-extinction, and is once again common in Florida parks.

Bees and wasps are rarely a problem, except for people allergic to their sting. Most bees and wasps are non-aggressive and only sting when disturbed. If you are stung, no treatment may be required (for a normal reaction). Or you may use remedies similar to those for fire ants. It helps to remove the sting, if it is still imbedded.

People allergic to stings, however, can suffer serious or even fatal reactions. It is very important to find out whether you are allergic to stings, and, if so, to carry the appropriate antidote. See a doctor to be certain.

Scorpions and spiders are rarely a problem, but are worth knowing about. Scorpions are uncommon, small, lobster-looking animals, one to two inches long and very flat, with two pincers in front of the body and a sharp sting at the tip of a slender, curving tail. The sting of a scorpion can be quite painful, though serious mainly to allergic persons. Scorpions live in many places, often hidden among vegetation and under rocks and logs. They are active largely at night.

There are only two dangerous spiders in Florida, the black widow and the brown recluse—neither of which is currently a significant problem for campers.

Black widows have a unique appearance: small, glossy black round body with long thin legs. The body is usually colored with a red or orange "hourglass" on the belly. There may also be spots, though, of white, red, or orange. Black widows spin exceptionally strong, messy webs in out-of-the-way corners, and prefer to avoid human activity. The one exception is worth knowing about. Black widows will spin webs across the opening in the seat of outdoor privies; most reported bites occur in these locations. If you are using an outdoor toilet, it's worth checking first before you sit down. I've never found one in a Florida camp, but I have found black widows in privy seats in parks in other states.

The brown recluse is a difficult spider to identify—moderate in size, nondescript brown, with a "violin" pattern on its thorax (shoulder area). Black widow bites need a doctor's attention. The bite of the brown recluse can cause a long-lasting wound and other complications.

Most spiders are harmless. Indeed, they are positively beneficial. Don't disturb them. They play a crucial role in the ecology of Florida, and are wildlife as fascinating as any bird—once you get eye-to-eye with them.

Ticks can be troublesome in certain seasons, especially in hot weather. If they bite you, the general advice is to remove them carefully, making sure to get out all of the head and mouth parts. Treat the wound with antiseptic.

Powdered sulfur and insect repellant help keep them off, but nothing is as effective as a thorough body-check, especially after hiking through brushy places. When checking your body for ticks, be sure not to overlook "seed ticks," which are about the size of a freckle.

Mosquitoes, biting flies, and sand gnats cause more misery in Florida than anything except inflation. The climate is ideal for them: hot, moist, lush, sub-tropical. You may as well make up your mind now not to do any serious camping in Florida unless you are thoroughly prepared—both mentally and pharmaceutically—for these biting insects.

Insect repellants work well for mosquitoes and most biting flies. Sand gnats ("sand flies," "no-see-ums") are harder to repel, and they can crawl through ordinary mosquito netting. Luckily, sand gnats are not found everywhere—mainly around beaches and sandy inland sites. If you study their feeding cycles, you may find times of the day or night when sand gnats are relatively rare. Their small size, persistence, and painful bite have driven many a camper to the nearest motel. Standing near a smoky fire is reported to help.

For sand gnats, lumberjacks around Cedar Key recommend an Avon product called "Skin So Soft Bath Oil." It is said to keep them away pretty well, and it makes for a lot of sweet-smelling lumberjacks. It's available through local sales representatives in most towns.

A number of people I interviewed said they take a balanced B-vitamin tablet, supplemented by extra B-2 for mosquitoes. Several recommended nutritional yeast and garlic. Most outdoors types, though, just recommended getting used to being bitten.

The Florida black bear is a large, shy creature rarely seen by campers. Bears are not the problem in Florida parks that they are in some other states.

Mosquitoes can appear anywhere in Florida, anytime. There are no sure methods of eliminating them. Indeed, that would be disastrous for all the birds, fish, and other insects that depend upon mosquitoes. Mosquitoes by the billions form the basis for one of the vital food chains of the Everglades. They, too, belong.

If you are prepared and do not panic, you can handle the mosquitoes without much problem. With one exception: Certain marshy, swampy areas become so mosquito-filled in hot weather that only the hardiest souls can stand it. The Everglades region and adjacent parks can be very difficult places in the summertime, especially the marshes and mangroves. Know what you're getting into. (See the description of Everglades National Park.)

Be observant of mosquitoes. Learn when they come out and where they stay. Look for ways to live "around" them, without relying heavily on chemical repellants except when unavoidable. Long pants and long-sleeved shirts help a great deal. Many sunny, breezy areas are mosquito-free, even in the summertime, while nearby shade can be thick with them.

Plan your mealtimes so they do not correspond to the peak of mosquito activity. You may want to eat earlier in the evening, before sundown, so you can be behind netting by the time it is dark. A screen-tent may be worth considering.

Don't spray your campsite with insecticide. It does not help much, and it may harm the park and even you.

Remember, insects are always with us. When you go camping, you are entering *their* world. Tread lightly, plan ahead, and adapt to some minor discomforts.

The eastern diamondback rattlesnake, one of the most dangerous snakes in the world, is common throughout Florida. Few people, however, are bitten, and deaths are rare. Though dangerous and worthy of great respect, poisonous snakes are a vital part of the economy of nature and should not be killed.

If you go off the paths, learn what *poison ivy* looks like and avoid it. In South Florida there are *poisonous tropical plants* to know about and avoid. Many parks have exhibits or labels to help you learn them.

Be careful of the weather. In hot weather, **sunburn, sunstroke,** and **heat prostration** can be real dangers. Even on a cloudy day, you can get a severe sunburn.

Lightning can be a serious hazard, especially during frequent summer thunderstorms—which can be awesome. Sensible precautions during a storm include avoiding open water, open areas, metal structures, and tall trees.

Hurricanes are potentially dangerous storms that usually come during the summer and fall. There is no way to anticipate them, so, if you are in Florida during hurricane season, listen to the news every day or two. Make no mistake: the winds, rain, and tidal surges caused by hurricanes can be devastating. If officials recommend that your area be evacuated, leave.

Alligators, after nearing extinction due to commercial exploitation, are once again common in Florida parks. They are rarely known to bother people. But don't push your luck. Don't swim near alligators, and most of all, don't feed them. They might not be too particular about where the candy stops and your hand begins. Incidentally, alligators will eat dogs. Watch your pet.

Bears are not the problem in Florida that they are in some other states. They are for the most part secretive, shy, and rare. You are unlikely to see one in a Florida park. But if you do, watch respectfully and give it a wide berth.

Snakes

Snakes are worth learning about if you plan to get off the beaten path in Florida. The vast majority of snakes in Florida are harmless, marvellous creatures who live in a primal, reptilian world of power and gracefulness. There are several kinds of poisonous snakes, however, and you should learn to identify them. Get a good snake book, or study the displays found in many parks. Almost every outdoors guide recommends that you take a snake-bite kit, and I can only reiterate that here. As a basic, common-sense precaution, watch where you walk, and don't go poking around holes, stumps, under logs, or other snaky places. Florida's poisonous snakes are:

Rattlesnakes: Poisonous. The eastern diamondback rattlesnake is one of the most dangerous snakes in the world. Learn this one. It has a dark, often heavy body with diamond-shaped markings on its back. Large diamondbacks may get to be over six feet long. Many parks have exhibits and specimens to help you in identifying them. Two other rattlers occur in Florida: the canebreak rattler and the pygmy rattler. The pygmy, though small, can inflict a dangerous bite.

Cottonmouth: Poisonous. Usually found in water and wetlands, the cottonmouth or "water moccasin," grows to be characteristically heavy-bodied and quite broad, from mottled brown to black in color, with a triangular head.

When disturbed, this snake often shows its threat posture: It opens its startlingly white mouth and hisses a loud harsh sound.

Copperhead: Poisonous. Found mainly in north Florida, the copperhead resembles a smallish rattlesnake without rattles, and with a copper-colored, mottled design across the length of the body.

Coral snake: Poisonous. Found primarily in central and south Florida, this smallish slender snake is marked by bands of black, red, and yellow.

The bite of any poisonous snake requires prompt medical attention. Complications can be extremely serious, and even fatal.

But to reassure you: A recent survey taken by the State Parks revealed that, out of the last 85 million visitors, there had been only five poisonous snake bites. And no deaths. More people are killed each year by lightning than by snakebite.

DO NOT KILL SNAKES. Not even poisonous snakes. If you find a snake you think dangerous, call a ranger to deal with it. It may be harmless. Or, if it is a poisonous snake, the ranger may elect to remove it to a remote natural area where it can continue to be a part of the economy of nature. Snakes matter; they belong; they, too, are part of the ecosystem. Even poisonous ones.

You will be lucky if you even see a snake in most parks. But if you do, observe with care these masters of survival and strength. Chances are, though, that unless you travel very quietly and look closely, you will see no snakes at all. They will see you first, and glide away.

The Seasons of the Day

Build your day around the rhythms of the day. Forget clock-time, and make time to respond to what the day presents you. The greatest symphony in the world happens as the pre-dawn light rises into day and the sun comes up to the songs of birds. Make time for it, often.

Nature's rhythms, because they are our own deepest rhythms, can be the greatest healer.

Consider this prescription for whatever ails you: Sunrise and sunset, each day, in silence and stillness, for two weeks.

Repeat as needed.

Night

At least once on your trip through Florida parks, get up in the middle of the night, somewhere around 2 to 4 in the morning. Carefully go out to the edge of your campsite, or as far as you know to be safe for you, and tune in to the deepest hours of the night, the hours of greatest stillness, the huge hollow hours before dawn. Listen. Listen to what your heart tells you then. (It is the traditional time worldwide for meditation.) Listen to the life of those creatures who make this hour their busiest noon—cicadas, singing crickets, the twitter of flying squirrels, solitary bats, echoing owls, nocturnal animals like raccoons, cautious deer easing down to the water's edge, ghost crabs scuttling along the beach . . . .

Good fishing is one of Florida's greatest attractions, and many parks have good places to fish.

Parks Need Your Help

Two things are happening at once to increase the wear and tear on parks in Florida. More and more people are visiting them. And each person is having a greater impact on the parks.

You can help greatly by reducing the impact of your visit.

Simple things: Don't litter. Clean up after yourself. Protect trees and vegetation. Don't kill snakes. Don't collect specimens. Keep noise down. Don't feed animals. Be considerate of nature and of other visitors. Know and understand the rules for each park you visit; follow them because you understand how they serve to protect the park and preserve the quality of your visit.

Learn to live more lightly off the land, for there are now a lot more of us, and a lot less land.

Many, many more people can have high-quality experiences in Florida parks. But only if we all make a conscious effort to protect those parks while we use them.

I Need Your Help

If you know of parks that should appear in this book (publicly-maintained parks that either have camping or preserve some outstanding natural feature), please write me about them, care of the publisher.

And when you find mistakes or misrepresentations, please write me about them too. I'll make corrections in future editions of this book.

While you are at it, let me know what you think of the book. Tell me what you liked or found useful, what was weak, missing, or bothersome. Otherwise, I won't know what to change in the next edition.

Thanks.

After Your Trip

One of the greatest advantages of a trip is that you get to see your own home with fresh eyes when you come back. Here are some questions you may want to ask.

What are the ecological habitats of your neighborhood? Where is the nearest unspoiled forest, marsh, shoreline, river? What native animals are still common? Which are gone due to loss of habitat? Where does your water come from, and is there enough for both people and nature?

Many parks in Florida owe their existence to the generosity of individuals or the dedication of citizens' groups.

What exotic plants and animals have displaced native species? Where can you go to see the stars? What long, dim tales does the geology of your region tell? Where can you see changes in habitat brought about by changes in elevation or moisture?

What do you need to do to re-experience some of the rhythms of nature where you live? (Even in cities, certain houseplants close at night.)

What green plants make your oxygen and your food? What animals share your habitat with you?

Where do the birds go when they leave your neighborhood?

How well, and how badly, have people in your area adapted to living with nature? What can you do to ensure that coming generations will have the opportunity to experience the natural beauty that is original to your area?

Remember, all life is life in nature. Without nature (even the version packaged in the supermarket), we could not live for five minutes.

A State of Mind

When you are home again, think back to your favorite place in natural Florida. Obtain a picture of it if you can—perhaps one you took, or a post card, or a drawing you can make yourself. Choose a place where you felt truly relaxed, alive, vibrant with your own possibilities, filled with the grace of the moment and the spaciousness of the setting.

Memorize this special place. Travel back to it in your mind. Relax, close your eyes, go there—and bask. Breathe that extraordinary air. Feel the fine hum of life renewing you.

Let this image of your favorite place become your own personal vacation, your private retreat. Go back often, until natural Florida becomes for you a state of mind.

Natural Habitats of Florida

In order to see more in nature and appreciate more, it helps immeasurably to have a few names. Labels can, of course, get in the way; it is easy to mistake naming for knowing. But naming can be a great help to knowing. If you know the names of some of the natural habitats of Florida, you can particularize your experience, see more, know more. Indeed, without some labels, the rich, lush vegetation of Florida tends to run together into a great mass of amorphous "woods."

It is especially valuable to learn to distinguish Florida's natural habitats from the man-made and man-altered habitats which cover more and more of the state. Man-altered habitats, such as farmlands, tree plantations, and landscaped parks, tell us about the values and pursuits of human beings. By contrast, in a natural habitat, each detail arises to your perception from the depths of the laws of nature. Each plant, animal, and insect is in place because of a rich, complex, fascinating series of interactions, barely understood, which underlie all life on the earth, including our own. In a relatively undisturbed natural area, you stand a much better chance of tuning in to, seeing, feeling, and knowing the deep rhythms of nature, which are, in turn, our own deep rhythms.

The fundamental tenet of this book is that perception heals, and nature helps us re-learn this. If you truly perceive natural Florida, no one will need to tell you why to value and protect it. You will know why. All you need to do is see.

As one small step in this larger seeing, what follows is a list of some two dozen natural habitats of Florida, brief descriptions, and some parks you can find them in. I have described Florida's habitats in terms of their plant life, because plants are the most stable and visible components of each natural community. Just as important, though, are animals, birds, reptiles, fish, insects, bacteria, fungi, soils, acidity, organic matter, light, the amount and timing of the water supply, and other factors such as the presence of salt breezes or changes in elevation. This list is respectably accurate and complete, though any naturalist could find something to change or add to it.

In the following descriptions, you will find the habitats of Florida divided into five contrasting groups:

1. *The Hardwood Hammocks:*
   —upland
   —lowland
   —coastal
   —cabbage palm
   —live oak
   —southern mixed
   —tropical

2. *The Swamps:*
   —cypress
   —dwarf cypress
   —mixed hardwood
   —floodplain
   —shrub bogs

3. *The Pinelands:*
   —pine flatwoods
   —longleaf pine sandhills
   —sand pine scrub

4. *The Coastal Zone:*
   —barrier islands
   —salt marshes
   —mangrove swamps

5. *Other Habitats:*
   —freshwater marsh
   —savannahs
   —Everglades
   —aquatic habitat
   —coral reef
   —native prairie

You can find examples of all these habitats in Florida parks, many of which have excellent exhibits, talks, or ranger-led walks which will introduce you to the natural features of the park. You may find it especially helpful to buy a guidebook to birds, insects, animals, trees, mushrooms, the stars, or other things that interest you in nature.

1. The Hardwood Hammocks

The hardwood hammocks are the most varied of Florida's native habitats, and also some of the most beautiful. You don't have to know the names of the big trees—oaks, hickories, beech, hornbeam, dogwood, sweetgum, magnolia, and others—to see that these are wonderful woods, immediately appealing, deeply satisfying as places to visit, hike through, and camp in. Major trees can grow to be columnar giants, rising to a closed canopy high overhead, while the ground may be rich with moss, ferns, and a thick, variegated carpet of fallen leaves. The understory is usually sparse, so you can walk through hammocks rather easily.

As you get to know Florida better, you will learn to distinguish a number of different hammock types. Here are the major ones, and some parks you can find them in.

The *upland hammock* (or "mesic" hammock) climaxes in central Florida, and can be seen in all its diversity and splendor in O'Leno, Highlands Hammock, Bulow Ruins, and San Felasco Hammock.

The *lowland hammock* ("hydric") spreads out in low-lying areas near both coasts. It usually has many cabbage palms in it, along with dense

A path through the twisting live oaks of a coastal hammock forest. Notice the ferns and epiphytes growing on the oak.

vegetation and many moisture-loving trees. Lowland hammocks can be found in Hillsborough River and Myakka River State Parks.

Behind some of Florida's beaches, you find the *coastal hammock,* where gnarled live oaks, dark red-cedars, and cabbage palms form a mottled shade among the older dunes. Outstanding coastal hammocks can be seen at Ft. Clinch, Tomoka, and Anastasia parks.

Hammocks dominated by a single species occur in places throughout the state. *Cabbage palm hammocks* are found throughout central and coastal Florida, especially in the Gulf Hammock region of the west coast. In Waccasassa Bay, for example, cabbage palm hammocks stand out like islands in the wide sweep of the marshes. They can also be seen at Myakka River and along many back roads of Central Florida.

Live oak hammocks occur in many places in the state, marked by stately stands of large, old, spreading live oaks—lifting their moss-draped limbs as the archetypal tree of the southeastern coastal plain. You will find live oak hammocks circling many Florida lakes, as in the Ocala National Forest.

Southern mixed hardwoods grow on the red clay hills of north and northwestern Florida, and may be seen in wonderful development at Florida Caverns and Torreya State Parks. These woods are essentially the Appalachian forest at the southernmost limit of its range.

Tropical hammocks occur in the southern part of the state and contain some of the most interesting of all Florida habitats. In tropical hammocks, familiar northern hardwoods (like live oak) mix with unusual Caribbean trees like gumbo-limbo, poisonwood, and mahogany. Outstanding examples have been preserved in Everglades National Park, Lignumvitae Key, and Matheson Hammock. The vast majority of the original tropical hammocks, though, have long since been cut, burned, or bulldozed away.

The word "hammock" may have derived from an Indian word meaning "shady place," or it may have come from a Spanish nautical term for "a prominent, detached mound of trees visible from sea" and used as a landmark for navigation. Today—its history, like so much Florida history, melting into obscurity,—the word is only used in reference to the hardwood forests.

Hardwood hammocks are home to a wide variety of wildlife, including deer, turkey, gray squirrel and flying squirrel, black bear, several kinds of woodpeckers, raccoon, opossum, quail, dove, various reptiles, and a wealth of songbirds.

2. The Swamps

Since so much of Florida consists of wetlands, the state hosts a tremendous range and variety of swamps. These are some of the most mysterious and beautiful habitats in North America.

Cypress swamps line many Florida creeks, rivers, and lakes and occur as isolated "domes" in the middle of pine woods, marsh, and pastures. These woods often stand in still, dark, mirroring water, where the bald-cypresses rise in buttressed gray columns to a thin canopy high overhead. Several parks—such as Highlands Hammock—have boardwalks that take you into the heart of a cypress swamp.

The most famous cypress swamp in the world is found in nearby south Georgia at the Okefenokee National Wildlife Refuge, while one of the most beautiful has been preserved in south Florida's Corkscrew Swamp Sanctuary.

In the remote interior of south Florida—the Big Cypress region—thousands of acres are covered with grassy marshlands interspersed with a scattering of *dwarf cypresses*. Though only six to twelve feet tall, these trees are often very old, stunted by the extreme conditions of soil and climate.

People now realize that Florida's many wetlands—such as this cypress swamp—play a vital role in the quality and quantity of the state's fresh water. A movement has just begun to save the wetlands.

Everglades National Park has a dwarf cypress forest near the Pa-Hay-Okee overlook.

Mixed hardwood swamps, more varied than cypress swamps, line wet areas throughout the state. They contain many wetland species, such as blackgum, sweetgum, and flaming red maple, and create a rich ambience along many of Florida's streams and rivers.

Floodplain swamps line flood-prone rivers of northern Florida (such as the Apalachicola). These swamps spend several months each year submerged when the river is full, then dry out when the river is low. They are much more open than mixed hardwood swamps, with little undergrowth. Here you find big tupelos, river birch, water hickories, along with familiar cypress and sweet-gum. The floodplain forest receives the river's load of nutrients and replenishes it with leaf-fall that feeds the rich estuaries downstream. Oysters, shrimp, and commercial fish downstream from these forests often depend on the health of the forest for their survival.

Shrub bogs consist of dense thickets of tangled trees, often occurring in a wet depression in a pine forest. Their names indicate the dominant species: titi bogs, willow thickets, pond-apple swamps, blackgum swamps, bayheads, and several others. Shrub bogs occur in many parks, usually in the middle of some other plant community.

Florida's swamps support many birds and animals, including deer, black bear, raccoon, elusive mink, many herons and egrets, fisheating osprey, endangered wood storks, rare bald eagles, limpkins, anhingas, colorful but shy wood ducks, pileated woodpeckers, prothonotary warblers, alligators, a variety of snakes, turtles, fish, frogs, and salamanders.

3. The Pinelands

Florida's most widespread habitat is the *pine flatwoods,* most often dominated by a variety known as slash pine. Although they vary a lot, these woods are unmistakable. Tall pines rise in close columns above a very flat terrain. The ground may be flooded part of the year, and so dry at other times that it regularly catches fire and burns clear.

In some locations the understory is an open and expansive carpet of low grasses. Palmettos, though, are the most common companion to the pines. And in swampier places, the slash pines rise above an impenetrable wall of hard, dense bushes: gallberry, fetterbush (aptly named), and others.

Flatwoods abound in the Apalachicola and Osceola National Forests, Lake Kissimmee State Park, Dade Battlefield, and (in the south Florida version) at Everglades National Park and Larry and Penny Thompson Park. Flatwoods are found throughout the state, though, except in parks, most natural stands have been replaced by intensive tree-farms that differ significantly from the original habitat.

The *sandhill community*, dominated by longleaf pines, once covered large stretches of the state, but has been reduced to a much smaller acreage. Virgin stands are almost unknown. These magnificent park-like woods consist of widely-spaced stately trees of longleaf pine with an understory of sparse wiregrass and many native wildflowers. As the name implies, these pine forests are usually found on rolling, sandy hills. Turkey oaks often grow with the pines—and these vary from stunted, scrubby things to great spreading trees.

Longleaf pine forests may be found at Gold Head Branch, Blackwater River, the Apalachicola and Ocala National Forests, and scattered throughout central and northern Florida. Much of the citrus belt was once a native sandhill forest.

Both flatwoods and sandhills are "fire-adapted," and can survive burning every few years. In natural conditions, fires were caused by lightning from Florida's frequent summer thunderstorms. Today, most such fires are carefully set by park personnel—because the pinewoods need regular fires to kill off the young hardwoods that would otherwise replace them.

Unique in all the world, the Florida *sand pine scrub* occurs on ancient seacoast dunes in the central Florida ridge and in sandy places along the coasts. This community is thought to be a remnant of an ancient desert scrub that once extended from California, through Mexico, and across dry portions of the Gulf, thousands of years ago.

This forest gets a lot of rain, but because of the extremely sandy soil, the habitat is desert-like. You can see many intriguing adaptations in the plants and animals to these harsh conditions. Ocala National Forest has the largest sand pine forest in the world. Other good examples may be seen at Rocky Bayou, Highlands Hammock, Blue Spring, and Wekiwa Springs.

The pinewoods provide a home for such wildlife as deer, bobcats, raccoons, gray foxes, fox squirrels, rabbits, diamondback rattlesnakes, skunks,

A campground in one of Florida's many pine forests.

quail, red-shouldered hawks, and several kinds of woodpeckers. The drier pinewoods include many burrowers, such as the gopher tortoise, indigo snake, and gopher frog. The sand pine scrub contains a number of rare and unique species, such as the Florida scrub jay.

4. The Coastal Zone

The "high energy" coasts of Florida—where strong waves come in all year—almost always have a stretch of open, sandy beach meeting the water. Many of these coasts are lined with *barrier islands*—long, thin, delicate, shifting islands (or spits) of sand that protect the mainland from the force of wind and storm. Many beaches are backed by a ridge of dunes, which owe their existence to the holding power of little plants no bigger around than a pencil. Pinelands and coastal hammock forests often grow behind the foredunes. These sea-oat-held dunes have survived hurricanes that obliterated reinforced concrete buildings nearby. Beaches and barrier islands survive by yielding. They move in slow waves in and out of the sea, up and down the coast, with a remarkable kind of shifting permanence.

Barrier islands line much of the Florida coastline, include many of the most famous beaches, and may be seen in a relatively natural state in parks like Gulf Islands, St. George, Little Talbot, Caladesi, and Canaveral National Seashore.

The "low energy" coastline of Florida—where the wave action is minimal—allows vegetation to grow right down into the ocean. Marshlands march across the land out into the shallows, sometimes many miles in width. Great *salt marshes* can be seen in the Gulf Hammock area, at St. Marks, in the Nassau Sound near Ft. Clinch, and along the Intracoastal Waterway in places like Washington Oaks.

In southwest Florida, a remarkable forest of *mangrove swamp* replaces the salt marshes at the water's edge. Perhaps the largest undisturbed mangrove swamp in the world, this is a fascinating and highly valuable habitat. Like salt marsh, the mangrove forms an indispensible link in the life-cycle of many important sport fish, commercial fish, and shellfish. Elsewhere in Florida, the once widespread mangrove swamps have largely been bulldozed away, but excellent samples may still be seen in Everglades National Park, Collier-Seminole, Ding Darling National Wildlife Refuge, and in the parks of the Florida Keys.

The coastal zone provides habitat for a large variety of shorebirds, terns, gulls, and pelicans. Crabs and other crustaceans are numerous near the shoreline. Some beaches serve as nesting sites for huge sea-turtles.

Forested areas behind the beaches give habitat for other birds, raccoons, bobcats, foxes, and skunks, while the salt marshes are home to many young fish and shellfish, as well as alligator, otter, diamondback terrapin, salt marsh snake, and many forms of waterfowl, such as elegant herons and noisy coots.

Few people realize that Florida is rimmed with mountains. Over millennia, whole mountains have travelled from the Appalachians, down the great rivers, grain by grain, to end in the transfiguration of a Florida beach.

Mangroves feed a wealth of underwater life and give homes to some of the most spectacular birds in the country.

5. Other Habitats

Florida's immensely valuable wetlands include several kinds of *freshwater marsh*—the spreading *marshes* of low depressions and riversides, the grassy *savannahs* that resemble pinewoods without pines, and the unique "river of grass" that forms the *Everglades*. Marshes support a rich food chain that culminates in many colorful wading birds, such as those seen at Paynes Prairie or the Loxahatchee National Wildlife Refuge.

Lakes, rivers, ponds, springs, sinkholes, streams, and estuaries all have native vegetation, fish, and animals of their own. This *aquatic habitat* is one of the most valuable and famous features of natural Florida, because it is where most people swim and fish. The Suwannee River and Lake Okeechobee are two of Florida's many aquatic habitats that are accessible through parks. Blue Spring State Park and a few other locations provide sanctuaries for the endangered manatee.

In the Florida Keys, the only *coral reef* in North America struggles for existence at the northernmost extremity of its range. The most profuse habitat on earth, the reef teems with an indescribable variety of colorful life-forms and may be visited at Coral Reef State Park and Biscayne National Park.

Central Florida has a unique *native prairie* that has been the site of cattle ranching (and rustling) for over a hundred years, making Florida an anomalous part of the Old West. Lake Kissimmee State Park is a good place to see this habitat, along with a last remnant of the original little tough scrub cows of centuries past.

The Value of Native Habitats

Native plants and animals are specifically adapted to live where they live. Native trees, for example, usually survive the normal variations in weather, flood, and fire. In times of recurring drought, many native plants and animals reveal adaptations for conserving water. Imported trees ("exotics"), on the other hand, usually need watering exactly when water is scarce, and often must be protected from flood and freezing. Lawns, subdivisions, and cities that are landscaped with exotics require more energy, water, time, and labor to maintain than those landscaped with the vegetation native to that site.

Unfortunately, Florida was developed for decades by "clear and replace"

In the freshwater marshes, multiple wildflowers bloom throughout their interweaving seasons.

methods. Typically, a choice site would be bulldozed of its native cover, built up (often with a building poorly adapted to the climate), and landscaped with decorative foreign shrubs and trees. But everywhere in the state, people are beginning to realize the value of native plants—and their deep, lasting beauty.

Several exotic plants and animals are causing serious ecological damage to the state, especially in South Florida. These include melaleuca, Brazilian pepper, Australian pine, water hyacinth, hydrilla, walking catfish, wild hogs, and a host of lesser ones. Without natural enemies to check them, these species are flooding over the landscape, crowding out native plants and animals, and, in places, reducing the terrain to a drab monoculture where little else can survive.

If you are building in Florida, consider leaving as much original vegetation as you can. And if you are planting trees and shrubs, consider using ones native to the setting. That way, you will expend less energy in upkeep and provide the kind of habitat essential for the survival of Florida's birds and animals.

Addresses

For more information on **State Parks, State Recreation Areas, State Preserves, State Historical, Archaeological, and Botanical Sites**, and **State Canoe Trails**:
> Information Office
> Department of Natural Resources
> Room 613
> 3900 Commonwealth Blvd.
> Tallahassee, FL 32399
> > 904/488-7326

For information on **hunting** and **fishing**:
> Information Office
> Florida Game and Fresh Water Fish Commission
> Bryant Building
> Tallahassee, FL 32399-1600
> > 904/488-4677

For the "Camping Packet" containing a list of private campgrounds, Florida attractions, and the official state map (currently free); also for a wide variety of brochures on Florida:
> Tourist Information
> Florida Division of Tourism
> Department of Commerce
> Tallahassee, FL 32399-2000
> > 904/487-1462

For brochures and camping information on the **State Forests:**
> Division of Forestry
> Forest Education
> 3125 Conner Blvd.
> Tallahassee, FL 32399-1650
> > 904/488-6727

For brochures and camping information on the **National Forests:**
> USDA Forest Service
> 227 N. Bronough St.
> Suite 4061
> Tallahassee, FL 32301
> > 904/681-7266

For brochures and information on the **National Wildlife Refuges:**
  U.S. Fish and Wildlife Service
  75 Spring Street SW
  Atlanta, GA 30303
        404/331-3594

Handicapped: Some information on access to parks for handicapped persons can be obtained from the Department of Natural Resources, from Tourist Information, and from the National Forests, at the addresses above.

Canoe and hiking trails: Information is available through the Department of Natural Resources, National Forests, State Forests, and the Florida Trail Association (see below).

Conservation Groups

Florida has many conservation groups, dedicated to the wise use and preservation of the state's natural features. Here are some of the more active ones:

Florida Audubon Society
1101 Audubon Way
Maitland, FL 32751

Florida Trail Association
P. O. Box 13708
Gainesville, FL 32604

The Sierra Club, Florida Chapter
1201 N. Federal Hwy.
North Palm Beach, FL 33408

Florida Wildlife Federation
2545 Blairstone Pines Dr.
Tallahassee, FL 32301

The Izaak Walton League
2807 SW 27th Ave.
Miami, FL 33133

The Nature Conservancy
1353 Palmetto Ave.
Winter Park, FL 32789

Florida Defenders of the Environment
1523 NW 4th St.
Gainesville, FL 32601

The Florida Native Plant Society
2020 Redgate Road
Orlando, FL 32818

Florida Conservation Foundation*
1191 Orange Avenue
Winter Park, FL 32789
*Publishers of *ENFO*

Your participation in these or similar groups will bring you information, field trips, outings, good company, and a chance to help protect natural Florida.

Updates to the Introduction

Fees. Prices have gone up for the Florida State Park System. Write or call them for a copy of their complicated new fee schedule (adopted in mid-1989 and still open to change).

Camping ranges from a low of $8 to a high of $19 per night in the state parks system. It costs a couple of dollars more for electricity, for waterfront sites, and for staying only one night. Florida residents get a $2 discount at parks charging $10 or more.

Many parks now cost more during their busy season—which is winter in South Florida and summer in North Florida. For example, St. Andrews State Park charges $15 per night from March through November, $8 in the winter. Some, like Blue Spring, charge the same $14 fee year round. State parks now cost about the same as nearby private campgrounds.

The cheapest state parks are in rural areas of North Florida, such as Blackwater River, Torreya, and Three Rivers. These are $8 year round.

The entrance fee to state parks is now $1 for the driver and 50 cents per passenger for Florida residents, and twice that for out of state residents.

Don't depend entirely on these figures. Park prices have been swinging up and down and may not have settled yet. Call them for the latest information at 904/488-7326.

Some **phone numbers** may have changed. Numbers are usually listed under the name of the parent agency, so you may have trouble getting them from the operator or a directory. If so, try this:

State parks, recreation areas, preserves, reserves, and historic sites are usually listed under "Florida, State of; Natural Resources, Department of; Recreation and Parks, Division of."

State Forests are usually listed under "Florida, State of; Agriculture and Consumer Services, Department of; Forestry, Division of."

National Forests are usually listed under "U.S. Government; Agriculture, Department of; Forest Service."

County Parks are listed under the name of the county and the parent agency, usually "Parks and Recreation," but often "Public Works."

The state parks no longer sell an annual camping pass, but they do offer reduced rates (to most parks) to the disabled and those over 65. Ask for an application at any state park or write the Department of Natural Resources (see *Addresses*).

Time Zones. Florida west of the Apalachicola River is in the Central Time zone (including Pensacola and Panama City).

Another type of park has sprung up since this book first came out. The **State Reserves** include some outstanding natural areas with minimal development. The most prominent of these (such as Tosohatchee, Rock Springs Run, Guana River, and Cape St. George) are managed jointly for hunting and other forms of outdoor recreation. Camping on Reserves is generally primitive.

Seashore Hazards. At many larger parks, you can pick up valuable information on sharks, jellyfish, stingrays, sea urchin spines, and other potential hazards of the seashore. The most common hazard still remains sunburn. Experts tell me not to worry about sharks; I still do.

Weather. Compared to most places in the U.S. and Canada, Florida's weather is balmy and semi-tropical, but Florida gets much hotter and much colder than the commercials lead you to believe. The weather is also unpredictable. A few years ago, many lakes went dry; the following year, some campgrounds were under a league of water. Some years, summer starts in April; yet, early one March, we threw snowballs in Tallahassee. When making reservations at a park during the winter, it's a good idea to ask what the weather is like.

Resource Alert. The Department of Natural Resources maintains a "watch line" you can call to report misuse of the environment or violations of state laws protecting Florida's natural resources.

Here are some examples of such violations: taking fish or shellfish out of season or under size; using illegal fish traps; destroying coastal dunes or protected plants, such a sea oats; building on the coast without the proper permits; harming or harassing the endangered manatee; molesting nesting turtles or stealing turtle eggs; harming or taking reef coral; illegal filling of wetlands; illegal timbering on public lands; cutting of mangroves; illegal hunting on public lands; taking plants from state parks. Resource Alert is also the place to report beached whales or saltwater fish kills, suspicious fires on state lands, spills of oil or pollutants, and unusual alterations to the shoreline.

If you think you saw harm occurring to Florida's natural resources, get as many details as you can and call 1-800-342-1821, day or night.

Youth group camping. About two dozen state parks reserve special areas for use by recognized youth groups (such as Boy Scouts, church groups, and non-profit service clubs). The Department of Natural Resources publishes an information sheet on these youth camping areas. Other information on youth camps is available from the national and state forests.

Swimming. Florida's beaches, lakes, rivers, and springs are wonderful places to swim. If you don't know how to swim, learn how. Even if you do know how to swim, learn the survival float known as "drownproofing." Too many people drown each year. Don't be one of them.

Since the last edition, hiking trails, bicycle paths, and canoe trails have grown in Florida. For **bicycling information**, phone 904/488-4640. For information on hiking trails, phone 904/487-4782.

Some of the most populous counties (such as Dade, Broward, Hillsborough, and Pinellas) offer interesting parks programs, including talks, films, guided walks, canoe trips, and trips to historic sites. If you are staying in one of these areas, contact the county parks and recreation department for more information.

PAM. An amoeba common in Florida lakes can, under certain conditions, infect people with a fatal form of encephalitis called PAM. In the past 20 years, less than one case per year has been diagnosed, which makes it a smaller hazard than lightning. Nevertheless, you may want to know about it. The PAM organism seems to become most dangerous in the sediments of fresh water bodies during the hottest weather. It appears to enter the brain by way of the nose. State epidemiologists suggested these precautions: If you go *swimming in fresh water during prolonged periods of hot weather* wear nose plugs or a face mask, and avoid stirring up sediment or swimming along the bottom. No one really understands this disease and very few swimmers get it. Still, many people do follow these precautions.

Hurricanes. The official hurricane season runs from early June through November, with most storms occurring in September. Recent large hurricanes, however, hit close to Thanksgiving. Remember: Hurricanes can be lethal. Don't take any chances with them.

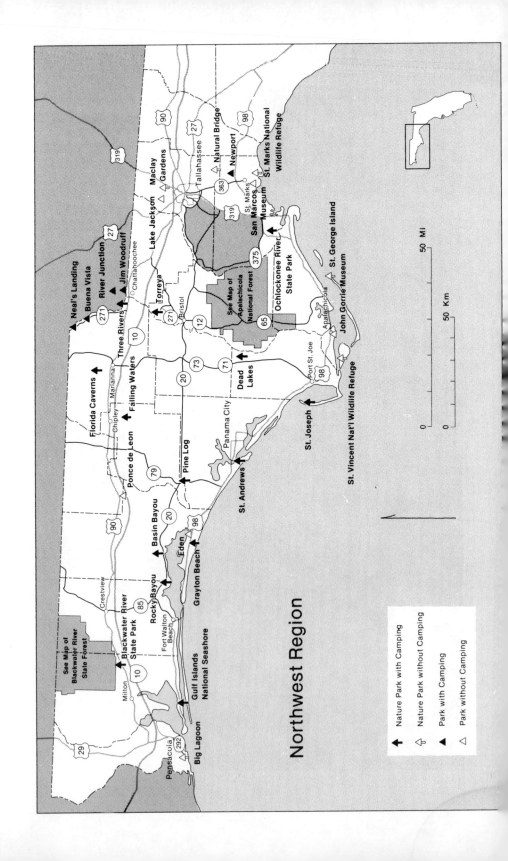

Northwest Region

Neal's Landing
Buena Vista
River Junction
Jim Woodruff
Three Rivers
Falling Waters
Florida Caverns
Ponce de Leon
Pine Log
Basin Bayou
Rocky Bayou
Eden
Grayton Beach
St. Andrews
St. Joseph
St. Vincent Nat'l Wildlife Refuge
St. George Island
John Gorrie Museum
Ochlockonee River State Park
San Marcos
St. Marks Museum
St. Marks National Wildlife Refuge
Natural Bridge
Newport
Maclay Gardens
Lake Jackson
Torreya
Dead Lakes
See Map of Apalachicola National Forest
See Map of Blackwater River State Forest
Blackwater River State Park
Big Lagoon
Gulf Islands National Seashore

Chattahoochee
Tallahassee
St. Marks
Bristol
Marianna
Chipley
Panama City
Port St. Joe
Apalachicola
Crestview
Fort Walton Beach
Milton
Pensacola

90
27
319
271
27
10
20
79
85
90
10
29
292
98
363
319
375
65
12
271
73
71

50 Mi
50 Km
0

- ▲ Nature Park with Camping
- △ Nature Park without Camping
- ▲ Park with Camping
- △ Park without Camping

Northwest

APALACHICOLA NATIONAL FOREST

One of the largest National Forests in the east, the Apalachicola covers half a million acres. Its sandhills and flatwoods stretch for mile after mile of longleaf and slash pines in all stages of development. Dense swamps of titi crowd the low areas in the pines. Along the drainage creeks, rich cypress swamps tower over honey-bearing tupelo and brilliant red maple. Bluffs along the two rivers support an extraordinary forest of mixed hardwoods and pines, where you can

Pinelands, such as these pine flatwoods, cover much of the 500,000 acre Apalachicola National Forest, but the Forest also contains a rich variety of other natural settings with camping facilities ranging from primitive to fully developed sites.

lose yourself in the rich insect life underfoot, the dogwoods at eye level, or the magnolias and hickories overhead.

Near the Apalachicola River, broad savannahs of open grassland come alive in the late winter and early spring with a different carpet of bloom each week. Orchids, wildflowers, sedges, wiregrass, and insectivorous plants—including the tiny orange sundew with its sticky arms—spread out in a carpet of living color.

Parts of Lost Creek, the Sopchoppy River, and the New River are practically wilderness streams, especially in their upper reaches. Sections of them can be canoed. The Ochlockonee is a fine-sized river, green and swampy and sometimes swift. A canoe trip requiring at least three days takes you through a long, wild stretch of Florida woods.

The Apalachicola River, though, is awesome. It is a huge brown muddy river, the largest single geological feature in north Florida. The rich waters it carries into the Gulf were gathered in the mountains and swept through the entire length of Georgia. It can also be canoed, but with more time and care, since crossings are scarce, and, once on the river, you have to go a long way downstream to get off again. Write for the National Forest brochure on canoe trails if you are interested.

Supplies are plentiful in the little towns surrounding the forest, but don't always count on finding the towns that maps show inside the forest. Some of these exist, others are ghost-towns from the old logging days, and may now be nothing but a crossroads. Though people live here and there on private land in the National Forest, most of it is remote and unpopulated woods or swamps.

The Apalachicola National Forest is administered in two sections, divided by the Ochlockonee River. If you need detailed information, plan to stop at both ranger stations, one in Crawfordville and one in Bristol.

Note: The Forest Service seems to be in the midst of re-numbering many roads. A new map has been issued showing these new numbers. Unfortunately, not all roads have their new numbers yet, and the old maps are still common. Buy the large folding map of the forest, but expect some difficulty finding your way around.

CAMPING

As in most National Forests, you can camp anywhere outside the restricted areas—which are around Lost Lake, near Tallahassee. If you do camp out in the woods, you'll have to supply your own water. Please be careful with fire, and pack out all your garbage. The luxury of camping where you like can only be possible if each of us leaves the campsite cleaner than we found it.

During hunting season, camping is restricted to designated areas, for your protection. Be careful then. Most hunters are. But accidents can happen. Hunting season varies, but typically runs from early November through January.

Designated camping areas are located in three separate sections of the Apalachicola National Forest. Silver Lake Campground is on the eastern edge, near Tallahassee. A line of campsites runs near the Apalachicola River, on the western boundary of the forest. And in the middle, five additional camping areas line the Ochlockonee River (pronounced o'*clock*-nee).

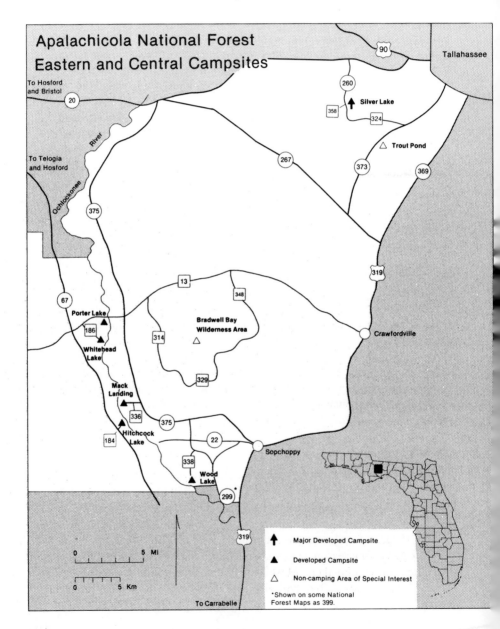

Three campgrounds in the forest are highly developed: Silver Lake near Tallahassee, along with Camel Lake and Wright Lake on the western edge.

The other campsites provide basic, minimal facilities: a place, a road, drinking water (usually a hand pump), and some type of enclosed toilet. There are tables, grills and fish-cleaning tables in some.

A fee is charged to camp at Silver Lake. The other campsites are free. Campsites in this forest are rarely filled, even though the cool months of the year here are permeated with a serene autumnal beauty—right through winter (except when it rains).

EAST CAMPGROUNDS

1. **Silver Lake** is the most highly developed camping area in the forest. There is a well laid out camping area with 45 designated sites that have tables and grills. Central restrooms have flush toilets and hot showers. There is a central dump station. A fee is charged for camping.

A nature trail goes along the moss-draped cypresses and pines that rim the beautiful, spring-fed 23-acre lake. There is a swimming area with a large white sand beach. A picnic area sits nearby in the shade.

Silver Lake is 8 miles west of Tallahassee, off Fla. 260. It may also be reached by going south on 373, west on 324 and north on 358, as shown on the map.

CENTRAL CAMPGROUNDS

Mack Landing and Wood Lake are located along the eastern side of the Ochlockonee River. Along the western side you find Porter Lake Landing, Whitehead Lake Landing, and Hitchcock Lake Landing. Forest Road 13 crosses the river on a series of very bad, rickety bridges that are being slowly upgraded.

Mack Landing was designed as a place to picnic and to put your boat into the Ochlockonee River for a fishing trip, but camping is allowed. It is a beautiful spot that provides only the bare essentials: a handpump that gives sweet, soft water, about a dozen cement picnic tables, grills, garbage cans, chemical toilets, a fish-cleaning table, and shade from sweetgums, small oaks, magnolias and spruce pine.

Take Forest Road 336 west from Fla. 375.

Wood Lake, a few miles south of Mack Landing, may be harder to find. You have to locate just the right dirt road, and hope the small signs have not been shot away. But the site is excellent: lush Southern mixed hardwoods shading a campsite much like that at Mack Landing, on a calm little oxbow lake that is connected on the far side to the river. Fine water for boating and fishing, woods rich with life. In warm weather, the air sings with bees, butterflies, mosquito-hawks and, alas, deerflies.

From Sopchoppy go west on 22, south on 340 and SW on 338.

Porter Lake, Whitehead Lake and **Hitchcock Lake** camping areas are quite similar to Wood Lake and Mack Landing. All three are located on tributary streams to the Ochlockonee River, amid the marvelous mixed hardwood forest and creek swamp that dominate these riverbanks. These three areas have similar facilities: handpump, vault toilets, access roads, picnic tables and a lovely natural setting.

Porter Lake is reached by Forest Road 13. Whitehead Lake is off Forest Road 13 on Forest Road 186. Hitchcock Landing is off Fla. 67 on Forest Road 184. Be careful of the bridges on F.R. 13 crossing the Ochlockonee River.

WESTERN CAMPGROUNDS

The string of camping areas near the Apalachicola River, in the remotest part of the forest, includes two that are well-developed (Camel Lake and Wright Lake) and three that have basic facilities only.

Camel Lake, in the northwestern corner of the forest, contains a nice open grassy area of longleaf pines that slopes down to a beautiful, medium-sized lake, surrounded by dense forest. The unattended campground has tables, grills, central faucets and a restroom with flush toilets. There is an outdoor shower near the (unsupervised) swimming area. *Take Fla. 12 south of Bristol, then go east on Forest Road 105. The way is well marked.*

White Oak Landing and **Cotton Landing** are quiet, wooded places to launch a boat, picnic, and camp on tributaries to the Apalachicola River. Facilities are basic: drinking water, enclosed toilets, garbage cans, tables. *White Oak Landing is off 379 on F.R. 115. To Cotton Landing, leave 379 on 123, take 123-B, and turn in at 193 to the landing.*

Wright Lake. *Take Forest Road 101 west off Fla. 65, and veer right onto 101-C.* Campsites here are shaded by tall pines. Some border the lovely little lake, which is fringed with cypress and live oaks. Sites have tables and fire pits. There are flush toilets and showers in the restroom. An area has been marked off for unsupervised swimming in the lake, and an especially nice picnic site can be enjoyed under shade at the lake's edge.

Hickory Landing. *Take Forest Road 101 west from Fla. 65, then veer left onto 101B.* The campsites are located on Owl Creek, and give boating access to the Apalachicola River. After passing through miles of pine flatwoods, you find a nice floodplain forest bordering the creek, consisting of tupelos and other trees well-adapted to the seasonal rise and fall of the river. The campsites nestle among oaks and hickories, with plenty of native vegetation separating the sites. A free-flowing mineral spring is piped out of the ground near the boat launch. Sites have tables and grills. Facilities are basic.

NON-CAMPING AREAS OF SPECIAL INTEREST

Some other areas are worth special mention, though lots of places in the National Forest have an unusual magic, especially along the unspoiled streams.

Fort Gadsden State Historic Site (day-use only) may be the only
accessible portion of the forest that is directly on the immense Apalachicola
River. It is a beautiful place to walk along the wide, rapid sweep of water at full
flood. You can feel the immense power of the river here. *From 65, take 129,
well-marked.*

The Apalachicola is one of the purest large rivers in America, but a serious
fight is shaping up about its future. Now, it conveys downstream a huge amount

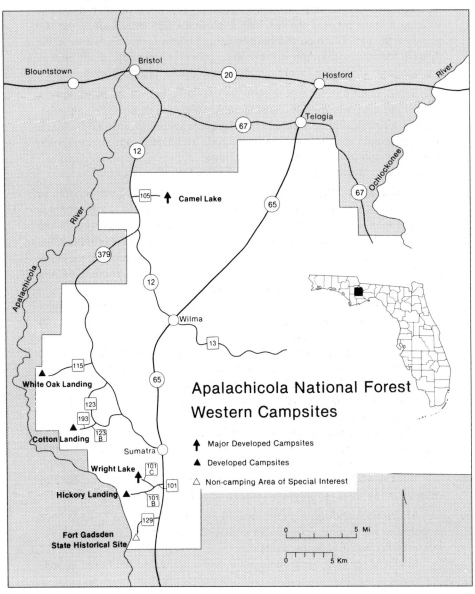

Apalachicola National Forest
Western Campsites

↑ Major Developed Campsites

▲ Developed Campsites

△ Non-camping Area of Special Interest

of precisely balanced and timed organic matter in just the right state to feed one of the most productive bays in the world. There is grave doubt whether this productivity could survive the damming, channelization, dredging, or heavy barge traffic that have been proposed.

Fort Gadsden itself was constructed inside the remains of an old British fort that was abandoned during the War of 1812 to a group of Choctaw Indians and runaway slaves. The original fort was brought under siege by American warships in 1816. During the opening shots, the fort's powder magazine suffered a direct hit, and the resulting explosion killed almost all of the 300 people in the fort. Gadsden was built by Gen. Andrew Jackson while invading Spanish Florida in 1818. You will find an excellent brochure at the site, and an interpretative kiosk gives more details of the history of Fort Gadsden.

Trout Pond has been developed for exclusive use by the handicapped. Wheelchair access is provided, and special markers guide the sight-impaired. There is a sheltered picnic area, swimming pool, restrooms, first aid building, fishing pier and a specially marked nature trail. Trout Pond is open from April to September, and by reservation at other times.
Off Springhill Road (Fla. 373) about 10 miles SW of Tallahassee.

Bradwell Bay Wilderness Area. The first Federal wilderness area in Florida, and still one of the few on the east coast, Bradwell Bay is a huge, dense swamp bordered by Forest Roads 314, 329, 348, and 13. A portion of the Florida Trail has been built through Bradwell Bay, but the trail is primitive, the area remote, and conditions highly demanding. Contact rangers before entering. Leave word of your itinerary, and be sure to carry a compass and emergency supplies. It's not a place you want to get lost in.

The heart of Bradwell Bay is a giant swamp, with standing water knee-to-waist-deep much of the year. It is too thickly wooded for a canoe. If you want to see it, you will have to slog for a few wet, slow, muddy miles. But if you do this, you will find another world. There is a group of huge virgin slash pines deep in the Bay—too deep for early loggers to get to—that stand like shadows of a primal world. A vast blackgum swamp spreads out around them. Ancient ogeechee tupelos suggest that this swamp has been developing steadily for thousands of years.

Check with the rangers before venturing in. Some seasons, it is too wet to camp. It's also quite easy to get lost. There are few natural landmarks to guide you out, and it's seven miles to the other side. That's a long wade.

Yet it is really no more inaccessible than Death Valley. You just have to know what you are doing, if you want to go into a big Florida swamp on foot.

Magnolia Landing, a picnic area, is part of a scenic area that has been proposed as the New River/Mud Swamp Wilderness. If this is approved, the spot may be closed to motor vehicles.

SPECIAL NOTE: Some maps show public camping facilities at Stouta-

An ecologically valuable floodplain swamp of tupelo, cypress, red maple, and other water-tolerant trees lines the big rivers of north Florida.

mire's Landing and Drake's Landing, on the Ochlockonee. This is an error. Those are privately operated fish camps.

Addresses. Main office: National Forests in Florida, P.O. Box 13548, Tallahassee FL 32308. Telephone 904/878-1131. Apalachicola National Forest: District Ranger (West), P.O. Box 578, Bristol, FL 32321. Telephone 904/643-2477. District Ranger (East), P.O. Box 68, Crawfordville FL 32327. Telephone 904/926-3561.

BASIN BAYOU State Recreation Area

On Fla. 20, seven miles west of Freeport.

You can camp, picnic, swim on the beaches of huge Choctawahatchee Bay, or launch your boat in nearby B   u for saltwater fishing. Twenty campsites sit close to the   der of the pine flatwoods and waterfront oaks. A natu   e dense, fast-growing planted slash pine woods that have re,   st of the native flatwoods in the state.

Since the bay is seve..ı miles wide at this point, it makes an exceptional place to watch the sun set over the water and listen to the wind in the pines.

Address: P.O. Box 278, Freeport, FL 32439. Telephone 904/835-3761.

BIG LAGOON State Recreation Area

Near Pensacola, on Fla. 292, just east of the intersection with 293, in the extreme southwest corner of the panhandle.

Opened in 1980, 700-acre Big Lagoon State Recreation Area has a large picnic pavilion and an area suitable for swimming on the lagoon (though there is no beach to speak of).

There is a campground of 120 units under construction.

This park contains several hundred acres of sand pine scrub, a well-preserved example of one of Florida's unique habitats.

Address: Big Lagoon State Recreation Area, Rt. 1 Box 350, Pensacola, FL 32507.

BLACKWATER RIVER State Forest

A large area northwest of Crestview and northeast of Milton. The main roads are Fla. 191 and Fla. 4. Forest Headquarters are located on 191, just south of 4.

Some of the most beautiful longleaf pine forests in the world can be seen along the numerous dirt roads of the Blackwater River State Forest. Dominating the more than 180,000 acres of the forest, these exquisite woods take on a cathedral appearance when the early morning sun fires up the grassy under-growth and lights the tips of the long needle-sprays. A wealth of wildflowers thrive in the sunny soil, which is kept open and clear by regular prescribed burning that duplicates the occurrence of natural fires. These "high pinelands" closely resemble the "sandhill community" of central Florida, except here the soil is a rich clay that shows up in road-cuts and ant-hills as a yellow-orange or bright red.

The high, rolling pinelands are laced with a series of pure, pristine creeks and rivers, whose dark waters meander past startlingly white, sparkling sandbars and high banks of sand. Along these rivers you will find lush growth of swamp hardwoods and the tall dark spires of "juniper"—as the Atlantic white cedar is called here. These rivers are world-famous among scientists because they are among the very few sandy-bottom rivers in the whole world that remain pristine. A unique system of life thrives on these pure sandy bottoms.

The rivers are also famous as canoe trails which take you for miles and miles without any sign of human habitation. Be sure to inquire about local conditions before you canoe. The rivers fluctuate widely during the year, and can rise and fall in a matter of hours.

In spring and fall, you can hike the 21-mile Andrew Jackson Red Ground Trail, a part of the Florida Trail system which traces an early trade route. There are shelters along the trail, and a trail guide is available at headquarters.

There are many miles of dirt roads in the forest that make beautiful places to drive or walk. However, these are rarely marked, and I recommend that you

Red Rock: a little camping and picnic area along the dark waters and brilliant white sands of the Blackwater River.

get a forest map and a county map before you start out, proceed with caution, and never leave the main roads at night.

Blackwater River State Forest is one of the most important recreational areas in northwest Florida, with a variety of sites ranging from fully-developed recreation centers to primitive camps. This is a listing of the most important. Note that camping is restricted to designated campsites. You cannot camp at large in the forest.

1. **Krul Recreation Area** (formerly Munson)—*Located off Fla.4, just east of 191.* A little manmade lake forms the focus, with a swimming area that has lifeguards in the summer season. It is too small for fishing or boating, though. Krul campground is presently one of only two fee-areas in the forest, charging average fees for campsites. There is a 2-week limit, and no pets are allowed here. (Pets are allowed elsewhere in the forest, on leash.) There are 33 campsites with water and electricity, and 33 with water only, in the woods near the lake. The area opens at 7AM and closes at sundown, when the gate is locked. There are flush toilets and hot showers.

2. **Bear Lake Recreation Area**—*Just east of Krul on Fla. 4.* Forty free campsites are located on a grassy slope under pines and scrub oaks, next to Bear Lake. There is a boat ramp, flush toilets, hot showers, no electric hookups.

Bear Lake also has two small primitive camping areas on the eastern side. These may be reached by taking the road marked "Hurricane Lake" and turning left at the first or the second dirt roads. The sites consist of a cleared area with a few picnic tables.

3. **Hurricane Lake**—*Follow sign from Fla.4, at the turnoff about 2 miles east of 191.* You will see turnoffs to "Hurricane Lake North and South Campgrounds". The north campgrounds are sunnier and have hot showers. There are twenty sites there, as well as twenty on the south shore directly across the lake. The south campground lies in a similar area, on sloping hillsides shaded with pines and small oaks, but the facilities are more limited. Both have launching areas and built-up berms for shore fishing. There are no hookups at either location. No electricity. Only electric motors are allowed on the lake.

4. **Karick Lake**—*Located east of Fla. 189, about 8 miles north of 4.* The north and south campgrounds at Karick Lake are quite similar, with 20 sites in each location. There are flush toilets, but no hookups at the sites. As at Hurricane Lake, grassy lawns slope down to the lakeside, shaded by pines and turkey oaks. No electricity.

5. **Coldwater Recreation Area**—*Reached by Fla. 191, where there is a marked turnoff a few miles south of Munson, or by Fla.4, at a turnoff some 13 miles west of Munson.* This is a specialized recreation area developed primarily for horseback riding and hunting-dog field trials. Four horse trails start from this area and go through the open pinewoods and hardwood forests. A large area of longleaf pine and oak was cleared of its built-up underbrush and is maintained in an open condition by regular burning, to provide a natural setting conducive to the field trials for bird dogs. At the frequent competitions, well-trained dogs locate and point live birds. (No shooting of these birds is allowed.)

Horse stables and dog kennels are available at Coldwater, and the campgrounds may be reserved in advance by groups, who may also rent the kitchen and dining hall.

The following campgrounds are less developed. Most are really picnic areas that permit primitive camping.

6. **Kennedy Bridge**, on the Blackwater River near Hurricane Lake, has 12 tables on a high bluff.

7. **Juniper Bridge**, on the north side of Juniper Creek where it crosses Fla. 191, has a few tables on the creek in a hardwood forest. No running water or toilet facilities. Good area for fishing and swimming.

8. **Bryant Bridge**, on the Blackwater River just northwest of Holt, is a well-used point for canoe expeditions. Eight picnic tables along the river constitute the only facilities.

9. **Red Rock Picnic Area,** on Juniper Creek, is a little harder to find. Eight tables, a hand pump, and chemical toilets are the facilities.

10. **Camp Lowry**, up Coldwater Creek about five miles north of Fla. 4, is

also difficult to find and poorly marked. This lovely, remote little campsite has no facilities except tables, woods and a beautiful stretch of the dark creek, where an old iron bridge crosses.

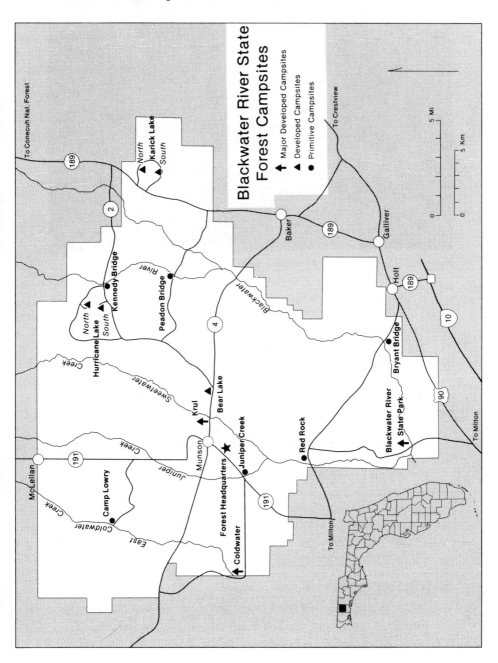

The swinging bridge on one of the hiking trails of the Blackwater River State Forest.

11. **Peadon Bridge**, on the Blackwater River about four miles north of Fla. 4, is being developed as a little picnic and primitive camping area similar to those above.

There is a group camp, **Camp Paquette,** limited to qualified organizations by reservation.

Bone Creek Recreation Area, north of Holt, is being developed as a recreation area. A large day-use picnic area is under construction and a dam is planned to provide a lake for swimming. When completed, its facilities will be comparable to those at Krul, except there are no campsites at Bone Creek.

Conecuh National Forest has campgrounds about ten miles across the Alabama line via Fla. 189.

Besides the campgrounds listed above, Blackwater River State Forest has plenty of places to fish, several hunting seasons, hiking trails, nature trails, picnic areas, swimming, canoe trails, horseback trails, stables, and many miles of remote and beautiful forest in a very rural part of Florida.

For information, contact State Forest Headquarters, Route 1 Box 77, Milton, FL 32570. Telephone 904/957-4111.

 ### BLACKWATER RIVER State Park

Fifteen miles northeast of Milton, off US 90.

It is impossible to describe the beauty of the Blackwater River. When you get near it, you feel it. Like all truly natural areas, it seems to give off some subtle essence that vibrates and hums through the human body, like the ringing of a distant bell.

Located in a corner of the Blackwater River State Forest, this beautiful little park contains prime examples of the habitat of the larger forest region. The almost-black water of the river (caused by dissolved tannin from leaves) creates a strikingly vivid contrast with the snow-white sandbars at each bend. The uplands of the park consist primarily of high longleaf pineland, while dark, rich stands of "juniper"—Atlantic white cedar—line the riverbank, along with the lowland hardwoods and cypresses.

Old river bends now separated from the channel form oxbow lakes, levees, ponds, swamps and ridges. The diverse vegetation of this rolling, rich terrain accounts for the wealth of wildlife in and around the park.

Blackwater River State Park offers camping, picnicking, swimming (off a wide sandbar in the river), fishing, nature study and excellent canoeing.

Various campfire programs and guided walks are offered by the park rangers.

Address: Blackwater River State Park, Route 1 Box 47-C, Holt, FL 32564. Telephone 904/623-2363.

BUENA VISTA LANDING
(Corps of Engineers)

On Lake Seminole, off Fla. 271, 15 miles north of Sneads.

Five campsites with table and grill nestle among the trees, at a beautiful, wooded, marshy arm of the lake. There is a handpump for water, chemical toilets, and a boat ramp. It is a primitive camping site used mainly by fishermen. Free.

DEAD LAKES State Recreation Area

West of the Apalachicola River on Fla. 71, two miles north of Wewahitchka.

Dead Lakes is said to have formed naturally when rising levees on the Apalachicola River blocked the tributary Chipola River. These levees were later stabilized by a dam which maintains the flooded swamp, where the bleached skeletons of thousands of dead trees give the lake its name, and stand in the still water as striking monuments to the ways the big river has shaped this terrain for thousands of years.

Most people come here to fish in Dead Lakes. If you camp, you will find 30 nice sites among hills of longleaf pine and wiregrass, next to a swampy thicket. A couple of manmade lakes still remain from earlier times when they were used as a fish hatchery.

A nature trail takes you around the little lakes through a bird-rich marshy area. Another curves through the longleaf pines along the edge of a swamp. Titi and other water-loving species have grown up along the border of the lake at the boat ramp.

Address: Dead Lakes State Recreation Area, P.O. Box 989, Wewahitchka, FL 32465. Telephone 904/639-2702.

Dead Lakes—a flooded forest, where the trunks of dead trees stand like bleaching bones—is a famous fishing spot in northwest Florida.

EDEN STATE GARDENS

Off US 98, in Point Washington.

In a setting of stately moss-draped live oaks, this 1895 plantation home recalls a prosperous period before the virgin forests of longleaf pine and cypress were exhausted in this part of the state. A close copy of an older plantation home in Mississippi, Eden houses antiques authentic to its period and conveys a poise and charm all its own.

The house is open daily from 9 to 5 during the summer season (May 1 through September 15). The rest of the year, it is closed on Wednesday and Thursday. Tours are offered every thirty minutes. A small fee is charged.

Address: Eden State Gardens, P.O. Box 26, Point Washington, FL 32454. Telephone 904/231-4214.

FALLING WATERS State Recreation Area

Three miles south of Chipley. Take Fla. 77 south to the turnoff going east on Fla. 77-A.

This little 155-acre park contains one of Florida's most appealing natural features: the state's only waterfall. And it is an unusual waterfall. Instead of starting high on a hill and dropping to ground level, this waterfall starts at

At Falling Waters State Recreation Area, Florida's only large waterfall starts at ground level and drops almost a hundred feet down a cool, fern-lined sinkhole.

71

ground level and plunges straight down a shaft in the rock for 100 feet, where it disappears into underground cavities. It is a remarkable and beautiful little place: a lush, moist, shady, fern-lined oasis in the stately, dry rolling longleaf pinehills. Here, you catch a glimpse of the mysteries that lie underground and shape the state.

Near the entrance station, there are 24 campsites in a forest of planted slash pine, next to shady hardwoods. The sites have water and electrical hookups.

A nature trail takes you through the first (unsuccessful) oil well in the state, along an area farmed by the Coosa Indians in 1776, near where a spear point was found that dated back to 7500 years ago, when mammoths still roamed the Florida swamps.

A small manmade lake provides a place for unsupervised swimming, and there is an excellent picnic area near the falls.

Address: Falling Waters State Recreation Area, Route 5 Box 660, Chipley, FL 32438. Telephone 904/638-4030.

FLORIDA CAVERNS State Park

Three miles north of Marianna, on Fla. 167.

This 1800-acre park has several outstanding features: a wonderful magnolia-beech forest, a fine example of a north Florida floodplain swamp, a river that disappears and reappears to create a natural bridge, and the mysterious beauty of the caverns.

First mentioned by the Spanish in 1693, the caverns were known to the Indians for centuries before, and have been the home or refuge for cave creatures for millennia. It is a place to ponder human time and geological time. Some sixty million years ago, this area was under a warm shallow sea. Slowly, slowly, over eons, billions upon billions of sea-creatures died, settled, and left their shells—from oyster shells you can still see embedded in the rock to untold numbers of microscopic organisms whose tiny shells fused to make the limestone rock itself that all of Florida rests upon. In many parts of America you can see volcanic rock jutting out of hillsides. Florida is organic. Its rock was created by creatures of ancient seas.

Large sections of the state have underground cavities, formed by water seeping from the surface. Most of these cavities are filled with water and some are the channels for underground rivers emerging as springs. Only in a few high areas of the state can you find dry caverns, and only dry caverns develop the intricate and beautiful formations that fascinate us underground.

As you take the cave tour with a ranger, you will see the kind of formations caves are famous for: hanging stalactites, rising stalagmites, columns, pillars, little hollow soda-straws, terraced rimstone pools full of clear cool water, smooth sheets of flowstone, and translucent, membranous draperies like the earth's dewlap. There are wonderful configurations with a cloud-like capacity to evoke images: pipe organs, wedding cakes, animals, curtains, proscenium stages, rice paddies, pin cushions, catacombs, balconies—all emblems of the way we continuously sift and project our images onto the mysteries of nature, to try to find some human resemblance to a geological process so vast and awesome that we are lost in a second of its enormous day.

And these processes are vast: it takes about a hundred years for one cubic inch of calcite to deposit, drip by drip, in a growing stalagmite. What you see is the work of eons, decorated by the transient art of millennia.

Yet it is a friendly, cozy place, shaped for human ease by the many hands of the Civilian Conservation Corps members who lived here during the Depression and dug out passageways for us to walk through today.

These wonderful little caves contain a number of creatures. Various bats live here, including the endangered Gray Bat and the common pipistrelle that you might see flickering around a streetlight at dusk. Like spiders, bats are commonly disliked creatures that are in fact a source of endless wonder for anyone who takes a little time to study them. They are also among our most valuable and least appreciated helpers in controlling insect pests.

In some of the remoter, more protected caves, there are extremely rare specimens of creatures that live only in caves, and have so thoroughly adapted

Florida Caverns State Park. The ground under most of Florida is hollow, swiss-cheesy, and filled with water. These lovely, small, dry caverns show all the fascinating features of limestone caves.

to total darkness that they are eyeless and ghostly white. These are the little cave crayfish with its long graceful antennas, and the startlingly eyeless cave salamander, almost skinlessly sensitive to its lightless environment.

The visitor center and guiding rangers will give you an excellent introduction to the ecology of caves and the surrounding woodlands. When I was last there, they presented one of naturalist Joe Kenner's superb slide shows introducing the park.

Around the caves, you find two outstanding north Florida habitats. Nature trails near the visitor center take you through the hilly terrain of a beautiful magnolia-beech forest of large, tall hardwoods, colorful leaf-fall, mossy trunks and limestone outcroppings. This is the southernmost range of the forest of the Appalachian foothills, and is not found in central or south Florida.

Another nature trail takes you alongside a floodplain swamp where you can see the rich, productive, and immensely important forest that grows along north Florida rivers. Here the trees are specially adapted to alternating periods of flooding and drought. It is striking to look down from the magnolia-beech forest, with its rich grassy floor of low herbs and shrubs, to the floodplain forest, where standing water stops all low growth except occasional small trees, and where, when it dries out, you can walk freely in any direction without hitting brambles or bushes.

Florida Caverns State Park also contains one of the rare "natural bridges" created by Florida's underground geology: the Chipola River vanishes underground, then reappears a few hundred yards downstream, after traveling through underground cavities like the ones you see in the caverns. Such natural bridges have been used by humans and animals for ages, and General Andrew Jackson crossed here with his troops in 1818.

The park has an excellent 43-unit campground located in overgrown pine woods, a developed swimming area at a spring called Blue Hole, several fine picnic areas, a visitor center with exhibits, tours of the caves, guided spelunking crawls through remoter caves, a boat ramp, lovely places to canoe, and fishing in the Chipola River.

This is a popular park, and the campgrounds are filled regularly in the summer. Camping fee: average. A fee is charged for the cavern tour. Reservations are accepted year-round.

Address: Florida Caverns State Park, Marianna, FL 32446. Telephone 904/ 482-3632.

GRAYTON BEACH State Recreation Area

About halfway between Ft. Walton Beach and Panama City, off US 98 on Fla. 30A.

If you leave the mile-long, wide, white sandy beach and climb the boardwalk across the high dunes, you can follow a trail into a little hobbit-hole made by gnarled coastal oaks and magnolias, a cool, shady tunnel behind the sunswept dunes. Beyond that, you can skirt the impenetrable scrub of the back-dunes, whose lichen-clad branches are rounded and sculpted by the stiff salt breeze. As you emerge onto hilltops, you alternately gain vistas onto the marshes around Western Lake and the wide Gulf to the south.

This trail is a good place to see how the wind-driven dunes are held securely in place by the roots of sea-oats and by large slash-pines and magnolias that have been almost totally buried—with only a fringe of leaves topping the sand. An extension of the trail descends to a swampy bayhead, and gives you an unusually good look at the natural habitat that lies behind and supports the open expanse of one of north Florida's finest beaches.

Near the entrance station, thirty-seven campsites with water and electricity are cut into the low scrub, with a few scattered pines overhead. (Average fees.)

During the summer you can buy the usual snacks and supplies at the concession building. Fishing is good in the surf and in Western Lake.
Address: Grayton Beach State Recreation Area, P.O. Box 25, Santa Rosa Beach, FL 32458. Telephone 904/231-4210.

GULF ISLANDS National Seashore
(Formerly Ft. Pickens State Park)

Offshore from Pensacola. Accessible by toll bridge from Pensacola Beach. Perdido Key and Johnson Beach, west of Pensacola Bay, are reached by Fla. 292.

This growing coastal park consists of several separate areas: Fort Pickens, Perdido Key, the Naval Live Oaks, the Santa Rosa Beach area, and other scattered sites.

(1) The main visitor area near **Fort Pickens** occupies the western end of Santa Rosa Island, a very long barrier island with a high foredune on the ocean side, capped with sea-oats and coastal grasses, and filled by an inland dune-field of rolling sands. It is a characteristic Florida barrier island, with stands of pine flatwoods in the protected places and a salt marsh on the bay side.

The long, wide beach is a popular place in the summertime. Many scuba divers use the offshore waters (strict safety rules are enforced by rangers). The dunes and inland forest offer the quiet of nature study and spaces for contemplation. Nature trails traverse the dunes and go into the rich estaurine marshes on the bay. Several places provide excellent salt-water fishing.

At Fort Pickens—an outstandingly preserved nineteenth century brick fort—the National Park Service offers a strong interpretive program that includes self-guiding tours, ranger-guided tours, a museum, campfire programs, brochures and living history enactments on summer Sundays. In the Sunday programs, rangers dressed as Civil War soldiers re-create daily life at the fort in the 1860's, demonstrating their equipment and firing their antique rifles.

In some of the coastal batteries, a few large mounted guns may be

Gulf Islands National Seashore not only has some of the finest beach in northwest Florida, but also preserves the remains of Fort Pickens.

inspected at close range, and in Fort Pickens there are mazes of chambers to explore (carefully).

Next to the museum, the "Sandbox" gives an ongoing series of environmental programs for children.

The park has biking and jogging trails along the bed of an old narrow-gauge railway.

A modern 165-unit campground is located near the fort in a partially shaded slash pine forest near the northern side of the island. Many sites have water and electric hookups. Average fees are charged. Pets can be kept in one area only.

The campgrounds usually fill up during the busy summer months and on all holiday weekends. Reservations are not taken. If you want to camp in the busy season, you need to arrive by 7:30 AM, get on the waiting list, and see if there is an opening for the day. During the busy season (March 15-Labor Day) camping is limited to 14 days. You can stay up to 30 days the rest of the year.

A concession store near the campgrounds offers more than the usual snacks, operates a laundramat, and rents bicycles. It has an overlook on top, where you may sit at tables and see out over the island.

Pets are strictly prohibited from the beach, for sanitary and health reasons—including the fact that roundworms, transmitted through pet feces, can infest humans.

(2) The **Perdido Key** section, a little west of Fort Pickens, but a 45-minute drive away, consists of popular *Johnson Beach* and a primitive area on the eastern end of the island. This seven-mile-long roadless area is accessible only by foot or boat. You can reach it from the Johnson Beach parking lot. Primitive camping is permitted once you are out of sight of the parking lot, but you will have to carry all your facilities with you. There is nothing on Perdido Key except sand, sea-oats, some marshy spits, and the husky breathing of the sea. You will have the unique experience of being in a wilderness area within plain view of the entire city of Pensacola across the bay.

During hurricane Frederick in September 1979, the island was battered by the full fury of the storm, flooded by six feet of water, and sheared of its seven-mile long, fifteen-foot high foredune. It looked as if it had been smoothed by a trowel. In taking the full impact of the storm, the barrier island acted as an effective barrier: it protected heavily populated developments on the bay from even more serious damage. Without Perdido Key, it is likely that the subdivisions along Big Lagoon would have been devastated.

(3) The **Naval Live Oaks** section of the park contains some large

This campsite at Gulf Islands National Seashore is typical of most beach campsites in northwest Florida—sandy, with partial shade from pines and little oaks.

77

moss-draped live-oaks in a site once planted with oaks to supply timbers for sailing ships. This section has a fine hiking trail and a large area of native sand pines. It is located on US 98 just east of Gulf Breeze.

(4) The park has recently acquired a large stretch of beach on Santa Rosa Island west of Navarre. Inquire about facilities.

(5) The National Seashore also administers some small historic forts on Pensacola Bay.

Address: Gulf Island National Seashore, P.O. Box 100, Gulf Breeze, FL 32561. Telephone 904/932-5302.

JIM WOODRUFF DAM
East Bank Public Use Area (Corps of Engineers)

On Lake Seminole, three miles north of Chattahoochee. Turn north in Chattahoochee at traffic light with the Coast Guard sign.

While this site is actually located in Georgia, it is so close I am including it here. Thirty sites sit close to the water—some directly on the big lake, others in that wonderful mixed hardwood forest that covers the banks of the Apalachicola River. There are hot showers and wash basins for clothes, a boat ramp, dump station and security gate. There are no electric or sewer hookups, and not all sites have water hookups in them. Campfires are allowed.

This site is within walking distance—about a mile—of Chattahoochee. A nature trail is being cut and interpretive activities have been planned.

There is access by water to the campsites.

Fee: Average fee during the summer (roughly Memorial Day to Labor Day). Half-price then to Golden Age Passport holders, and free to everyone the rest of the year.

JOHN GORRIE State Museum

In Apalachicola.

Like Cedar Key, Apalachicola is one of those deeply charming little fishing villages that outlived a former age of booming prosperity. Once a major Gulf port, Apalachicola first lost the cotton trade to the railroads, then underwent a second boom that died with the exhaustion of the pinewoods. Now it has settled onto the more stable base of its seafood. It is one of the finest places for oysters, shrimp, saltwater fish and blue crab—although even that resource is being threatened by proposed alterations of the river upstream.

The town has many late nineteenth century buildings and an ambience that has drawn people and held them since this was a remote and marshy wilderness.

The history of the town and exhibits on the river may be found in the John Gorrie State Museum, just off US 98. Gorrie has been immortalized as the inventor of the ice-making compressor, the essential elements in modern air conditioning units. The museum charges a small fee.

Address: John Gorrie State Museum, Apalachicola, FL 32320. Telephone 904/653-9347.

LAKE JACKSON MOUNDS State Archaeological Site

A few miles north of Tallahassee, off US 27, at the end of Crowder Road.

This site contains two of the principal mounds of a large Indian ceremonial center of the Fort Walton period. It is now a place of quiet retreat among lovely trees and a grassy picnic area. From the top of the large mound, you can look out on Lake Jackson, which is especially beautiful in the early morning.

The original Indian site contained six mounds. Only two of these are on the state site. Two others have been destroyed for fill dirt. As one was being bulldozed, archaeologists who were allowed to excavate made some of the most important discoveries about Florida prehistory. The rest—like a lot of Florida history—disappeared into pavement.

Perhaps history should be considered an endangered species.

The mounds are open daily from 8 AM till sunset. Free.

Address: 1313 Crowder Road, Tallahassee, FL 32303. Telephone 904/385-7071.

MACLAY STATE GARDENS
(Formerly Killearn Gardens)

In Tallahassee on US 319, just north of I-10.

This is one of the finest ornamental gardens in the southeast. Extensive plantings of showy exotic plants rest in a setting of native pines and oaks. Many native trees and shrubs have been planted as ornamentals. The US champion flowering dogwood shows off here each spring, along with thousands of azaleas and camellias and hundreds of types of ornamentals.

Over half the azaleas and camellias in the gardens are no longer commercially available, so the stock here provides an invaluable gene-pool for the creation of new varieties and the maintenance of older, hardy species.

The gardens are best seen in early spring, which some years can start in late January. A separate admission fee is charged for the gardens, which includes admission to Maclay House, with its family history and lovely antiques.

All year you can go to Lake Hall for swimming, fishing, canoeing, sailing on small boats and picnicking. (Only electric motors permitted on boats.) Some particularly impressive pines dominate the picnic area on the lake.

The nature trail from the swimming area gives you a fine opportunity to visit the kind of mixed hardwood and pine forest that grows on the red clay hills of north Florida.

Until recently, Maclay Gardens lay alone in a rural area surrounded by undisturbed forest. As Tallahassee expands, housing developments are pressing up to the park boundaries. Soon, when you look up from the azaleas, you will

Early each spring, the camelias, azaleas, dogwoods, redbuds, and dozens of other showy flowers burst into bloom at Maclay State Gardens near Tallahassee.

not see dense native forests, but houses, yards and cars. This is a sad example of the way a park seems to shrink when it becomes surrounded by development.

     Open daily, 8 AM to sunset. There is a small entrance fee. No camping.

     On summer weekends the swimming area is sometimes full by noon. *Address: Alfred B. Maclay State Gardens, 3540 Thomasville Road, Tallahassee, FL 32303. Telephone 904/385-4232.*

NATURAL BRIDGE BATTLEFIELD State Historic Site

Six miles east of Woodville, off US 319.

     Near the end of the Civil War, a battle fought here between invading Union troops and a motley collection of old men, young boys, and wounded Confederate soldiers saved Tallahassee, and kept it the only Confederate capital east of the Mississippi uncaptured.

     The setting for the battle is one of those remarkable features of the Florida landscape that has played a role in human affairs since time was first reckoned here: a natural bridge, where the St. Marks River disappears underground, then reappears some yards downstream. Sinkholes in the nearby woods give further evidence of the unusual (but typically Floridian) geography.

Today, the scene of the battle is a few acres of exceptional woods along the cool, dark waters of the river, with remnant earthworks, a few markers, and a monument.

In recent years, the battle has been re-enacted by armies of volunteers dressed in Union and Confederate uniforms, usually on the first Sunday in March.

The area is unstaffed, and admission is free. No camping.

For further information, write the Department of Natural Resources, Commonwealth Building, Tallahassee, FL 32303.

NEAL'S LANDING
(Corps of Engineers)

On Lake Seminole where Fla. 2 crosses the Chattahoochee River, on the west bank.

This is a more developed area than nearby Buena Vista. Twelve sites are widely spaced in a shady planted pine woods with a grassy floor—and the area can handle at least twice that many. There are no hookups, but there is a dump station. The campground has central water faucets and chemical toilets, but nearby at the boat-launch and picnic area, you will find a modern restroom with flush toilets, electricity, and hot showers. No reservations.

The landing is located on lovely bluffs on an open area overlooking the river. An average fee is charged from about Memorial Day to Labor Day. Half price then to holders of Golden Age Passport, and free to everyone the rest of the year.

NEWPORT TOWER Camp Site
(Div. of Forestry)

On US 98 at the St. Marks River, south of Tallahassee.

Twenty developed sites, a boat launch, and picnic tables sit on a couple of acres next to the wonderful St. Marks River. Since this campground is located at the entrance of the St. Marks Wildlife Refuge and near the Aucilla Wildlife Management Area, it is packed to overflowing during hunting season (usually November through January). An average fee is charged. No reservations are taken. Basic supplies and good seafood may be purchased in nearby towns.

OCHLOCKONEE RIVER State Park

South of Sopchoppy, off US 319.

On the scenic drive and along the nature trail, you will pass through some of the most beautiful pine flatwoods you can ever hope to see. These lovely, open woods are kept in a natural state by periodic controlled burning, which duplicates the effect of natural fires. As a result of the burning, the woods are open and grassy, with thousands of beautiful wildflowers in the warm months and scenic sprays of dried weeds in the winter. Other communities interspersed in the pinewoods—little grassy ponds, dense swampy bayheads and live oak thickets—provide the diversity needed to support the park's wildlife. Many birds can be seen here, including the endangered red-cockaded woodpecker, which can only nest in old, tall pines that suffer from heart-rot. Deer, fox, squirrel, bobcat, gray fox, a wealth of insects, and all the small crawling life of the forest may be observed by the patient visitor.

A small campground of 30 sites is nestled amid beautiful little oaks near the river. Many of the sites have water and electricity. Reservations are advised during the busy summer months, though the cool fall and mild winter are by far the finest seasons here.

There is a picnic area, boat ramp, and nature trail along the pristine Ochlockonee River (pronounced o'CLOCK-nee), which flows into the Gulf of Mexico some five miles downstream. Both fresh and saltwater fish are caught near the park.

Quiet, unspectacular, pristine: this park is a superb sample of the beauty of unspoiled north Florida woods and streams.

Address: Ochlockonee River State Park, P.O. Box 5, Sopchoppy, FL 32358. Telephone 904/962-2771.

PINE LOG State Forest Campground
(Div. of Forestry)

One-half mile south of Ebro, on the west side of Fla. 79.

A small campground in an unusual area, with two ecologically contrasting lakes. An open "sandhill" lake provides a good place to swim (no lifeguards) and camp. Nearby, there is an older cypress-lined lake topped with lily-pads that offers a good place to canoe or fish.

The unattended campground is free at present, but it may be upgraded to a fee-area in the future. There are 20 sites and a picnic pavilion. Water and electricity are available in a central location.

A three-mile loop nature trail takes you through the surrounding forest. *Address: District Forester, 715 W. 15th Street, Panama City, FL 32401. Telephone 904/763-6589.*

PONCE DE LEON SPRINGS State Recreation Area

Off US 90, just east of Ponce de Leon.

A lovely little spring has been developed into a pleasant day-use area. A nature trail takes you through fine mixed hardwoods and floodplain swamp. Along the Sandy Creek trail, you can see a stand of very tall and conspicuous spruce pines, with their dark, oak-like bark. On a recent walk, I surprised a pair of wood ducks, who leapt up in an explosion of brilliantly colored flight.

Picnicking, swimming, fishing, and nature study. No camping.
Address: P.O. Box 126, Ponce de Leon, FL 32455. Telephone 904/836-4281.

RIVER JUNCTION
(Corps of Engineers)

Just over the line into Georgia, along Lake Seminole, above Chattahoochee.

Ten shady sites with water access, hot showers, but no water, electric or sewer hookups. Not locked at night. Boat ramp.

Fee: Average; same schedule as Jim Woodruff Dam area.

ROCKY BAYOU (Fred Gannon) State Recreation Area

Three miles east of Niceville, north of Fla. 20.

In Rocky Bayou you can see some of the finest sand pine scrub in north Florida. An excellent nature trail winds along the sloping border of Puddin Head Lake, where mature sand pines rise above the low scrubby oaks, lichens and rolling sandy hills. Pick up one of the excellent trail guides at the trail head.

The fifty campsites are located among sand pine, oaks and magnolias that

Camping at Rocky Bayou State Recreation Area.

grow along the scenic Bayou, which is a sizeable arm of the immense Choctawatchee Bay. Some campsites are open to the water, and have a fine view.

You can launch a boat here for saltwater fishing in the bay or freshwater fishing in nearby Rocky Creek. There is a swimming area with a thin sandy beach, and a lovely picnic area sits among red cedars and magnolias on a bluff overlooking the water.

You will find plenty of space here for quiet walks (there are two other nature trails), fishing, boating, and afternoons along the peaceable expanse of waters.

Address: Rocky Bayou State Recreation Area, P.O. Box 597, Niceville, FL 32578. Telephone 904/897-3222.

ST. ANDREWS State Recreation Area

In Panama City, 3 miles east of Panama City Beach. Turn South off 98 onto Fla. 392 two lights west of the bay bridge. Watch for signs to Treasure Island Marina; the park signs are hard to see.

St. Andrews is one of Florida's most heavily-used parks. Its 1000 acres contain over two miles of exceptionally beautiful beach on the Gulf of Mexico, in addition to water frontage on the bay. Inland you will find the high rolling dunes typical of a barrier island, giving way to low marshes, ponds, damp pine flatwoods, and higher sandy hills of sand pine scrub. Though this area has long been used, timbered and turpentined, it remains in unusually fine and natural condition, and provides a healthful contrast to the cluttered, high-density commercial beaches of Panama City. Only in sizeable parks can you still find the natural setting which gives depth and meaning to these beautiful strips of beach.

There are 184 campsites spread over two areas near the Grand Lagoon,

St. Andrews State Recreation Area is one of the most popular parks in the state. Its long, curving, white sand beach is typical of the beaches in northwest Florida.

with some facing the water. Located in pine flatwoods, most of the low-numbered sites are relatively open and exposed to one another. Sites 77 and above offer greater privacy.

Besides ample facilities for camping and enjoying the beach, an excellent nature trail winds through seasonally-flooded pine flatwoods, along a shallow lily-dotted pond, through sand pine scrub. Another trail passes through marsh as well, where birds are plentiful in winter months.

A fishing pier juts out into Grand Lagoon, on the north side of the park, with a boat launch next to it. Two other fishing piers and a rock jetty provide excellent saltwater fishing all year. Boats can be rented during the summer, and a small store sells the usual limited supplies.

The park service has reconstructed an old turpentine still in the pines near the fishing pier. This two-story structure houses a very impressive replica of the kind of equipment once found throughout the pine woods of Florida. If you take a few minutes to stand in the shade and read the signs, you can imagine the intense activity of this industry, that, until recently, commonly thrived from converting pine-sap into turpentine and resins known as "naval stores." This kind of small-time local industry has been increasingly displaced, in recent decades, by centralized, petroleum-based industry.

Along one shoreline of the park, you can see stumps of a 1000-year-old forest, and offshore in the ship channel divers recently located stumps of a slash pine forest dating back 40,000 years—now submerged by the rise in sea-level. It is worth taking a moment to stand on the beach, look out over the Gulf, and try to imagine how the sea and shore have oscillated into one another over the centuries. Only 12,000 years ago ice covered much of North America, and human beings had not yet invented the alphabet. There are individual trees almost as old as recorded history. We are newcomers on the earth. Messy ones, at that.

Increasingly, it is parks alone that preserve some remnant of the nature and history that made us. They offer us a place to pause and realign with the roots of our own flowering in the sun.

Address: St. Andrews State Recreation Area, 4415 Thomas Drive, Panama City FL 32407. Telephone 904/234-2522. Reservations accepted year-round. Summer is the busiest season.

ST. GEORGE ISLAND State Park

By toll bridge from Eastpoint, east of Apalachicola.

As you cross the bridge, you may see oystermen out in numerous two-man boats, lifting the oysters off the shallow bottoms with long "tongs." Pause a moment to realize that you are speeding across some of the richest, most productive waters on the face of the earth. If the Apalachicola River is left in its natural state upstream, this bay will continue to pour forth its harvest year after year, with no effort on our part.

Long, curving slender St. George graphically shows the fragility of the barrier island habitat. In places dunes have blown away or washed out. Some dunes have migrated across the island and run against tall pines, almost burying them as they stop the sand. On the way to the park, you pass houses built on stilts, a reminder that the tidal surge of a large hurricane would probably wash right across the island, sweeping many of the structures with it. This is the common fate of most of Florida's developed barrier islands. Their dynamic, changing, wind-blown, wave-worn, storm-tossed shores have little patience for the walls and foundations we place there. Yet, as natural systems, these frail islands endure and endure, held together by the roots of plants no bigger around than a pencil, flexing where they are hit, and continuously shifting in response to the blows of the sea.

The 1900-acre park is open for swimming and fishing along its nine miles of undeveloped beaches and dunes. There are boardwalks, overlooks, picnic tables and a series of nature trails. A three-mile hiking trail has been opened to a primitive campsite on the tip of the island, on the bay side among the pine flatwoods and oak-magnolia coastal hammock. Family campsites have been planned, but won't be built for a few years.

Like all Gulf coast parks, St. George Island is a wonderful place of shifting light and shadow, thin, graceful windblown grasses, the gnarled hair of tough scrub, struggling pines, the whale-like humps of sleeping dunes, and the unfathomable mystery that takes place at the edge of the sea. In hot weather, it is also home to hoards of sand-flies and dog flies, who busily take their ounce of blood.

St. George Island is even more fragile than most of the barrier island parks, so please take care that your visit causes no additional stress on a natural system already living at its limit.

Address: Dr. Julian G. Bruce St. George Island State Park, P.O. Box 62, East Point, FL 32328. Telephone 904/670-2111.

ST. JOSEPH PENINSULA State Park
(T.H. Stone Memorial Park)

Near Port St. Joe, off US 98 on Fla. 30.

Climb the boardwalk to the overlook and you will stand on a sudden scarp of dunes that rises in a long bluff over miles of clear Gulf water and some of the finest beach in north Florida. Along the beach you may see some of the many shorebirds that live or stop here. In spring or autumn, you may see why this park is known as one of the best areas in the East to observe migrating hawks, and, if you are very fortunate, you may see one of the rare, regularly visiting peregrine falcons.

There are 115 campsites with water and electricity, divided into two locations. Campground one is located in a sparse pine flatwoods area bordering a small marsh. Most of the sites are open and sunny. Campground two is in a

Hikers in the wilderness section of St. Joseph State Park can get away from it all among the high dunes and white sands of the peninsula, but must carry their own water.

shady flatwoods where native undergrowth provides privacy. You can get to the beach easily from either campground.

On the bay side, there is a boat ramp and marina that sells supplies during the summer (only). Nearby waters are well-loved for deep-sea fishing, surf-fishing, floundering, scalloping, shelling, crabbing, and scuba diving. The fish, of course, have a mind of their own, and bite when they are good and ready.

More adventurous visitors can hike into a 1650-acre wilderness preserve on the north half of the peninsula and set up camp near the tallest dunes on this coast.

The number of hikers is limited to protect the preserve, so you must make reservations in advance. There is no drinking water in the preserve.

Two nature trails take you through territory typical of a Gulf coast barrier island. One passes through sand pine scrub, salt marsh and bayside shoreline. The other gives you a good experience of the dunes, scrub, flatwoods, and hammock.

You probably won't notice it all summer, but when the wind is northerly (as it frequently is in winter) the acrid smell of the papermill blows across the bay into the park. Fall and winter here offer cold winds and a rare solitude.

As in all Florida coastal parks, you should be prepared for mosquitoes and biting flies, mainly in shady places during hot weather. But also be prepared for the experience of an unspoiled Florida beach.

There are a number of curious, pushy, hungry and utterly fearless skunks in this park. You will see them scavenging campsites around dusk. Give them a wide berth.

Address: T.H. Stone Memorial St. Joseph Peninsula State Park, P.O. Box 909, Port St. Joe, FL 32456. Telephone 904/227-1327. Reservations accepted during the summer season only.

 ## SAN MARCOS DE APALACHE State Historic Site

Off Fla. 363 near St. Marks.

An amazing amount of early Florida history intersected at this sleepy little junction of the St. Marks and Wakulla Rivers. The museum has interesting exhibits that tell of the jockeying among the Spanish, Indians, English, Americans, pirates, and even a self-proclaimed King for possession of this once-strategic marshland and its little fort. Small towns nearby offer superb seafood.

A nature trail and boardwalk take you beyond the museum to the fort site, and on to the point between the two rivers. Birding is excellent, and the view out onto the marshes of the St. Marks National Wildlife Refuge must be the same one homesick soldiers stared at over those centuries of hazardous duty here.

Open daily 9 AM to 5 PM. A small fee is charged.

Address: Box 27, St. Marks, FL 32355. Telephone 904/925-6216.

 ## ST. MARKS National Wildlife Refuge

South of Tallahassee off US 98. Entrance via Fla. 59, across the St. Marks River from Newport.

This large refuge provides an easily-accessible place for seeing birds and wildlife, especially in winter months. Little of its 64,000 acres can be visited by car, but a bumpy road goes through the middle of the refuge to an old lighthouse on the coast. Wide sweeping salt marshes, low tidal flats and creek estuaries, pine woods, hardwood swamps and oak-palm-cedar hammocks provide the space and variety that give habitat to numerous species of birds and wildlife. Like all refuges, this one is carefully managed to maintain habitat for wildlife, including regular controlled burning of the pinewoods and restoration of certain areas that were logged or farmed before acquisition. The refuge has several hunting seasons in wintertime.

Alligators are common here and may be seen most easily in the late spring and early fall. Birds are numerous any time, especially early and late in the day. In the wintertime, large numbers of migrating waterfowl stop here and can be seen easily from the road.

The refuge has an observation tower near the lighthouse, interpretive displays, boat ramps on the bay, and a self-guiding nature trail (with booklet). There are presently three foot-trails for observing wildlife, and additional interpretive facilities have been planned. Visitors interested in longer hikes can stop at the office (west of Newport on 98) for a map of the fire-lanes. A segment of the Florida Trail is being developed through the refuge which will give access to some of the remotest sections.

You will find restrooms and drinking water along the road at a nice picnic area. A new visitor center is under construction.

Note: Very buggy in warm weather, like all coastal marshes.

The coastal woods along the drive contain many examples of the Florida state tree, the cabbage palm, in its natural setting.

Address: St. Marks National Wildlife Refuge, Box 68, St. Marks, FL 32355. Phone 904/925-6121.

ST. VINCENT National Wildlife Refuge

Near Apalachicola. Access by boat only.

Like other National Wildlife Refuges, St. Vincent is open only for day-use—except during the brief annual primitive-weapons hunts. This 12,000-acre barrier island remains remarkably preserved in its native state, except for roads and a small herd of enormous Sambur deer, imported from Asia early in the century.

Native wildlife thrives here: Deer, turkey, nesting loggerhead turtles and a profusion of birds makes this a rich area. Many species of shorebirds, water birds, wading birds, ducks, gulls, terns and pelicans live here or visit. Bald eagles and golden eagles regularly appear in season, porpoises can be seen playing offshore, and rare peregrine falcons pass overhead during their migrations. As in other National Wildlife Refuges, the managers here are working to maintain a natural habitat and manage it for the benefit of species that are disappearing in other parts of the country.

A chain of ponds in the interior of the island hosts a number of alligators, and freshwater fishing is permitted from March 1 through October 31. Saltwater fishing is permitted all year. The sparse funds allocated to the refuge are almost all used for wildlife management and maintenance of equipment. But when time and money permit, the refuge staff gives a first-rate tour to organized groups with a special interest in nature.

More than in most parks, you are on your own here. St. Vincent Island has 14 miles of white sandy beaches along the south and east shores, which make a rare, deserted place to walk, swim, fish, collect shells, watch birds, or listen to the suggestions of the sea. The interior of the island is a wild place of dense palmettos, scrub oaks lining old sand dunes, hammocks of cabbage palm and magnolia, forests of moss-draped live-oaks, willow-thickets, cattail ponds, and slash-pine flatwoods growing in damp swales.

St. Vincent National Wildlife Refuge is famous for its rugged interior, wildlife, great natural beauty—and for its snakes, mosquitoes, and ticks.

Miles and miles of primitive roads crisscross the island for the more adventurous hiker. An excellent nature trail starts at the eastern end of the island and runs about two miles through a variety of habitats. But note this: drinking water and restrooms are not available on the island. There are no visitor facilities. St. Vincent is locally famous for its ticks, chiggars, biting flies and poisonous snakes (which are protected). By advised, be prepared, be safe.

You have to arrange transportation by boat—either from Apalachicola over nine miles of water, or across narrow Indian Pass from the end of Fla. 30-B.

A little out of the way, with few conveniences, St. Vincent National Wildlife Refuge is a place of wild beauty that offers the rare solitude and depth of a Florida wilderness island and gives habitat to some of the vanishing creatures that grew up on this earth with us.

Address: P.O. Box 447, Apalachicola, FL 32320. Telephone 904/653-8808.

THREE RIVERS State Recreation Area
(Formerly Jim Woodruff State Park)

Off Fla. 271, one mile north of Sneads.

This park offers access to a large lake and marvelous north Florida woods. Its 800 acres extend for four miles along the shore of Lake Seminole, created by a dam in 1956. The tops of dead trees sticking out across the wide lake hint of the vast floodplain swamp that once occupied this lowland. Now it is a popular lake for fishing and water sports.

Three Rivers State Recreation Area is an excellent place to see the southern mixed hardwood forest that so much resembles the woods of the Appalachian mountains. These woods, in a setting of rolling hills and steep ravines, are quite different from what you will find in south and central Florida parks.

Camping area No. 1, on the lake, holds 26 sites amid the shade of mixed pines and oaks. Some sites are directly on the water, and all have water and electricity.

Camping area No. 2, a short walk from the lake, is located in beautiful mixed hardwoods—large hickories, various oaks, flowering dogwoods, shortleaf pines—and contains sites 27-64. Some have electric hookups. Both campgrounds have modern restroom facilities.

A large picnic area on a grassy, shaded slope overlooks the lake. Swimming is permitted in the lake, but there are no lifeguards.

There are two fine nature trails here that give you a chance to hike over this unusual and unusually beautiful terrain—through a forest of tall mixed hardwoods, across ravines, along the lakefront. You pass among a very rich diversity of plant life in these hilly woods and may encounter some of the corresponding diversity of animal and insect life, including fox squirrel, deer, grey fox, raccoons, and large alligator snapping turtles that live in the lake.

A boat ramp is provided, and there is a fishing dock in the picnic area.

Three Rivers State Recreation Area is located in one of Florida's most rural counties—a place of winding roads, little towns, friendly people, farmlands, a recent pioneer past, and mysterious woods. A drive through some of the nearby back roads will take you through an authentic area of Florida, unperturbed by the frenzy of large-scale development or tourist boom.

Address: Three Rivers State Recreation Area, Route 1 Box 15A, Sneads, FL 32460. Telephone 904/593-6565.

TORREYA State Park

Between Bristol and Greensboro, on Fla. 271, off Fla. 12.

It is truly startling to hike the trail down these steep bluffs and slicing ravines and find what looks like a forest out of the Appalachian Mountains. It is even more surprising to learn that you are witnessing evidence of the last ice age. Naturalists say that about 12,000 years ago the advancing ice pushed northern trees and animals into the South, and when they followed the receding glaciers back north again, a few pockets remained in Florida—one preserved in this park.

Because of the unusual terrain and unique history, these bluffs contain a number of plants and animals that are found nowhere else in the world. Most famous are the Torreya tree and Florida yew. But there are other plants, animals, and insects that are rare or unknown elsewhere.

You don't have to be a scientist, though, to see that it is a beautiful place. There is magic enough in the bubble of numerous streams cutting through the hillsides over mossy rocks, near rare little needle-palms. In the floodplain forest near the river, columns of fullgrown trees tower majestically above the bare mud and leaf litter of the often-flooded floor. Water hickory, swamp-chestnut oak and American ash loom large above ironwood and winged elm.

In old channels abandoned by the changeable river, swamp forests of large bald-cypress thrive, accompanied by dark tupelo, Virginia willow, and the few other trees that can grow in standing water.

The uplands of the park spread out into pinewoods mixed with scrub oaks. In places, the abandoned fields of pioneer farms have grown up into a forest with tell-tale signs, such as the presence of loblolly pines. The highest bluffs are crowned with great magnolias, beech and hickories. In the late autumn, this is one of the most colorful forests in Florida.

In this unusual topography, plant communities shift dramatically with small changes in elevation. The trees on the bluffs differ from those on the slopes, and the flat floodplain hosts yet another community. The narrow ravines hold unique habitats, such as the last stands of the Torreya tree. Everywhere, you can see how each species is growing in a location specifically suited to it—at the elevation and in the moisture conditions that fit the needs of that species. Although very diverse, these forests are not random; the more you look into them, the more you glimpse basic principles of ecology at work. Nature has shaped these woods, with relatively little human interference; look into them and you learn about nature's methods. That is part of the irreplaceable value of a natural area—something no cultivated forest or landscaped park, however beautiful, can provide.

A plantation house dating from the 1840s sits on the high bluff overlooking the broad Apalachicola River. This is the Gregory House—originally built across the river, but saved and moved here in the 1930s. This beautiful structure has been restored close to its original design, and its antique furnishings help

The Gregory House at Torreya State Park: a restored antebellum mansion from the heyday of riverboat trade on the Apalachicola River.

you imagine the life of these sometimes prosperous, sometimes bankrupt (but necessarily hardy) settlers. Standing on the porch of the Gregory House, you can begin to imagine the more than two hundred steamboats that paddle-wheeled up and down this river in the late nineteenth century, ferrying cotton and supplies, transporting hopeful adventurers, trading with settlers, and making possible those rare but memorable balls that are still emulated here and there in the South.

Like all great rivers, the Apalachicola has borne the efforts of many ages. Indians, Spanish, British, French, Americans, Federals and Confederates ploughed it with their "immortal purposes." And it will no doubt bear patient witness to whatever follows us.

The 35 campsites sit in a loop amid shady hardwoods. The sites have water and electricity, and there is a dump station nearby. There are marvellous picnic places, some overlooking the river from a high bluff. The river, though, is too far downslope and too swift for safe swimming. A small store operates in the park, and other supplies are available in Bristol, 13 miles away.

Torreya State Park has an exceptional backwoods camping trail for those who want to hike a couple of miles to a primitive site on the lower bluffs near the

93

river. Nature trails, fire roads, and a segment of the Florida Trail lead through all the important plant communities and scenic features of the park.

I remind you not to collect any plants or animals, though it's fine to fish in the river. More than in most parks, the natural life in Torreya is fragile and unique.

Some of the most delicate, beautiful, and irreplaceable examples of natural Florida exist precariously in the "steephead" ravines found outside the park. But at this writing none are on protected land—which is a shame.

Address: Torreya State Park, Star Route, Bristol, FL 32321. Telephone 904/ 643-2674.

At Torreya State Park, high river bluffs and cool, isolated ravines contain a forest that looks like part of the Appalachian Mountains and is the protected home for a number of extremely rare animals and plants.

Updates to Northwest (NW) Section

Apalachicola National Forest. New addresses—Main Office: USDA Forest Service, 227 N. Bronough Street, Tallahassee, FL 32301. Phone 904/681-7265. Ranger for East section: Hwy 319: 2.3 miles north of Crawfordville. 904/926-3561. Ranger for West section: Hwy 20 in Bristol. 904/643-2282. Activities at Trout Pond (the recreation area for the handicapped) have diminished due to budget cuts; phone before going there. There are no hookups or hot showers at Wright Lake, but there are flush toilets. Magnolia Landing is now part of the New River/Mud Swamp Wilderness Area, closed to motor vehicles.

Apalachicola River Estuarine Sanctuary. Several agencies are managing large tracts of public land near the mouth of the river. Public use is minimal at present into this undeveloped natural area of estuary, floodplain, and forests, but there are opportunities for hiking, boating, nature study, and tours for organized groups. For information on access, call 904/653-8063.

Basin Bayou State Recreation Area has been *closed* (the Air Force took it back).

Big Lagoon State Recreation Area has developed to include a large, 104-site camping area, a pavilion that can be reserved by large groups, and a 500-seat amphitheater with a meeting room and full kitchen. There are three swimming areas, a dock, and a boat ramp onto both Big Lagoon and the Intracoastal Waterway. Three miles of boardwalks and trails lead to scenic areas of the park. Open year-round, 8 AM till sundown. 10 miles west of Pensacola. 12301 Gulf Beach Hwy., Pensacola, FL 32507. 904/492-1595.

Blackwater River State Forest. The Peadon Bridge site is closed now. Bone Creek Recreation Area is open for heavy day-use; no camping. Camp Paquette is open only to scouts and similar groups.

New Listing: **Cape St. George State Reserve** (Little St. George Island) is a beautiful, natural 10-mile barrier island next to St. George Island that you can reach only by boat. A (very) primitive camp site sits at each end of the island, and the middle contains an old lighthouse. For more information, call 904/670-2111.

New Listing: **Eglin Air Force Base**, east of Pensacola, has 16 primitive camping areas located on the bay, or along creeks, ponds, or rivers in natural areas on this former national forest. These sites have no facilities, not even drinking water. They are inexpensive, but you must get a permit that says exactly where you will be and when, and you have to pay in advance by cash or certified check. During the winter hunting season, many of the sites will be full of hunters. For the latest camping brochure, contact: Natural Resources Branch, 3200 SPTW/DEMN, Eglin Air Force Base, FL 32542-5000. Phone 904/882-4164.

Florida Caverns State Park has added 8 miles of horse trails and holding pens for camping near your horses.

Gulf Islands National Seashore. Fees now average. 14 day limit. More outlying areas have opened, including Santa Rosa beach, the Naval Live Oaks area, and the the Pensacola Forts area, where you can tour 2 old fortifications. New numbers—Information: 904/932-9994; campground: 904/932-5018.

New Listing: **Henderson Beach State Recreation Area** is now open 11 miles west of Grayton Beach. Another fine beach, though without Grayton's high dunes. No camping here.

Updates to Northwest Section (cont'd)

Hopkins Landing Campground. A quiet, isolated little Gadsden County campground and boat landing on the north shore of Lake Talquin. 60 sites on about 7 acres, with water and electricity. Fees below average. No reservations. On County Road 105, south of Fla. 267, about 20 miles west of Tallahassee. Rt. 3, Box 2606, Quincy, FL 32351. 904/875-4236 or 627-3498.

The campground at Lake Seminole's **Jim Woodruff Dam** (called "East Bank" on some signs) has grown to a fully-developed recreational area with 120 sites and now charges average fees. Phone for all Corps of Engineers sites on Lake Seminole: 912/662-2814

Lake Jackson Mounds. New phone: 904/562-0042.

New Listing: **Lake Stone Park** has opened 3.3 miles south of Century, off Fla. 4., in the extreme northwestern corner of the state (follow the signs from Century). This Escambia County park has about 75 sites for either tents or RVs, hot showers, a playground, boat ramps, a resident manager, and a gate that is locked at night. Fees are below average. For information, call 904/256-5555.

Lake Talquin (near Tallahassee). At the Lake Talquin State Recreation Area, the **River Bluff picnic area** is open for day-use, and can be reserved by large groups. Phone 904/575-4071. Leon County operates three small, free camping areas on the big lake. All are off Fla. 20 on the south side of the lake (look for the signs). **Williams Landing, Coe Landing** and **J. Lewis Hall Landing and Park** all have 10 to 20 campsites, boat ramps, picnic shelters, restrooms with cold showers, security lights, and fish cleaning stations. No electricity or dump stations. Hall Park also has a nice nature trail and boardwalk (handicapped accessible), but only allows tent camping: no RVs. All have a time limit of 10 consecutive days and 30 total days per year. As at most county camping areas, no alcoholic beverages are allowed here.

The **Museum of Florida History** in the Gray Building in Tallahassee grows more impressive each year.

The visitor center at **St. Marks National Wildlife Refuge** has excellent exhibits. The refuge has expanded its guided nature trails, the Florida Trail now extends across the refuge, and a new 16-mile bike trail connects to Tallahassee on a former railroad bed.

St. Joseph Peninsula State Park now has several family cabins available for rent.

Note: **Sunset Landing** on Lake Jackson is now closed to camping.

Torreya State Park. Remember: there is no store in this wonderful, remote park. Also, you must register as a camper before backpacking on the primitive trail.

New Listing: **Wakulla Springs**, one of Florida's greatest springs, has just become a state park. No camping, but there is an elegant old hotel and restaurant in this former resort. The spring water is deep, cold, and refreshing to swim in. The entertaining boat tours are a great way to see alligators, birds, and other wildlife, especially in the winter. 12.2 miles south of Tallahassee. Take 319 (Crawfordville Hwy.),follow signs. Entrance is on Fla. 267. 904/222-7279.

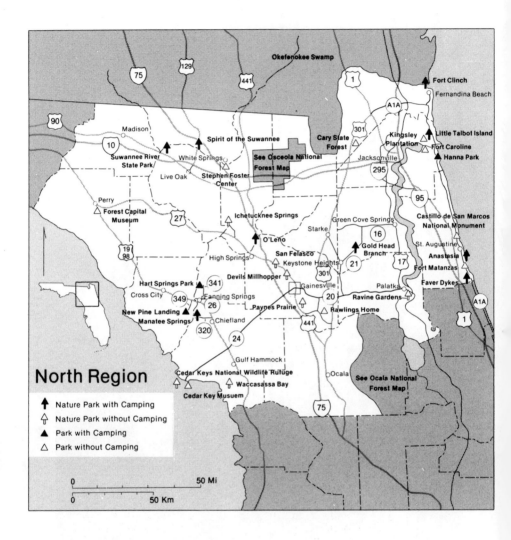

North Region

- ↑ Nature Park with Camping
- ⇧ Nature Park without Camping
- ▲ Park with Camping
- △ Park without Camping

0 ————— 50 Mi
0 ————— 50 Km

Okefenokee Swamp

Fort Clinch
Fernandina Beach

Madison

Spirit of the Suwannee

Cary State Forest

Kingsley Plantation
Little Talbot Island
Fort Caroline
Hanna Park

Suwannee River State Park
White Springs

See Osceola National Forest Map

Jacksonville

Live Oak
Stephen Foster Center

Perry
Forest Capital Museum

Ichetucknee Springs

Green Cove Springs

Castillo de San Marcos National Monument

O'Leno

Starke

St. Augustine

Gold Head Branch

Anastasia

High Springs
San Felasco
Keystone Heights

Fort Matanzas

Hart Springs Park
Cross City
New Pine Landing
Manatee Springs

Devils Millhopper

Faver Dykes

Fanning Springs
Chiefland

Gainesville

Palatka

Ravine Gardens

Paynes Prairie
Rawlings Home

Gulf Hammock

Cedar Keys National Wildlife Refuge
Waccasassa Bay
Cedar Key Musuem

Ocala

See Ocala National Forest Map

98

North

ANASTASIA State Recreation Area

On Florida A-1-A, at St. Augustine Beach.

Like all the State Recreation Areas, Anastasia offers a high-quality environment with easy access for outdoor recreation. In this case there are over two miles of beautiful beach—wide, white sandy stretches with blowing dunes and swaying sea-oats, wind-sculpted scrub, and the whole face of the Atlantic opening in the morning. There is also a large camping area—139 campsites (with water and electricity) in a beautiful coastal hammock, set among twisting live-oaks, red cedar, red bay, yaupon, beautyberry, and climbing carpets of wild grape. The sites are well separated by native vegetation, and the area offers you that rare chance to camp close to the heartbeat of a living forest.

Anastasia State Recreation Area, with its fine wide beach and rich coastal forest, is also the last known home of the endangered Anastasia Beach Mouse.

An excellent nature trail extends back into a fine region of coastal hammock. After climbing a relic sand dune, you pass through a prime section of Florida coastal woods—with several hundred species of plants flourishing around you, the whole place buzzing, crawling, singing, humming with life. You might see golden orb weavers spinning their great webs, or greenfly orchids in bloom.

Besides, camping, swimming, and activities on the beach, you can fish in the surf or the saltwater lagoon. (This lagoon contains one of the northernmost black mangrove swamps.) Shaded picnic tables nestle under windblown oaks. Birdlife is abundant, especially in the winter. Anastasia is one of the busiest parks in Florida. Reservations are a must.

There are a few problems visible at Anastasia that afflict other parks around the state. Although a bypass road was completed to replace it, a county road still slices through the park, permitting uncontrolled access day or night. As a result, vandalism along the road has been severe: outdoor showers ripped down, restrooms busted out with sledge hammers, trees cut down, dunes rutted and eroded. That road (like similar roads in parks around the state) needs to be closed in order to protect the public recreation facilities in the park.

Nearby development has begun to press flush against the park's fencelines. It would be terrible to see this park become another Birch Park—a last-overused green patch in a sea of concrete development. At this writing, the beach north of the park remains undeveloped, and would, in its natural state, be a thing well worth preserving.

Because of local tradition and politics, people are permitted to drive their vehicles on the beach inside the park. Much of the value of a wide, white, windblown stretch of ocean is lost when someone can drive a car (or even a semi cab) a few feet from where you are sunbathing. It's the only state park I've ever been in with a traffic jam on the beach.

Like other state parks, Anastasia offers interesting programs. Its most recent addition has been a campfire cooking class. When I was last there, the class featured Dutch oven techniques, clay-baked chicken, and biscuits cooked over an open fire—methods the superintendent learned when he took his doctorate at Hobo University during the Depression.

Address: Anastasia State Recreation Area, P.O. Box 167, St. Augustine, FL 32084. Telephone 904/829-2668.

CARY State Forest

Northeast of Jacksonville on US 301, halfway between Callahan and Baldwin.

This 3400-acre state forest is open to the general public for day-use only. There are no camping facilities. The nature-study trail takes you through a typical north Florida pine flatwoods along the transition zone with a swamp-lined pond. There is a first-rate guidebook for the trail, which is an excellent place to see native vegetation and experience the dramatic shift in natural habitat that is brought about in Florida by only a few inches change in elevation.

Turn at the "Division of Forestry" sign next to mailbox No. 60, and follow the dirt road east about half a mile to the parking lot and trailhead.

For information or to reserve the nature center for group use, contact *District Forester, Florida Division of Forestry, 8719 Beaver, Jacksonville, FL 32220. Telephone 904/781-1434.*

CEDAR KEYS National Wildlife Refuge

Offshore from Cedar Key a group of islands forms this refuge, which is classified as a Wilderness Study Area and allows only restricted access. Hunting, camping, and fires are not permitted. There is no entrance fee, but you need a boat to get there, if you want to go for shelling, picnicking, beachcombing, birding, photography, or watching the sky cross the water. Seahorse Key does not allow visitors beyond the beach line, for a very good reason. The island has an extraordinarily large population of poisonous cottonmouth snakes.

Remarkably unmolested by man's activities, these islands are surrounded by shallow sand and mud flats which make access difficult. The shallow bays and lagoons are an excellent place to see mangrove swamps near the northern limit of their range.

For information, contact the refuge manager at Chassahowitzka National Wildlife Refuge.

CEDAR KEY State Museum

In Cedar Key. Follow signs.

The town of Cedar Key has that special patina found only in old fishing

Cedar Keys State Museum chronicles the colorful history of this little town.

villages. History has come and gone here in great waves, yet throughout the changes a basic quality of the town has remained: close to the sea. Besides housing a fine sea-shell collection, the museum at Cedar Key catalogues the large history of this little town, from its first settlement in the 1840s, through its boom days after the Civil War, to its decline down to the basics that continue to maintain it now. It is a resonant place, with lots of sky, Gulf breezes, and great smoked mullet.

A single quote from the museum explains the decline of Cedar Key. According to the local newspaper of 1860, "The Suwannee River is inexhaustible in its timber resources and easy of access." "Inexhaustible" has been a fatal word for the environment. By the late 1800s, the multitudinous cedars had vanished into pencils; the big virgin pines and cypresses were stumps. Without conservation, the industry died, almost taking the town with it. It's a sadly familiar American story—the tale of a lot of Florida: Take it while you can get it, and when it's gone, leave. Here, too, people had to learn that the earth and the goodness thereof are not inexhaustible. You can still sense the bafflement of those nearsighted pioneers who logged their way through the forests, then stood in a wasteland, wondering where all the riches went.

It's a mistake we are still making with other resources.

The museum charges a small entrance fee.

Address: Cedar Key State Museum, Cedar Key, FL 32625. Telephone 904/ 543-5350.

DOWLING COUNTY PARK (Suwannee County)

Although this park is still shown on most Florida maps on the Suwannee River at Fla. 250, there are no longer any facilities there. Restrooms and water pump were removed several years ago, due to repeated vandalism. A small area still may be used by self-contained campers.

DEVIL'S MILLHOPPER State Geological Site

Two miles northwest of Gainesville on Fla. 232 (Millhopper Road).

The Millhopper is a special place. You park in the pinewoods, then descend the boardwalk, 120 feet down, into another world. Unlike the bright, dry pines above, everything below hums with a moist, shady, green profusion—modulated by the low, glad sound of numerous little waterfalls that seep out of the steep walls of this immense, deep depression in the earth, this ancient and enormous sinkhole. There are plants and animals here that do not exist elsewhere; others which are found again only when you get as far north as the Appalachians. The air is cool and sweet with ferns. You know at once you are in a special place.

Yet it was almost not so. When the state park system acquired and restored it in 1974, the Millhopper was run-down, badly eroded, almost clogged with litter and garbage, some of the slopes stripped of vegetation. Even now it is threatened: visitors leaving the boardwalk start the inexorable fissures of erosion on the steep slopes; heavy, silted runoff slices down a ravine and pumps sand into the sinkhole.

Precarious, delicate, different, fragile, special: the Millhopper remains open for your visit and your special care. There is no camping here. The excellent exhibit building and the sink are open during daytime hours. All plants and animals here are protected; some are irreplaceable.

A small entrance fee is charged.

Address: Devil's Millhopper State Geological Site, 4732 NW 53rd Avenue, Gainesville, FL 32601. Telephone: 904/377-5935.

FAVER-DYKES State Park

Fifteen miles south of St. Augustine, off US 1.

The dirt roads through the park look like old country roads—narrow, winding through dense forests. You can't see very far ahead. On all sides, the woods thrive in the sun and rain. Imagine a path instead of a road, and you see this part of Florida the way the first Europeans saw it—rich pinelands and hammocks; spreading marshes, open to the sun; a winding, many-fingered oxbow creek for their cautious canoes. By air, Faver-Dykes State Park is less than 10 miles from the busy beach coast of east Florida. But by mind, it is more than 500 years away.

Faver-Dykes does not have "outstanding" features. There are no champion trees or Spanish gold or stunning vistas. Instead, the whole park is "typical": Here a portion of original Florida has been captured in all its variety and usualness. There are fine wide spans of flatwoods, dominated by spreading pines and thick palmetto. There are excellent stands of hardwood hammock: magnolia, oaks, hickory, with an occasional palm.

You will not be struck with wonders. But here is a rare and vanishing place of common Florida woods, old dirt roads, minimal development, no bustle—a place of quiet immersion and retreat.

To appreciate Faver-Dykes State Park, just remember that all it takes to transform your life forever is the right light falling at the right moment on the right leaf—and a ready heart.

When you come to any Florida park, come ready.

Facilities in this 750-acre park include a campground (30 sites with water and electricity), nature trails, a large picnic area by the creek, a boat ramp and excellent fishing. Pellicer Creek, which runs through the park, is a Florida canoe trail. Camping fees are average.

Almost all the present park was donated by Hiram Hall Faver, in memory of his parents, with the stipulation that it be kept in as natural a state as possible.

Address: Faver-Dykes State Park, RFD 4, Box 213-J-1, St. Augustine, FL 32084. Telephone 904/794-0997.

Faver-Dykes State Park: a place of quiet woods, dirt roads, good camping, canoeing, and fishing.

THE FLORIDA STATE MUSEUM

Gainesville. Take US 441 to the University of Florida campus, where there are signs.

A visit to this museum is one of the best ways to become acquainted with natural Florida. It is organized around a series of outstanding permanent exhibits which display major Florida habitats and give an in-depth introduction

Personnel at the Florida State Museum put the finishing touches on one of the realistic habitat exhibits that give an excellent introduction to natural Florida.

to the ecology of the plant and animal life found in them. The Florida Cave exhibit is stunning: It is like being underground. Other exhibits cover the savannah, mangroves, and coral reef. At one point, you walk through a life-like reconstruction of a mesic hammock and Indian village. There are intelligent, interesting signs and taped programs arranged around the subject of "adaptation"—how plants, animals, and people adapt to the specific conditions of their setting. This is an outstanding exhibit, and gives you a powerful conceptual tool for continuing to learn about nature. Admission is free.

In addition, the museum separately features a cataloged collection of specimens, on display for systematic study.

Open 9 to 4, Monday through Saturday. Sundays from 1 to 5. Telephone 904/392-1721.

FOREST CAPITAL State Museum

On US 19/27 just south of Perry.

This is a nice place to stop for a picnic in the shade of pines and oaks. Then visit the little museum, which has vivid displays on forestry, plant communities, common animals, and products made from trees. The park also includes an old pioneer log house, furnished (somewhat elegantly) from that period. The cool breeze from the "dogtrot" and the soft warm light in the wooden rooms will tell you about something that got lost as we sped up our pace of life in the past hundred years.

A small admission fee is charged.

The Florida Forest Festival is held in this area each year, and if you catch it, you will find a lot of down-home fun.

Address: 304 Forest Park Drive, Perry, FL 32347. Telephone 904/584-3227.

FORT CAROLINE, CASTILLO DE SAN MARCOS, AND FORT MATANZAS (National Monuments)

The oldest European history in America is commemorated by these three forts, and it is a bloody history of struggle, hardship, battle, shipwreck, hunger, storm, siege, and execution. Coming for gold, the Spanish were unable to appreciate the incredibly rich land of semitropical Florida. Instead, France established the first real settlement by building Fort Caroline in 1564, near present-day Jacksonville. The following year, the Spanish attacked, building the Castillo de San Marcos at St. Augustine as their base of operations. After the counter-attacking French were wrecked in a storm, the Spanish intercepted the survivors at a narrow inlet, took the captives across in small groups, and, out of sight of the rest, put them to the sword. Over 250 captives, who were mostly French Huguenots, met their death in this way. The inlet still bears the name "matanzas," meaning "slaughters."

The following centuries saw a continual struggle on these coasts among the Spanish, French, British, Indians, and Americans, with pirates entering the fray when the opportunity presented itself.

The original buildings still stand at Castillo de San Marcos and at Fort Matanzas. At Fort Caroline, the walls have been reconstructed on the plain of the St. Johns River. Interpretive programs are offered at all three sites.

Fort Caroline is 10 miles east of Jacksonville. Take Fla. 10, turn north on St. Johns Bluff Road, right on Fort Caroline Road.

Castillo de San Marcos is in downtown St. Augustine, and can be reached by US 1 or A-1-A. Rangers here give "living history" programs in the old fort.

Fort Matanzas is on Fla. A-1-A, 14 miles south of St. Augustine. All are well marked with road signs.

FORT CLINCH State Park

In Fernandina Beach, off Fla. A-1-A.

Fort Clinch is an outstanding park for both nature and history.

Walking through the very well preserved fort (begun in the 1840s), you will meet rangers dressed in the uniforms of the Union Army that occupied it during the Civil War. As they carry on their chores of maintaining the fort, cooking meals, and performing guard duty, you can talk to them—but they will only reply to you as if you both were living in 1864.

These "Union soldiers" give a guided tour of the fort as well, which is a good chance to see its vaulted passageways, brick bastions, cannon, and many other features of a working fort. The thin straw mattresses on rough wooden bunks speak volumes about the life and lice of the common soldier in any era.

From the walls of the fort, you can see out into wide, beautiful Cumberland Sound, and back into the forested hammocks of the park. Gnarled live-oak, cabbage palm, red-cedar, and a wealth of hardy undergrowth grow on

107

A ranger at Fort Clinch State Park, dressed in a Civil War uniform, answers a question for a visitor from another century.

old sand dunes that were once the outer edge of the advancing island. A walk through them takes you into one of Florida's most lovely and interesting plant communities—one that is seizing land barely rescued from the mouth of the sea. Most of the park roads tunnel through the hammock on lovely canopied drives.

Aside from the fort, most people come to this park for the wide, long strip of beautiful beach on the Atlantic Ocean. In the summer, it is a popular place for beach activities, and in cooler weather the beach offers excellent birding and some solitude.

There are two camping areas at the park. The Beach Camping Area lies behind the foredune in the northeast corner of the park, near the swimming area and fishing jetty. It is a shadeless, open area with 21 sites on bare grass, with water and electric hookups.

The River Camp has a variety of sites, from shady to sunny, cut into the lovely coastal hammock, with many sites under spreading oaks. This camp contains 41 sites, some with water and electricity, and is near the boat launch on the wide Amelia River estuary.

Camping fees are average. A small entrance fee is charged to non-campers.

Fort Clinch State Park has a wide range of natural attractions, besides the historical attraction of the fort. Beach, dunes, beach scrub, coastal hammock, a marshy freshwater pond and extensive salt marshes provide habitat for a wide variety of native animals and migratory birds. The surrounding waters offer excellent fishing.

When the breeze is westerly, you get a powerful dose of paper-mill smell, an acrid and sulphurous odor.

Address: Fort Clinch State Park, 2601 Atlantic Avenue, Fernandina Beach, FL 32034. Telephone 904/261-4212.

GOLD HEAD BRANCH State Park

(Mike Roess Gold Head Branch State Park)

Six miles NE of Keystone Heights on Fla. 21, about halfway between Gaines-ville and Jacksonville.

As at Devil's Millhopper and Ravine Gardens, the ravine of Gold Head Branch appears quite suddenly in the middle of a wide expanse of arid longleaf pine forest, and descends abruptly into a richly forested, cool, shady wonder-land of ferns, murmuring streams, and towering trees. It is an oasis in a dry land, where oaks and pines, with dry, crunchy leaf-fall lying on a desert-like earth, suddenly yield to verdant hickories, live oaks, sweetgums, and huge bay trees. In this unlikely and soothing place, you may come across the rare, moisture-loving needle palm. The earth underfoot grows rich, brown, deep, and soft from the heavy leaf-fall—so unlike the thin sandy earth only a few yards above you.

Besides the cool fascination of the ravine (cut by clear streams), this 1500-acre park offers a highly popular lake for swimming, canoeing, and fishing, and a small deep lake usable by experienced scuba divers.

The lake is so popular in summer that the park is often filled to its parking capacity on summer holiday weekends.

There are three camping areas. Areas one and two have water and electric hookups in a turkey oak forest of partial shade, where the native longleaf pines are slowly growing back from grass to giants. There are 37 sites here.

Area three sits closer to Lake Johnson on an open and grassy hillside, with some shaded locations. There are 73 additional sites here, some with electricity. This area is open all year. Camping fees are average.

Fourteen modern cabins, partially furnished, may be rented by the day or week, and accommodate up to six persons.

There are picnic pavillions, plenty of tables, bathhouses for swimmers, and a softball field. A small store is open from May 1 through Labor Day, and sells the usual limited groceries. It also rents canoes. Motors are not permitted on shallow Lake Johnson.

A primitive camping area is open, by reservation only, to those willing to take a short hike through the woods to a site overlooking the lake.

One of the chief functions of state parks is to preserve and restore native plant communities. Some areas in this park contain large, old-growth longleaf pines, marked with the "cat face" scar of early turpentining. This kind of forest, once common in Florida, is now almost never found in anything resembling its natural condition. Everywhere, longleaf pine forests have been cut and replaced by slash-pine tree-farms, citrus groves, or suburbs. Though most of this park was logged, it is slowly returning to its natural state, and in fifty years this may be one of the finest sandhill forests in Florida.

There are good trails and fire roads you can use to hike through the park's varied habitats. Much interesting wildlife, including the threatened scrub jay, may be observed by the quiet and patient walker.

Address: Route 1 Box 545, Keystone Heights, FL 32656. Telephone 904/473-4701.

HANNA PARK

On Wonderwood Road, at the southern boundary of the Mayport Naval Station, on the Atlantic Ocean.

This 450-acre city/county park features a mile and a half of beach on the Atlantic near Mayport. With parking for upwards of 2,000 cars, it can handle very large crowds for those hot summer weekends and holidays that draw people to the ocean.

A large campground has 300 fully developed shaded sites, with water and electric hookups, laundramat, and central hot showers. A convenience store and two concession stands provide supplies and rent bikes, boats, and surfboards.

A separate area of 50 acres has been set aside for tent and primitive camping, and may be reserved by groups. Camping fees are average.

The park maintains part of its acreage in a natural area, where several miles of footpaths and nature trails take the visitor through the oaks and palms of the native coastal forest.

Plenty of picnic areas and a stocked, 60-acre freshwater lake round out the features of this well developed, heavily used municipal camping and beachfront park.

Lifeguards are on duty during the busy season, from April through September. A small entrance fee is charged.

For camping reservations, call 904/249-0952. For other information, call the resident manager at 904/249-4700.

HART SPRING County Park (Gilchrist County)

Off Fla. 344 at the Suwannee River, six miles from Fanning Springs.

This 275-acre park has 35 campsites and a picnic area. Six hundred feet of freshwater beach on the spring run and the river make it a popular swimming spot.

The park floods each winter when the river rises, making it unusable then.

This park is already so heavily used by local residents (I was told), that visitors may have better luck finding a place in nearby private campgrounds.

ICHETUCKNEE SPRINGS State Park

Four miles NW of Fort White, reached by Fla. 47 and 238.

Ichetucknee Springs State Park is one of the most popular natural attractions in Florida. Crystal-clear water boils out of a large headspring and

With up to 3,000 visitors per day going down its chilly waters on floats and tubes, you won't find many solitary moments on the Ichetucknee River—unless you come in mid-winter to walk the hardwood forests along the banks.

numerous side springs to create a beautiful wild river of cold, pure water, flowing through prime hardwood hammock and imposing river swamp. The headwaters and 3.5 miles of the river are in the state park, and with this protection it is one of the clearest, purest rivers in Florida.

A place of such beauty was bound to attract settlement throughout history. Numerous Indian sites have been found nearby, and a Spanish mission was once located on one of the side springs. Wildlife has been drawn here for millinnea, as shown by the numerous fossils found in the springs.

The Ichetucknee River rose to sudden fame in the early '60s, and now thousands upon thousands of people converge on it each year to float downstream on inner tubes. It is a thrilling experience to be so nakedly close to such a safe wild place. But the flood of tubers almost drowned the river.

The charter of the state park system—to provide outdoor recreation while preserving the natural resources of the park—is nowhere challenged more than at Ichetucknee Springs, where sheer pressure of appreciation threatens to obliterate the frail beauty thousands come to see. The park now hangs suspended between intelligent management and exuberant overuse.

The river itself is the main attraction. Besides tubing in the summer, it makes a fine canoe trip in colder months. The surrounding park contains 2250 acres of springheads, sinkholes, dense river swamp, open longleaf sandhills, and the dappled shade of hardwood hammock paralleling the river. There are long canopied trails through the lush beauty of the forest.

The park is open for day-use only, 8 AM to sunset, year round. There are picnicking areas, but no camping facilities. A small entrance fee is charged.

Tubing and snorkeling cause measurable damage to the aquatic plants along and in the river, as well as erosion to the banks. For this reason, there is a limit to the number of persons who may use the river at any one time. Ichetucknee Springs is as fragile as it is beautiful, and each visitor must be careful that his use does not damage the park. Food and drink are prohibited on the river, because so many people left so much litter for so long. Please understand these restrictions, and obey them out of your understanding.

Any park this heavily used may sustain damage that can only be repaired by closing all or part of it, to give it time to recover. Do not be surprised if you find the park closed to tubers, or portions closed to divers. Every footstep causes a little damage.

Most natural areas can recover from many, many footsteps. But imagine hundreds of thousands of people each year stepping on the same banks, grasping the same limbs, pulling at grasses in the same river bend. Beyond a certain point the park cannot recover, and begins to disintegrate. That is why limits are set.

In the presence of these magnificent springs, it is worth pondering whether our increased use of water will someday lower the aquifer to the point that such springs diminish, or dry up. Human beings now have that kind of influence on the environment in Florida. One of the most important labors of our time is to understand the ecosystem well enough to assess our impact upon it, so we may devise ways to thrive in a thriving environment.

Special note: The water is *cold*.

Address: Ichetucknee Springs State Park, Route 1 Box 173, Fort White, FL 32038. Telephone 904/497-2511.

KINGSLEY PLANTATION State Historic Site

Entrance off A-1-A in Fort George.

The history of Fort George Island, which goes back to the Spanish days of 1562, centers on the outstandingly preserved Kingsley Plantation house (built in 1817). A small museum and guided tours interpret the big house (furnished with antiques), slave quarters, and stable.

Kingsley Plantation is a good place to ponder life in early Florida—a strenuous existence that attracted independent (even outrageous) individualists like Kingsley. A multifaceted man of powerful opinions and accomplishments, Kingsley was married to an African princess, with whom he raised a family until public pressure drove him to move them to Haiti shortly before his death.

It is interesting to compare the picture of southern plantation life suggested by the Kingsley Plantation with the image memorialized at the Stephen Foster Center. Kingsley Plantation suggests a hard life full of mosquitoes, Indian raids, devastating fires, and raging epidemics, while the Stephen Foster Center celebrates a nostalgic myth of riverboat balls, gallant gentlemen of leisure, easy existence, and contented slaves. Since we so readily project myth onto history, it is an interesting challenge to sort them out again and learn more about how the early settlers really lived.

A small entrance fee is charged.

Address: P.O. Box 321, Fort George Island, FL 32226. Telephone 904/215-3122.

LITTLE TALBOT ISLAND State Park

Seventeen miles NE of Jacksonville, on A-1-A.

Little Talbot Island is an exceptional example of an unspoiled barrier island. Walking it, you can easily imagine how the first sandbar formed offshore thousands of years ago, grew, became covered with the thin tough hair of sea-oats, and captured sand from the tides until there was a dune. Then another dune formed seaward, another, and another, so that now you can see the parallel ridges of old dunes ripple across the island like a washboard.

You can also see the signs of plant succession, from the pioneering grasses on the dunes of the ocean side, to the slow, gnarled growth of picturesque live oaks on the older dunes.

Like all barrier islands, Little Talbot preserves the interior coastline from

Little Talbot Island State Park, northwest of Jacksonville, is large enough to offer some solitude, particularly in the middle of the beach in the cooler months.

the constant wear of wind and waves, by constantly shifting, yielding, thinning, and reappearing, in a long-term stability based on constant change.

Except for the corridor occupied by highway A-1-A, Little Talbot Island State Park includes the entire island. There are over five miles of beautiful, wide, white sandy beach on the Atlantic Ocean, plus a rich estuarine maze of salt-marsh and tidal creeks on the west, teeming with the miniature life that supports the great fisheries of the ocean.

The campground consists of sixty sites set into the shade of a coastal hammock, many with water and electricity. Although across the island from the beach, the campsites are unusually beautiful, and a short walk will take you to the salt marshes and a lingering expanse of sunset. Fees are average.

The fine, wide beach has two points of access, one on the north and one on the south part of the island, both with parking lots and bathhouses. The long stretch of beach in between gets little use, and offers some solitude even on busy days.

Little Talbot Island is an exceptional place to observe migratory birds, and in early summer sea-turtles nest on the undisturbed stretch of beach. Fishing is excellent in the ocean, Ft. George River and adjacent estuarine creeks. A new nature trail has been opened on the northwest part of the island, through some of the finest coastal hammock forest in Florida.

Reservations may be made all year.

Address: Little Talbot Island State Park, P.O. Box 246, Fort George, FL 32226. Telephone 904/251-3231.

MANATEE SPRINGS State Park

On Fla. 320, six miles west of Chiefland.

Over 80,000 gallons of crystal-clear water pour up per minute out of Manatee Springs and flow through a thousand-foot-long run down to the wide

Manatee Springs State Park pours out a huge flow of clear, cool water into the wider reaches of the lower Suwannee River, and offers a place to camp amid the owls and deep shade.

reaches of the lower Suwannee River. You can swim in the cold, pure water of the spring-head, and an area has been terraced to provide shallow water for youngsters. Certified divers can explore the extensive underground caverns that link a chain of sinkholes in the park.

The campground is nestled under the shade of a dense, lovely hardwood hammock. Red-shouldered hawks may pass near your campsite, and barred owls may echo through the night with their soft hoots and cacophonous cackles.

Take the boardwalk along the spring run. You will pass through a fine river swamp of cypress, ash, gum and red maple, with white spider-lilies and clusters of the eggs of apple-snails. For unknown reasons, the endangered manatee is almost never seen here anymore—perhaps two days a year.

Some 2,000 acres of shady hardwoods and dry upland pines surround the spring. If you ask directions, you can hike for hours along the fire roads through this area. It's a good place to see the ecology of fire at work. But watch out for ticks in hot weather.

The concession stand near the spring sells snacks and rents canoes. A fine nature trail interprets the shady hammock and takes you along several wooded sinkholes. Ranger-led activities are offered during busy seasons. Camping fees are average.

Address: Manatee Springs State Park, Route 2 Box 362, Chiefland, FL 32626. Telephone 904/493-4288.

 ## MARJORIE KINNAN RAWLINGS State Historic Site

On Fla. 325 between Fla. 20 and US 301, twenty-one miles south of Gainesville.

In this house you can see that mixture of ready practicality and inexplicable love that characterizes all human greatness. The old nineteenth-century "cracker" house with its rambling porches, breezeways, rough wooden siding and hopeful windows reveals everywhere that touch of simplicity and depth that is so moving in the writings of Marjorie Kinnan Rawlings. Home for 13 years, and regular retreat for the next 12, this house anchored Marjorie Rawlings to the Cross Creek region that she immortalized in her work, the most famous of which is the Pulitzer Prize winning novel, *The Yearling,* set in a nearby section of what is now the Ocala National Forest's "Big Scrub."

The house is kept as it was when she lived here. Her garden still grows. Oranges still ripen on her trees. In a "living history" reenactment, a woman ranger who bears a striking resemblance to Ms. Rawlings tends the garden, does chores and gives tours of the house, dressed in the attire that Ms. Rawlings might have worn.

It is as human a piece of history as you will find in Florida. Open daily from 9 to 5. A small entrance fee is charged.

Address: Marjorie Kinnan Rawlings State Historic Site, Route 3, Box 92, Hawthorne, FL 32640. Telephone 904/466-3672.

In part of a living history presentation, a park ranger does chores around the house and garden, just as Marjorie Kinnan Rawlings might have done when she lived here.

NEW PINE LANDING (Dixie County)

On County grade off SR 349, south of Old Town, on the Suwannee River.

A boat landing with 30 campsites, a picnic area, and ramp. About 3 acres of park give excellent access to the wider end of the lovely Suwannee, and offer canoeists a place to stop for the night.

OCALA NATIONAL FOREST

The 380,000-acre Ocala National Forest comprises a large and varied setting. Beautiful, pristine streams meander through lush swamps to spacious lakes. Trees in all stages of development fill the productive forest land. Cypresses and bayheads dominate the low areas, while rich mixed hardwoods grow on the slopes. Moist flatlands are populated by pine flatwoods, and the rolling hills hold large, well developed expanses of longleaf pines.

But the main feature of the forest is the Big Scrub—an ancient, immense spread of sand pine scrub, unique in all the world, that covers the central and western portions of the forest. This highly unusual habitat is thought to be a remnant of the desert scrub that once extended from California through Mexico across the lower Gulf into Florida. Its plant and animal life is adapted to a tough, hardy existence of heat and dryness. Many of the mammals, lizards, and insects burrow into the ground to seek moisture and relief from the sun-baked sands overhead.

The dense scrub covers such a large area in the forest that the spacious longleaf pine forests stand out in it like islands—and they are named that way:

117

Pats Island, Hughes Island, and others. This terrain was immortalized by Marjorie Rawlings in her novel, *The Yearling*.

Portions of the forest have been set aside because of their great scenic value, but most of it is engaged in timber production. Do not be surprised if you encounter logging, controlled burns, tree planting, or other activities of forestry. And because it is a working forest, the Ocala National Forest changes from year to year. You may return to a spot to find that is has been thinned or harvested. You will understand Florida parks better if you contrast this situation with the state and national parks in the state. In the state parks, trees are not harvested and hunting is excluded, in an effort to perpetuate a few segments of original Florida in their native condition. By contrast, many parts of the state and national forests consist of previously abused land which was reclaimed and built into productive timberland. State and national forests offer easy access to large outdoor areas. State and national parks offer more regulated access to more pristine natural areas.

CAMPING

The Ocala National Forest is one of the most heavily used recreation areas in Florida. With the recent acquisition of Salt Springs, the forest now has nine "major" recreation areas, as well as eight "developed" areas. Fees are charged in most of the major areas, and three of them—Juniper, Salt, and Alexander Springs—have resident rangers and concession stores.

National Forest campsites are designed to provide a beautiful setting for your enjoyment. Facilities vary from nothing to full development. It is rare, though, to find electricity or sewer hookups in National Forest campsites. Many of them contain only the basics. In these forests, it is the location that matters most, not the amenities, and you may have to provide for more of your own comforts than you would in a private, city, or county campground.

Except for certain restricted sections, you can officially camp anywhere in a National Forest, although you may have some trouble locating a site that is dry, clear enough, accessible, or near enough to water. Most campers use designated camping areas.

If you do explore on your own, be careful that you are not trespassing on one of the sections of private land within the National Forest. And remember, if you want to maintain the privilege of hiking and camping in the forest at large, take care of it. Pack out your litter; protect the trees and animals.

A.   The **MAJOR RECREATION AREAS** in the Ocala National Forest are:

1. *Johnson Field Campground*—on ⌐⌐7, off Fla. 19, near the northern edge of the forest. Eighteen ⸱⸱ ⟍ very shady, somewhat boggy hammock that slopes dc **CLOSED** River. Beautiful trees make an almost complete shade co ⸱⸱⸱on. There is no resident ranger and no supplies are available for some miles. Free.

2. Just outside the National Forest, the Army Corps of Engineers main-

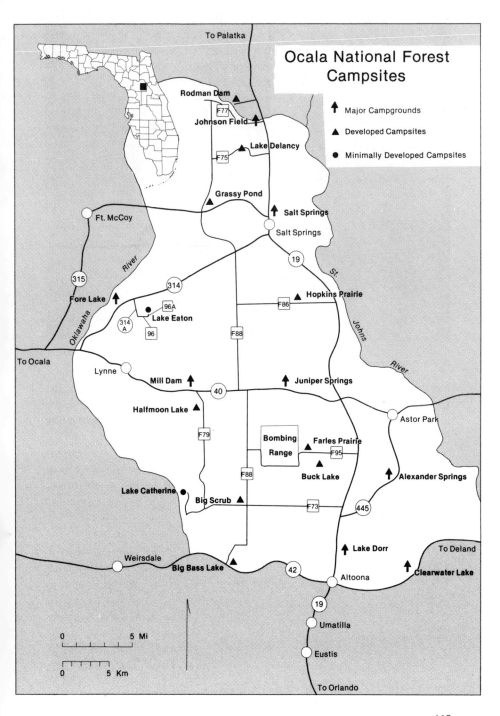

Ocala National Forest: Big Scrub is the largest stand of sand pines in the world.

tains two recreation sites as adjuncts to the disastrous Rodman Dam and Cross-Florida Barge Canal. These can be reached by an access road going 6 miles west from Fla. 19, between Fla. 310 and F77. The **Rodman Dam Recreation Area** is a medium-sized campground in a pine forest located for easy access to the lake. A fee is charged. The *Oklawaha Recreation Area,* located at the dam itself, has no camping facilities, but is worth mentioning because a specially equipped fishing pier has been built there for access by the handicapped.

3. **Salt Springs,** near Lake George, was a huge private campground with full facilities and a large overflow area, but has recently been purchased by the National Forest. The nearby town of Salt Springs provides any needed supplies. Though this may be changed, the present sites are largely cleared and grassy, and lack the undergrowth that gives privacy. Dense forest borders the camping area on several sides. Fees are average. The springs themselves are surprisingly salty, because the water rises from the deposits of an ancient seacoast underground.

4. **Fore Lake:** Twenty-seven campsites on a sizeable lake, in a setting of live oaks, palmettos and a few very tall slash pines. Swimming, boating, camping, and picnicking. An average fee is charged to camp or swim. Located off Fla. 314 a few miles NE of the intersection with Fla. 40.

5. *Mill Dam Campground:* Fifteen campsites on large Mill Dam Lake, a popular spot for fishing and boating. There is a swimming area at the campground. The sites themselves are shaded by medium-sized live oaks over a mowed grassy cover. They are set in a ring around a small sinkhole. An average fee is charged for camping. Non-campers are charged a small fee to swim.

6. *Juniper Springs.* Off Fla. 40. One of the major recreation areas in the forest, Juniper Springs offers 87 campsites in three different areas. The main

Less-developed campsites in the national forests offer only the basics: a handpump, a pit or chemical toilet, road access, and the great outdoors.

121

camping area (Tropic) is dominated by tall slash pines with lots of undergrowth. Sites are paved for RV parking. The Sandpine camping area gives you an excellent look at this unique forest, with semi-private sites. The Hammock tent camping area offers dense shade, dirt roads, and the most isolated location. There are good vegetation buffers between most sites at Juniper Springs and lots of trees and shrubbery around. It is a lovely natural setting, developed into an excellent campground.

Juniper Springs itself is a beautiful clear spring whose cool waters make it a refreshing place to swim. A first-rate nature trail with excellent signs begins

A lone boater heads for home as twilight approaches Mill Dam Campground in the Ocala National Forest.

near the spring pool and takes you along the crystal-clear spring run, where you will find lowland hammock species such as red maple, black gum, the rare needle palm, bays, rich ferns, the crooked pond pine and tall straight moisture-loving loblolly pines. You will also have the rare opportunity to see a well-labled poison-sumac tree. Under the bridge over Fern Hammock Spring, numerous clear circles in the dark bottom-growth mark the places where water boils up through white sand to fill the clear bluegreen pool.

Juniper Springs Run is the start of a fine canoe trail down Juniper Creek for a four-hour trip. Canoes may be rented and rehaul service arranged at the spring. To reserve, phone 904/236-2808.

There are large, modern restrooms with showers, a laundramat, and a concession store selling the usual snacks, supplies, and light groceries. An average fee is charged for camping or swimming.

7. **Alexander Springs,** with 67 campsites, has a full range of activities—swimming, camping, picnicking, boating, nature study. It offers full facilities, including a concession and canoe rentals. An average fee is charged for camping or swimming. The spring head is larger than Juniper and boils up in a sunny swimming area, fringed by a sandy beach on one side and nice swamp on the other. Rental canoes cannot be reserved, so plan to arrive early in the morning if you want one. Canoe trips on Alexander Spring Creek take from one and a half to four hours, depending on the take-out point. There is an interpretive trail with interesting signs that tell how early man used the natural environment for his survival.
Located in the southeastern part of the forest, on Fla. 445.

8. **Lake Dorr** offers camping, picnicking, swimming, a boat launch, as well as restrooms and showers. It is located off Fla. 19 at the southern end of the forest. An average fee is charged for camping.

9. **Clearwater Lake,** located on the southeastern border of the forest, on Fla. 42, is a camping area where longleaf pines slope down to the small live-oaks that so frequently rim Florida lakes. It is a good area for swimming, boating and fishing. The campsites are grassy, with vegetation separating most of them. An average fee is charged. Clearwater Lake has a short nature trail.

B.   **DEVELOPED SITES.** The following campsites are less developed than the first group, and are free. Unless otherwise noted, they have good access, drinking water, non-flush "vault" toilets like the one pictured in the introduction, tables, and grills (or fire rings).

1. **Big Scrub,** located amid the startling, rolling sand dunes of the ancient coastline, offers partial shade from the pines, adequate indoor restrooms with flush toilets, central water faucets, and seventy-five grassy, open sites with little undergrowth. A few sites have tables and grills.

2. **Farles Prairie** has a handpump, vault toilets, and an area where undergrowth has been cleared beneath the pines.

3. **Big Bass Lake,** with some sites under longleaf pines and some lakeside sites under live oaks, has basic facilities: a hand pump, vault toilets, room for about seventy-five sites, the shallow grassy lake, and access to a lovely outdoor setting.

The following sites are at about the same level of development as those just mentioned (see map):

4. *Lake Delancy*
5. *Grassy Pond*
6. *Hopkins Prairie*
7. *Buck Lake*
8. *Halfmoon Lake*

A quiet moment at the spring and old mill house at Juniper Springs in the Ocala National Forest.

C.   **MINIMALLY DEVELOPED CAMPSITES.** These areas have no water. There are vault or chemical toilets, however, and road access is good. There are usually no tables—just a cleared area for primitive, self-contained camping.

    1. *Lake Eaton* (off 314, take 314A, 96, and 96A)

    2. *Lake Catherine* (take F73, go north on 91)

D.   **GROUP CAMPS.** Two areas in the Ocala National Forest may be reserved by groups. For information, contact the district ranger.

E. The **OCALA TRAIL** crosses the forest and provides 66 miles of hiking through highly varied terrain. It is largely a dry trail, with boardwalks across the swampy and wet areas. Established camping areas are maintained along the trail. For information and a brochure, contact the district ranger or the Tallahassee office.

    Good brochures are also available on the canoe trails.

    SPECIAL NOTE: Recent Florida road maps contain several errors concerning the Ocala National Forest. The maps notwithstanding, there are no camping facilities at Ryals Camp, Bills Branch, Dry Camp, Long Point, Lake Dexter, Baptist Lake, Beakmon Lake, or at the unnamed sites north of Mill Dam and south of Lake Dexter. These may be beautiful locations and you may want to visit them, but don't spend all night looking for a developed campground when there is not one there.

Address: National Forests in Florida, P.O. Box 13548, Tallahassee, FL 32308. Telephone 904/878-1131. District Rangers: (North) P.O. Box 1206, Ocala, FL 32670. Telephone 904/622-6577. (South part of forest:) 1551 Umatilla Road, Eustis, FL 32726. Telephone 904/357-3721.

O'LENO State Park

About 15 miles south of Lake City, off US 41/441. Ten miles north of High Springs.

Amid the tall, shaded woods of a beautiful hardwood hammock—oaks, magnolias, hickories, and dogwoods—the dark Santa Fe River disappears in a large, slowly swirling tree-lined pool. After appearing intermittently in scattered sinkholes, the river rises three miles downstream in a big boil, then continues on to meet the Suwannee and the sea.

Old log structures built by the Civilian Conservation Corps blend with the outstanding hardwood forests and beautiful dark waters of the Santa Fe River, at O'Leno State Park.

This unusual "natural bridge," like the one in Florida Caverns State Park, has been a river-crossing for man and beast since the earliest times. An Indian trail and later a stagecoach line crossed here. Around 1850, a thriving pioneer town stood near the river, with a sawmill, general store, post office, and telegraph. This town—thought to have been called Keno, then Leno, then Old Leno, and finally O'Leno—disappeared soon after it was bypassed by the railroad around 1900, and the little-disturbed forests reclaimed their own.

The river and its forests give the park its main attractions and make it one of the finest nature parks in the state. Besides the truly impressive hardwood hammocks, there are stands where cypresses mirror themselves in still waters, walls of dense river swamp, sudden sinkholes rich with ferns, and expanses of open longleaf pinelands in the rolling hills. The varied natural plant communities support a wide range of animals. The deer, which have lived free of hunting since the park's inception in 1936, have no fear of humans and will approach quite close to look at you. (As tempting as it is, don't feed them; they are much better off eating their natural food.)

Two nature trails give convenient access to the River Sink area, a wonderful segment of the hardwood forest, and a small, stately cypress swamp (crossed by boardwalk).

O'Leno's camping facilities consist of 65 sites divided between two separate campgrounds. These rustic sites are fairly well separated from each other, and the setting is exceptionally beautiful: You sleep close to the heartbeat of one of Florida's great forests. Most sites have water and electrical hookups, and there is a sewage dump station. Fees are average.

Boats can be launched outside the north boundary of the park, upstream, at a county launch. Fishing on the river is said to be excellent.

Eighteen rustic cabins, with a pavilion, meeting building and dining hall may be reserved to accommodate groups of up to 140 people.

The diving platform marks a good place to swim in the soft, cool waters of the Santa Fe, and canoeing up this dark river is like travelling back to original Florida. The park has scenic places to picnic, and a lovely wooden footbridge over the river—built by the Civilian Conservation Corps in the 1930s—invites you to contemplate the passing of time and the renewal of nature.

River Rise State Preserve, adjacent to the park, contains an additional 4000 acres of this wonderful terrain. Trails from the park loop through the Preserve for day-hikes and overnight backpack camping. Inquire at the park for further information.

Address: O'Leno State Park, Route 1 Box 307, High Springs, FL 32643. Telephone 904/454-1853.

Each winter, volunteers reenact the major battle of the Civil War in Florida, at Olustee Battlefield.

OLUSTEE BATTLEFIELD State Historic Site

Two miles east of Olustee, off US 90.

This park has become famous because of the yearly re-enactment of the battle fought here by scores of volunteers dressed in Yankee and Confederate uniforms. This event usually takes place in late February of each year.

An outstanding little museum introduces the major battle of the Civil War in Florida and gives you some feeling for the weight of human presence and human suffering in that vivid and crucial war. If you want to begin to understand the South, you'll need to learn what you can about the Civil War.

Olustee Battlefield is a good place to start.

Open daily, daylight hours only. No camping. Free. The battlefield amid the original pine flatwoods, palmettos, and bayheads (this is what survives great battles) is accessible by a trail and well marked by signs along the battle lines.
Address: Olustee Battlefield State Historic Site, P.O. Box 40, Olustee, FL 32072. Phone 904/752-3866.

OSCEOLA NATIONAL FOREST

West and north of Lake City, off US 90. Leave I-10 for US 90 at the Lake City or Sanderson exits.

There is one major camping area in the Osceola National Forest: *Ocean Pond Campground,* located off US 90, eleven miles east of Lake City.

Fifty campsites sit along the northern shore of a large lake, a number of them facing the water, others in the nearby pines and oaks. While there are no electrical or sewer hookups, there are central restrooms and water faucets, as well as a sewage dump station.

You can swim and launch your boat here, or at the day-use area on the south side of the lake. The Osceola Trail, which runs nearby, gives you a chance to get into the backcountry. The trail is likely to be wet except in the driest times of the year.

Isolation, a large lake to the south of you, miles and miles of uninhabited pinewoods: these are the features of Ocean Pond Campground.

A below-average fee is charged. Stay is limited to 14 days, and pets must be kept on a leash.

Contrary to some road maps, the south side of Ocean Pond does not contain a campground. It is a day-use recreation area.

The 157,000-acre Osceola National Forest itself is composed almost entirely of pine flatwoods, growing in the endless array of subtle variations caused by changes in moisture and soil. The undergrowth beneath the tall slender pines ranges from low palmetto to high thick walls of fetterbush and gallberry. A few running streams show themselves by their borders of cypress and blackgum. Titi bogs, cypress stands, flatwoods ponds covered with lilypads, bayheads, open expanses of recently cut trees, dense stands of thick woods—these are the marks of the forest.

There is one different and outstanding area. Big Gum Swamp is a thick, varied, wet area of enormous beauty and difficulty that has been proposed for wilderness status. Forest Road 235 passes near this swamp.

Conditions on National Forest roads are variable. One day when I was there, a bridge was out on a major forest road, another was flooded, and a third had lost its markers.

The two *fire towers* have developed campsites nearby, with water, flush toilets, and open space.

The primitive campsites here are really primitive—just some space underneath the pines that is dry part of the time. There may not be drinking water or toilets. But these boggy, buggy areas are blessed with crickets, owls, and solitude, though mostly only hunters use them. They are not marked, so you'll need an official forest map to find them. They are *Cobb, Ocean Pond Boat Camp, Seventeen Mile Camp, Wiggins & Big Camp.* During hunting season, many of them will be filled.

All intersections of dirt roads in the forest are well marked and you can find your way around if you have the official map, and if the markers have not been shot away. Many of the smaller connecting roads, though, are pretty boggy and sandy. I wouldn't try them without a four-wheel-drive.

Osceola National Forest has been the site of a bitter controversy in recent years. Companies holding mineral leases to about a third of the forest have petitioned to begin strip-mining the forest for phosphate ore. Such operations

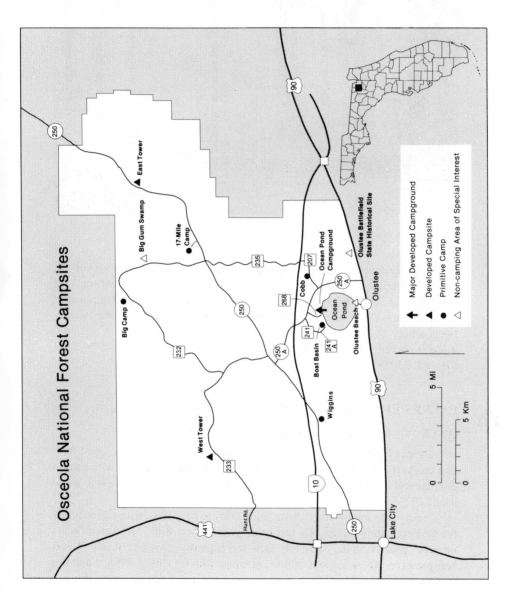

Looking south from Ocean Pond Campground in the Osceola National Forest.

would utterly devastate the plant and animal communities of the lands involved, and these are unlikely ever to return to their natural state. At this writing, the outcome is unclear—but the issue underlines the kinds of conflicts that can arise when different elements of the "multiple use" approach come into irreconcilable conflict.

Address for map: District Ranger, U.S. Forest Service, P.O. Box 1649, Lake City, FL 32055.

PAYNES PRAIRIE State Preserve

Off US 441, immediately south of Gainesville, in Micanopy.

Paynes Prairie is not a place you go to see. You go to see the coral reef: you snorkel down from the boat and—bam!—it's there. It hits you with a maze of color and movement. But you don't see the prairie. You wait for it to show itself.

It may be a long wait, so bring something to keep busy with—binoculars for birding, nature guides. Or just bring your senses: walk, sit, watch, wait. Immerse yourself in the unusually slow and expansive rhythms of this 18,000 acre preserve, where seasons of flood alternate with seasons of drought and fire to keep this rich land treeless and waving with grasses. Immerse yourself in the

130

expanse of insect sounds, birdsong, frogs croaking, wind blowing in long rippling waves, herons frozen in concentration, and the ongoing drama of the sky. It's a place where you can watch the approach of distant rain or find soft new toadstools. Like all natural areas, it is deep: the more you look, the more there is to find.

And, if you are lucky, while you are giving yourself to the observation of some sparkling dragonfly, the prairie, naked of its long reticence, may show itself to you; and, for a moment, you may know the mystery that has brought human habitation to this place for almost 10,000 years. You may sense the unthinkably intricate web of interconnections, the delicate dependencies, that make this one of the finest wildlife areas in the country. You may suddenly know, as if through a new sense, just how this grassy plain could be the most important sandhill crane wintering ground in the East, the home of eagles, hawks, egrets, meadowlarks, white ibis, deer, turkey, pileated woodpeckers, squirrels, and more and more. You may see into the ecosystem itself, the background against which all these individual creatures crystallize: the humming web of water, fire, climate, minerals, soil, grasses, and time that gives off such a huge array of life.

Visit the overlook off 441. After walking a half mile through live-oak

A school group pauses at the edge of Paynes Prairie State Preserve, one of the most important, impressive, and subtle natural areas in Florida.

hammock, you emerge onto the prairie basin at a fire lane. What confronts you there will be different every week of the year—as the multiple grasses, plants, and flowers of the prairie emerge through their interweaving seasons.

Or visit **Lake Wauberg,** where plans have been made to construct one of the most impressive nature exhibits in the state. Lake Wauberg is a very popular spot for swimming, fishing, picnicking, and boating and is open from 8AM to sundown daily. A small entrance fee is charged.

Nature is always changing. In 1871, the gigantic Alachua Sink became plugged, and Paynes Prairie turned into a lake. A new commerce sprang up. Paddlewheel steamers chugged across the miles of water, carrying oranges, vegetables and supplies. Then, one day in 1891, the sink opened again, and by the next day the steamers were stranded on the drying bottom of the prairie.

The buffalo (bison) once common to this region of Florida have been reintroduced onto a closed portion of the Preserve. They appear to be thriving and may soon spread to areas where they are visible to visitors.

Paynes Prairie is home to an unusually large number of species of snakes, even though these have been reduced by decades of over-collecting. Now, all plants and animals in the Preserve are protected.

(See update for information on new campground.)
Address: Paynes Prairie State Preserve, Route 1 Box 41, Micanopy, FL 32667. Telephone 904/466-3397.

RAVINE State Gardens

Off Twigg Street in Palatka. Follow signs from 17.

A breath of coolness, green and color. A secret garden down in the earth. More than a large city park, Ravine State Gardens contains a steep cut made in the earth by two large natural ravines fronting the St. Johns River. The upland pines look down on a world of native oaks, magnolias, sweetgum, elderberry, a multitude of ferns, herbs and shrubs—a lush, grassy green richness. In this steep valley with its grassy floor and flowing stream, its tall columns of large trees, its mossy shade and lush undergrowth, its hidden birdsong and private butterflies—here a garden of palms, jasmines, azaleas, ferns, orange trees, mimosa, banana—a multitude of exotic flowering and ornamental plants have been carefully placed and ordered by their size and seasons. As at Maclay State Gardens, a beautiful natural forest has been left in place, with a structured garden added around it.

Most of this was developed in 1933 by the Federal Works Project Administration during the Depression. The ampitheater, log cabin meeting room, and picnic areas were also built at that time.

A jogging "parcours" has been added recently to the rim drive.

Open 8 AM to sunset daily. A small entrance fee is charged.
Address: Ravine State Gardens, P.O. Box 1096, Palatka, FL 32077. Telephone 904/328-4366.

SAN FELASCO HAMMOCK State Preserve

Northwest of Gainesville, on Fla. 232, a few miles west of Devil's Millhopper.

One of the recent Environmentally Endangered Lands purchases, San Felasco Hammock preserves a remarkably wild and natural region on the edge of a major metropolitan area.

Here, one of the largest remaining examples of Florida's climax forest— the mesic hammock—still precariously thrives. Steep ravines, rocky hills, lakes, sinks, caves, ponds, swamps, varied woodlands, and Indian sites give an immeasurable value to this wonderful area—which is small for a preserve (5500 acres). Over a hundred small springs seep out of the hills and ravines. Most of

This "hardwood hammock" forest along the Ichetucknee River gives a hint of the great undisturbed forest in San Felasco State Preserve, which was too shady to photograph well when I was there.

them soon disappear back underground through the many "swallows"—small openings into the aquifer underground, where hidden water flows.

The mesic hammock is a marvel. Over 1000 species of plants luxuriate here, including over 150 species of trees alone. You can hardly begin to name them—swamp chestnut oak, southern magnolia, pignut hickory, spruce pine, Shumard oak, bluff oak, sweetgum, the ironwoods, the flowering dogwoods, the hollies, and on and on. No species dominates. Instead, there is a continuously changing modulation of thriving diversity. There are big trees everywhere—many a hundred feet tall—and a few live oaks that are true giants. Except for places logged in recent years, the forest floor is almost free of vegetation, due to the heavy shade.

It is a magical place. If you look at spots only a few yards apart, the forest is different. And if you go back week after week to the same place, it will be different each time. There are few places so immediately appealing or so thrilling to the human senses as a fine hardwood hammock. This is one of the best in existence.

Activities are necessarily limited—for this area is primarily for nature, not for intensive recreation. A day-use nature trail has been developed into the preserve (at the parking lot on Fla. 232), ranger-led walks are offered regularly, and guided nature-study trips can be arranged with the personnel of Devil's Millhopper, who oversee the preserve.

Preserves like this capture and protect Florida's extraordinary inheritance of natural diversity. Elsewhere in the state, this diversity is being bulldozed, disked, plowed, and converted into monocultures of slash pine, citrus groves, farms, or sugar cane; or built over with the concrete of shopping centers; or converted into little, isolated plots that do not offer the space for many species to survive.

Once a preserve is established, only a few things can seriously harm it, and at this writing San Felasco Hammock is threatened by one of those. A large chunk of land cutting from the southern boundary into the heart of the preserve, almost a fifth the size of the preserve, is in the hands of a developer. As far as I can determine, it would be well-nigh impossible to develop this particular plot of piney uplands without weakening the unique, diverse, and exceptionally fragile woodlands downslope from it, not to mention the streams and sinks and swamps that will receive the added burden of runoff from every square inch of roof or pavement built above. Natural systems have only so much resilience. Beyond a certain amount of stress, they break down. Preserves deserve the maximum protection we can extend to them.

With luck, the state may be able to purchase this "out" and incorporate its diversity into the preserve. Without luck, our children's children will never know San Felasco Hammock—only a degraded version of it.

Clearly, there must be places for people to live. But we need wild nature as much as we need the air we breathe. We cannot have viable preserves without agreeing to exclude development from them. Preserves are our gift to the future. Without them, our descendants will not even know how much of nature they have lost.

No camping. San Felasco Hammock State Preserve is accessible only by ranger-guided walks or the nature trail. It is patrolled to prevent trespass, hunting, collecting, and misuse. *Address: through Devil's Millhopper.*

SPIRIT OF THE SUWANNEE County Park

Four miles north of Live Oak, on US 129.

If you hike the river trails, you will pass along the natural levee, cross the river's rich floodplain forests, and feel the cool shade of the hardwood hammock's large oaks and sweetgums. Inland, the trails will take you through a couple of miles of longleaf pines and dense turkey-oaks to a little cypress-ringed fishing lake. Behind the cypresses, you will notice another ring of live oaks, on higher ground circling the pond, where live-oaks are so often found in nature.

This lovely 500-acre park is now developing into a major recreational facility for the region. It has 71 fully developed campsites with water and electric hookups, a separate tent area that is more remote and shady, lots of hiking trails, several picnic areas, and playgrounds. You will find two miles of paved roads that make excellent bike paths, and a beautiful white sandbar beach on the Suwannee. (No swimming because of swift currents.)

The park takes reservations year round, charges average camping fees, and allows pets on leash. There is a 14-day limit, and trailer maximum of 40 feet.

Restrooms have hot showers; there are washers and dryers. A little store is operated at the entrance, and supplies are available in nearby towns.

The park plans to add a community center, swimming pool, and playing fields. But the main attraction will always be the quiet beauty of the natural setting.

Address: Route 3 Box 215, Live Oak, FL 32060. Telephone 904/362-5145.

STEPHEN FOSTER State Folk Culture Center

In White Springs on US 41, near where I-10 and I-75 cross.

This is one of the most popular parks in Florida, developed around Stephen Foster, who brought the Suwannee River into national prominence with a song. In an atmosphere of old Southern charm, you can visit a museum where colorful dioramas depict the action of ten of Foster's best-loved songs. There is an impressive tower housing carillon bells, which play each day.

Like Foster's songs, the park is built around a celebration of the myth of the Old Plantation South, supposed to be a peak of American culture just before the Civil War. A stately courtesy, profound guilt, and fragile grace still haunt the Southern imagination, giving it both charm and stiffness.

If you would like a very different look at the Old South, read the classic *The Mind of the South* by W.J. Cash. It will help you understand Southerners today.

Other facets of the Southern character erupt here during the annual Folk Festival each Memorial Day Weekend. Then, the raucous resilience and tough joy of the pioneer South bursts out again and hoots its enduring vitality above the somewhat stodgy melancholy of the lost Plantation culture.

The Suwannee River—as darkly beautiful as it is famous—is the center of a growing struggle
between those who would develop or strip mine around it, and those who want to see it protected.

As you visit the fine exhibits, it is worth asking what harsh realities of
pioneer existence are overlooked in the sweet nostalgia of the songs and the
myth. Come and enjoy. Think about it too.

The park is in a beautiful natural setting along the Suwannee River. There
are ample picnic facilities and many shaded walks. No camping.

A small entrance fee is charged. Open daily from 9 to 5.

Address: P.O. Box 265, White Springs, FL 32096. Telephone 904/397-2192.

 ## SUWANNEE RIVER State Park

13 miles west of Live Oak, on US 90.

With all the names in the world, who would think Florida had to name two
rivers "Withlacoochee"? But it did. One runs through central Florida in a state
forest of that name, and the other comes out of Georgia to end in the Suwannee
River at this state park.

At one time, steam boats toured up and down these rivers, carrying
visitors, cotton, and supplies. Confederates built earthworks in the present park
to protect the railroad bridge at a crucial period in the Civil War. A completely

vanished town—Columbus, Fla.—stood here, leaving only a graveyard as its memorial. One of the state's early governors had a stately mansion near where the two rivers meet. Archive photographs trace its progress from grand columns and sculptured gardens to a rotting ghost-house hidden in the fullgrown live oaks that took over the abandoned yard.

A visitor to this park can watch the beautiful Suwannee curving its dark waters around high limestone bends, from which springs (in high water) gush to the river below. Lovely longleaf pinelands cover much of the park, with dense floodplain swamp and rich hardwood hammock near the rivers.

It is a good place to stand on the Confederate earthworks, look at the two rivers coming together, and ponder the long history rivers have, compared with the short history we call our own.

As you camp here, picnic, launch your boat, canoe silently past the high banks, drop down a patient line for fishing, or hike the wooded nature trail along the river to see the rare little cedar-elms, you may hear in your mind thoughts that seem to take their rhythms from the rhythms of the river. Perhaps then the long, enduring flow of time and the water will not make our time seem quite so small any more, when you can offer something back to the river.

This is one of the less-travelled parks in Florida, yet it lacks nothing. Camping (32 shady sites with water and electricity), picnicking, boating, fishing, varied nature walks, the long shadow of history, the cricket-symphony of a rural night, and the endless breathing of the river make this as real a Florida park as you will find.

Average fees are charged.

Address: Suwannee River State Park, Box 220, Route 1, Live Oak, FL 32060. Telephone 904/362-2746.

WACCASASSA BAY State Preserve

Headquarters in Cedar Key. Boat entrances near Cedar Key and Gulf Hammock.

What can you say about a salt marsh? Except that it is one of the most important ecological habitats in the world. It absorbs the shock of waves and protects land from the storm and sea. It slows down arriving rivers and spreads out their nutrients so they can be absorbed and utilized more fully. It harbors and protects enormous numbers of little fish, shrimp, oysters, and crabs, which later become commercially valuable catches. It filters out of the water pollutants, fertilizers, agricultural runoff, and other contaminants, and converts them into one of the most productive biological habitats on the earth: the marsh-lined, mangrove-crowned estuary bay.

Over two-thirds of the 30,000 acres of Waccasassa Bay State Preserve consists of an enormous salt marsh. Its horizon-to-horizon stretches of waving grass are broken up with dense tree-islands of red cedar, cabbage palm, and live oak. Where the marsh meets the land, a solid wall of coastal hammock forest

One of the remotest areas in Florida, Waccasassa Bay State Preserve consists of an immense, sweeping salt march, punctuated by little islands of trees and intertwined by twisting estuary creeks.

rises to meet it—the tall palms marching as far as they can into the prohibitive salt mud. In places, wide coastal savannahs of saltwort and glasswort spread their sparse cover across the exposed flats. Ramifying like tendrils from the slow river, little snake-tongued estuarine creeks interweave their way slowly to the sea.

Uncluttered, unspoiled, pristine: this is a large segment of Florida wilderness as it has always been. Wildlife is unusually abundant here, especially birds. And the preserve provides one of the last homes for those species that need an extensive range—such as the Florida panther, bald eagle, and black bear.

Waccasassa has the added distinction of containing one of the northernmost mangrove forests in Florida, giving essential habitat to large numbers of water birds that breed in the preserve.

Large salt marshes are not particularly hospitable places for people, but many, many other species thrive there, need those expanses, and arise as animate expressions of the way sea and shore communicate through the waving fields of black rush.

Present activities are quite limited in the preserve, because it's so hard to get to. Fishing is the major pursuit, out of the fish camps near Gulf Hammock. Periodically, the preserve offers ranger-led canoe trips. An access road was recently acquired by the state, and someday there may be a visitor center.

But meanwhile, Waccasassa Bay remains as 30,000 acres where the original natural conditions of our wild heritage are still able to go on, undisturbed.

It's simply good to know it's there.

Address: Waccasassa Bay State Preserve, P.O. Box 187, Cedar Key, FL 32625. Telephone 904/543-5567.

Updates to North (N) Section

Just north of Little Talbot, all of **Big Talbot Island** is now a state park. At this writing, it is not developed, but miles of beaches are open. Phone 904/251-3231.

Florida State Museum. This outstanding museum has expanded its exhibits to include more Florida habitats and a time-line of Florida history.

Fort Clinch State Park. During the summer, you pay an additional fee to see the fort (worth it). Nice new 1500 foot fishing pier.

New Listing: **Gores Landing County Park** (Marion County) has 15 RV sites at a small park on the Oklawaha River, with picnic tables and a boat ramp. Midway between Silver Springs and Fort McCoy. Take County Road 315, turn east on NE 105th St. For information, call 904/694-5868.

Ichetucknee Springs State Park has more put-in and take-out points for tubing, which gives you the option of a long or a short trip in this cold water. From some of the tubing points, you can return to your car by a shuttle bus. Address is now: Route 2, Box 108, Fort White, FL 32038.

Lower Suwannee River National Wildlife Refuge. Located at the mouth of the Suwannee River on the Gulf. 40,000 acres of varied terrain—dry scrub, bottomland hardwoods, swamp, coastal salt marshes, and estuarine islands, fronting 26 miles of the Gulf of Mexico. This area is rich in wildlife (258 species of birds have been reported).

The Shired Island Tract is located north of the mouth of the Suwannee. You can camp there at a Dixie County Park at the end of Fla. 357. South of the Suwannee River, you can camp in the Shell Mount Tract at a Levy County park and boat ramp, at the end of Fla. 326. (They have a phone: 904/543-5627.) The main part of the refuge, the Ocala Tract—located at the mouth of the river—is accessible by boat only.

For information, contact the refuge at 904/493-0238. Headquarters is 17 miles south of Chiefland, off Fla. 347.

Hanna Park Located just southeast of the Naval Air Station in Mayport. Address: 500 Wonderland Drive, Atlantic Beach FL 32233. New phone: 904/249-2316.

Marjorie Kinnan Rawlings State Historical Site is open 10-5 but closed Tuesdays.

Updates to the North Section (cont'd)

Ocala National Forest. Johnson Field campground has been closed. Mill Dam has been closed to camping, but enlarged as a picnic and swimming area. Salt Springs, now a part of the national forest, contains more than 200 developed campsites, over half with electricity. Salt Springs phone: 904/625-2520. New phone number for canoe rental at Juniper Springs: 904/625-2808. Rehaul service is now available.

Address change: Ocala National Forest District Ranger, Rt. 2, Box 701 (just east of) Silver Springs, FL 32688. 904/625-2520.

Osceola National Forest. New mailing address: District Ranger, U.S. 90, P.O. Box 70, Olustee, FL 32072. Phone 904/752-2577. In a tribute to local history, Ocean Pond Boat Camp has been renamed Hog Pen Landing. Strip mining in the forest was recently restricted by the Florida Wilderness Bill, but that was a close call.

Paynes Prairie State Preserve. A superb center has been opened at Lake Wauberg, along with a new 60-site *camping area*. Phone: 904/466-4100.

Peacock Spring has been acquired by the state and should open as a state park in the early '90s. It starts about 10 miles north of Mayo, a few miles east of Fla. 51, and flows into the Suwannee River.

New Listing: **Guana River State Park** has opened, on the Intracoastal Waterway, south of Jacksonville. No camping, but this is a beautiful, varied coastal habitat with fresh and saltwater fishing. Several miles of beach on the Atlantic. Phone 904/824-2163.

San Felasco Hammock. Wonderful news! The large holding in the middle has been purchased and added to the preserve. Call Devil's Millhopper for information about guided hikes.

New Listing: **Shell Mound County Park** is a small, out of the way park on the marshy part of the Gulf. Location: off County Road 347 at end of County Road 326, 6 miles north of Cedar Key.

Silver River State Park should open in the next few years in the river below Silver Springs, east of Ocala.

Spirit of the Suwannee Park, after being closed, has re-opened as a private "music park," featuring bluegrass on Friday and Saturday nights. It has camping, canoe rentals, and the other facilities described in the main entry, and there is swimming nearby. Address change: Route 1 Box 98, Live Oak FL 32060. Phone 904/364-1683.

Stephen Foster is open daily from 8 till sundown. New phone: 904/397-2733.

New Listing: **Yankeetown County Park** has restrooms, a saltwater beach, picnic tables, and primitive campsites for tents or RVs. There is a small fee. Located on the Gulf at the mouth of the Withlacoochee River, at the west end of County Road 40. Attendant's phone numbers: 904/447-9465 or 2907.

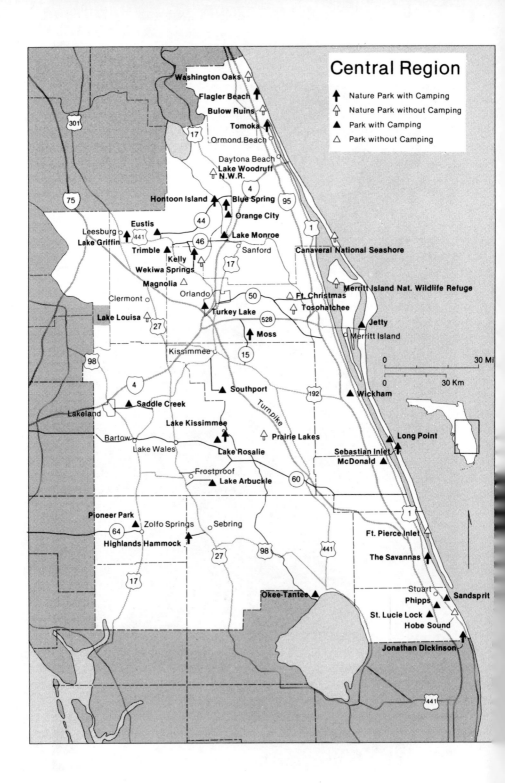

Central Region

- ⬆ (filled) Nature Park with Camping
- ⬆ (outline) Nature Park without Camping
- ▲ (filled) Park with Camping
- △ (outline) Park without Camping

Washington Oaks
Flagler Beach
Bulow Ruins
Tomoka
Ormond Beach
Daytona Beach
Lake Woodruff N.W.R.
Hontoon Island
Blue Spring
Orange City
Eustis
Leesburg
Lake Griffin
Trimble
Kelly
Wekiwa Springs
Lake Monroe
Sanford
Magnolia
Clermont
Orlando
Lake Louisa
Turkey Lake
Canaveral National Seashore
Merritt Island Nat. Wildlife Refuge
Ft. Christmas
Tosohatchee
Jetty
Merritt Island
Moss
Kissimmee
Southport
Wickham
Saddle Creek
Lakeland
Turnpike
Lake Kissimmee
Bartow
Lake Wales
Lake Rosalie
Prairie Lakes
Long Point
Sebastian Inlet
McDonald
Frostproof
Lake Arbuckle
Pioneer Park
Zolfo Springs
Sebring
Highlands Hammock
Ft. Pierce Inlet
The Savannas
Stuart
Okee-Tantee
Sandsprit
Phipps
St. Lucie Lock
Hobe Sound
Jonathan Dickinson

0   30 Mi
0   30 Km

Central

C

BLUE SPRING State Park

Two miles west of Orange City, off I-4 and US 17-92.

Although it is a beautiful and gracious place for people to visit, swim, camp, canoe, hike and picnic, Blue Spring State Park exists primarily for the endangered manatee. These large, gentle mammals cannot survive the cold winter waters of the rivers and ocean, and must enter the warmer waters of the springs during that time. An observation platform allows you to stand over an area in the spring run where manatees gather in the winter. They may usually be seen here from November through April. A television special on the manatee, produced in 1970 by Jacques Cousteau, provided an important impetus for the acquisition of this park by the state.

Blue Spring is a marvelous first-magnitude spring, pouring forth from a steep-sloped springhead surrounded by magnificent lowland hammock trees. You can swim at the spring or downstream at a dock. Below the dock, there is a concession store that sells snacks and supplies, and rents canoes and rowboats.

A 44-unit campground (recently moved from its original position near the

In the summer, it is a cool place for people to swim. But in the winter, Blue Spring becomes a life-saving refuge for the slow, gentle, endangered manatee—one of which is shown here wearing a tracking device on its tail. (Photo courtesy of Courtland Richards.)

concession) is located in a pine forest, a short walk from the spring and the St. Johns River. Fishing is excellent in the river. Boats may be launched, but (to protect the manatee) motors are not permitted upstream in the spring run itself.

One of the newer parks, Blue Spring has modern facilities. But if you leave the developed area, you can canoe past swamp forests that look much the way

John Bartram saw them in 1766. A ranger-guided canoe tour into nearby waters is offered regularly by the park, and there is an overnight canoe trail from Blue Spring to a primitive camp on Hontoon Island. The old Thursby House—now the superintendent's residence—still stands prominently in the park, as it has since it was built in the heyday of St. Johns River traffic in 1861.

An excellent self-guiding nature trail takes you by boardwalk through the lush hydric hammock. Tall oaks, sweetgums, magnolias, palms, and hickories preside over a rich array of vines, ferns, and flowers. The park also has a fine stand of sand-pine scrub, growing along the dunes of an ancient seacoast.

Special note: Swimmers sliding down the banks of the spring have caused extremely serious erosion problems. This seemingly harmless activity, repeated so many thousands of times, is ruining the vegetation of the slopes, eroding the banks and threatening the spring itself with a cave-in. Understand the rule against climbing on the banks, and follow it—please. As more and more people use parks, each person must reduce the environmental impact caused by his visit, or we will have no parks left.

Special note: Blue Spring State Park usually fills up on summer weekends. *Address: Blue Spring State Park, Star Route 3, Orange City, FL 32763. Telephone 904/775-3663.*

BULOW PLANTATION State Historical Site

Nine miles southeast of Bunnell, near Flagler Beach, off King's Highway (Fla. 201).

The young John Bulow, who had inherited his father's 4700-acre plantation, opposed the U.S. Government's plan to send the Seminole Indians to reservations west of the Mississippi. During the Seminole Wars of the 1830s, Bulow actually resisted the troops that were sent down to subdue the Indians, but his plantation (which thrived on sugar cane, cotton, rice, and indigo) was taken as headquarters. The troops, however, were unable to cope with this wilderness outpost. With most of them sick with dysentery and yellow fever, the commander withdrew to St. Augustine, and Bulow, realizing he had lost his friendly relations with local Indians, abandoned his immense plantation. Along with the other settlers of the area, he left with the troops.

In January of 1836 the settlements of this area were all destroyed by the Seminoles. In their long war against the encroaching tide of settlers, the Indians won that round. But fifteen years later, they would be reduced to a remnant fleeing to the Everglades, where they still remain.

Today, the site of Bulow Plantation holds a few stark reminders of that era—the most impressive being the thick stone ruins of the old sugar mill, made of Florida coquina rock.

A little museum at the ruins interprets the history of the plantation. There is a picnic area overlooking Bulow Creek, where both saltwater and freshwater fishing are available in the brackish water. Bulow Creek itself is a beautiful slow mirroring stream, and a state canoe trail.

But the life of the park today lies mainly in the magnificent, rich stand of hardwood hammock that permeates the area. Driving into the Bulow Plantation down the one-lane dirt road, you tunnel through one of the most impressive forests in a Florida park. The road is walled and canopied with rich hardwoods. Around you lies the ever-changing rich diversity of a fine hardwood hammock, studded with old Indian sites and pioneer artifacts.

The road to Bulow Plantation ruins passes through a wonderful hardwood forest.

Day-use only. No camping. A small entrance fee is charged.
Address: Bulow Plantation State Historic Site, P.O. Box 655, Bunnell, FL 32010. Telephone 904/439-2219.

CANAVERAL NATIONAL SEASHORE

Main entrance and headquarters: Take Fla. 406 east of Titusville, then go east on 402 to beach.

Canaveral National Seashore contains the longest stretch of undeveloped wilderness beach in Florida. Twenty-five miles of white sand and rising dunes span the coast north of the space station at Cape Canaveral. This pristine wilderness beach is the invaluable home of nesting loggerhead and green turtles in the summer months, stopping place for thousands of migratory birds, and a refuge for the human spirit.

Playalinda Beach is the main visitor area, located at the south end, within sight of the NASA rocket installations. Here, five miles of beach have protected swimming areas. The other twenty miles of beach contain some of the most solitary sandy shores in Florida.

Camping is not allowed at Canaveral National Seashore, but there are private campgrounds nearby. Please note that vehicles are not permitted on the beach.

West of the beach, the park includes a large, highly productive, completely undeveloped estuary, aptly named Mosquito Lagoon. The park's beaches, coastal scrub, tree-covered hammocks, marshes, and stands of mangrove provide habitat for an abundance of wildlife and birdlife, who may pursue their needs largely without human interference. Fishing is good both in the surf and the lagoon.

Note: Ocean currents are very strong here. Be careful. It would be best to swim only in supervised areas.

Address: Canaveral National Seashore, P.O. Box 2583, Titusville, FL 32780. Telephone 305/867-4675.

DONALD McDONALD PARK

From I-95, take Fla. 512 east. Go two and a half miles north on Fla. 505.

Twenty-five campsites in a high, dry sand-pine area, maintained by the Division of Forestry. There is a boat ramp on the brackish Indian River, which leads through Sebastian Inlet to the ocean. This out-of-the-way campground contains about 38 acres of nice, wooded terrain, with a nature trail, well-developed sites, hot and cold showers, and boating access. As in most marsh areas, mosquitoes can be fierce in hot months.

An average fee is charged for camping. No resident ranger.

Address: c/o Vero Beach Work Center, Division of Forestry, 4330-4th Street, Vero Beach, FL 32960. Telephone 305/562-2079.

ERNA NIXON PARK (Brevard County)

Evans Road, in southwest Melbourne.

With the surrounding area being converted into housing and shopping centers, Brevard County wisely set aside this little park to preserve some of the area's original woods in a 52-acre nature center. A 2700-foot boardwalk provides access to an unusually fine hardwood hammock, with stops, overlooks and signs along the way. The park is used by nature-lovers of all kinds, from those seeking a moment's quiet to serious students and photographers. Tours available by appointment.

Hours: 10 a.m. to 6 p.m., Wednesday through Saturday. No camping.
Park telephone: 305/725-0511.

EUSTIS RECREATIONAL VEHICLE PARK

In Eustis, adjacent to Fairgrounds on County Road 452A.

This is a well-run, high-quality, high-density city park developed for RV campers and popular with RV clubs as well as individual travellers. A cleared grassy area of 44 acres (with a 30-acre extension) contains full hookups for over 600 recreational vehicles, arranged close to one another in neat rows. Though there is little shade, the restrooms are air conditioned. There are laundry facilities, the city maintains a rentable clubhouse with kitchen, and the nearby fairgrounds may be rented by large groups. A recreation hall has been built for square-dancing and other activities. Pets are allowed on leash.

This is definitely an RV park. Tent camping is allowed only with special permission.

Average rates charged, with reduced rates for extended stays and groups of 20 or more.
Address: Box 509, Eustis, FL 32726. Phone 904/357-8882.

FLAGLER BEACH State Recreation Area

On Fla. A-1-A at Flagler Beach, 30 miles south of St. Augustine.

Flagler Beach is famous for the campsites, which are located right on the top dune, overlooking the beach and the Atlantic Ocean. The sites are open and

Flagler Beach State Recreation Area is immensely popular because you can camp on a site overlooking the ocean.

148

sunny, and may be too hot for tents much of the time. It is a very popular campground, booked solid most of the year. Fees are average.

The park extends all the way across the barrier island to the Intracoastal Waterway on the western side. There, you can find an excellent boat basin and picnic area. A nature trail takes you through the coastal scrub—a dense, varied plant community that is kept pruned and rounded by the constant salt breeze. If you look closely, you can see how top-shoots are killed off by the salt wind, leaving the densely branched main body of the plant.

Coastal scrub like this is one of the main habitats of the threatened Florida scrub jay, a cocky, friendly bird that might come out to take a look at you. As adjacent scrub is cleared away for real estate developments, the jays may not be able to survive on the habitat that remains in the park alone.

This is a state-wide problem. Wildlife knows no park boundaries, and depends on neighboring wild areas as well. As these wild areas disappear, you will see less wildlife inside parks—or anywhere, for that matter.

Address: Flagler Beach State Recreation Area, P.O. Box 717, Flagler Beach, FL 32036. Telephone 904/439-2474.

FLAGLER PARK

The official Florida map shows a Flagler Park north of Bunnell. There was at one time a Forest Service campground here, but it has been closed.

Reconstructed Fort Christmas houses a fine little museum.

C

FORT CHRISTMAS MUSEUM (Orange County)

At Christmas, Fla., on Fla. 420, two miles north of Fla. 50, 12 miles west of Titusville and 23 miles east of Orlando.

Like Fort Foster in Hillsborough River State Park, Fort Christmas is a fine replica of a Seminole War fort, from about 1840. Exhibits inside present a poignant picture of the war, including the Indian point of view. One section of the fort is devoted to the history of the local area. In photographs, old plows and tools, hand-made furniture, quilts, old letters and artifacts, you can see how close many little Florida towns are to their recent pioneer days.

On the grounds there are picnic tables, a playground, and ball fields. No camping.

Admission free. Museum hours: Wed. through Sat. 10–5, Sun. 1–5. Guided tours available by calling 305/568-4149.

For information, write Orange County Parks, address under Magnolia Park. Park telephone: 305/568-4503.

FORT PIERCE INLET State Recreation Area

Four miles east of Ft. Pierce, off A-1-A.

This park includes four separate areas. ***Fort Pierce Inlet*** itself is the main visitor area—with a long stretch of fine white beach, shaded picnic sites, and a jetty for fishing. Two bathhouses open onto the beach, and the inland shoreline contains fine stands of mangroves. A new nature trail takes you through an excellent example of coastal hammock.

Across a stretch of private property, ***Pepper Beach*** continues with more fine sandy beach, boardwalks, bathhouse, and picnic area.

St. Lucie Museum, located at Pepper Beach, houses small, excellent exhibits of Spanish gold salvaged offshore, and is the little sister to the McLarty Museum at Sebastian Inlet. In its cool interior, you can travel to another age—an age of pirates, plunder, vast treasure fleets, and gold on the Spanish main.

Just north of Pepper Beach and across the road, a small sign marks the drive to ***Jack Island,*** which could not be more different from the beaches you have just enjoyed. Jack Island is a 600-acre mangrove island that has been impounded for mosquito control. Walkways take you several miles through the seagrapes, mangroves, and small coastal hammock of this sanctuary. Birds and wildlife thrive here, in spite of the drainage canals. If you go quite early in the morning (especially in winter), you may witness thousands of wading birds— egrets, herons, ibis—rising off the island for their day's foraging in nearby waters. Imagine how much duller the surrounding towns would be without a wild sanctuary like this to provide home for native birds.

At low tide, you can also find an abundance of fascinating birds along Dynamite Point at Ft. Pierce Inlet. Gulls, terns, skimmers, stilts, sandpipers, willets and pelicans crystallize on the mudflats like brilliant, flighted dreams of the shore—that border where land and water have for millennia shaped one another's sleep.

No camping; day use only. Surfing is popular here, and is permitted outside the swimming areas.

Address: Ft. Pierce Inlet State Recreation Area, North Beach, 2200 Atlantic Beach Boulevard, Fort Pierce, FL 33450. Telephone 305/461-1570.

HIGHLANDS HAMMOCK State Park

Six miles west of Sebring, off US 27-98. Turn west at the sign onto Fla. 634.

Highlands Hammock is one of the most famous nature parks in the southeast. Its 3800 acres preserve a magnificent hardwood forest containing some trees over a thousand years old. One of the few virgin hammocks left in Florida, it appears much as it did when Spanish conquistadores first arrived looking for gold.

Nature trails give convenient access to the hammock and its immense oaks, hickories, sweetgums, cabbage palms, and accompanying ferns, bromeliad airplants, and rich shade. Other nature trails give access to several other important Florida plant habitats. You can cross boardwalks into a bayhead, a gum swamp, and the reflecting mystery of a large cypress swamp. Pine flatwoods ring the hammock, and a special trail has been marked to show you what happens to pinewoods in the absence of natural fire. If you walk a fire road north of the campground, you will come to a large area of sand pine scrub, growing on ancient seacoast dunes.

Ask at the entrance station for a copy of the superb guide to the park's trails.

The size, diversity and undisturbed nature of the park combine to create a splendid habitat for many wild creatures. A large deer herd lives here with little fear of man. Alligators can be seen easily from the cypress boardwalk. Florida scrub jays often appear in the sand pines and scrubby flatwoods. Bald eagles and even Florida panthers have been sighted. As in most natural areas, wildlife is most active at dawn, dusk, and at night.

The hammock was saved from development by local residents, aided by the Roebling family, who purchased a section of it and donated it as a park in 1931. A few years later, the young men of the Civilian Conservation Corps established camp here and developed many of the facilities still standing today.

The Visitor Center has exhibits on the park, and rangers give guided walks and campfire programs. Every day except Monday a concession-operated tram tour gives you a good overview of the park. A small store sells basic supplies and serves breakfast and lunch. There is a gigantic shopping area only a few miles away. (Increasingly, parks are islands of nature in a sea of development.)

The campground contains 138 sites, most with water and electricity, plus

One of the huge, ancient oaks in the virgin forest of Highlands Hammock State Park.

16 primitive sites in another area. Many of the pine-shaded sites are open to one another, but a few offer more privacy. The park is busiest in the winter months, when reservations are a must.

Address: Highlands Hammock State Park, Route 1 Box 310, Sebring, FL 33870. Telephone 813/385-0011.

HOBE SOUND National Wildlife Refuge

Four miles north of Jupiter, off US 1.

This little refuge, donated by residents of Jupiter Island, preserves one of the last examples of its coastal habitat in south Florida. The nature trail takes you over the high dunes paralleling US 1—fifty feet or more above sea level—through scrub oaks, palmetto, and sand pine on the upper elevations, down through a forest of exotic Australian pines, to mangroves along the shore. Here a peaceful atmosphere awaits you only a quarter-mile from the busy highway.

Pelicans, ospreys, and shore birds are common along the sound. Endangered manatee swim here and are sometimes killed by the propellers of speeding boats.

A little nature center at refuge headquarters serves as a local environmental education center.

For more information, write: South Florida Refuges, Box 510, Big Pine Key, FL 33043.

HONTOON ISLAND State Park

Take Fla. 44 south of DeLand. Go south on Old New York Road, then south on Hontoon Road. Follow sign onto River Ranch Road. Remember the way back.

Suddenly, you reach a vacant lot in the beautiful suburban homes that line the St. Johns River. Then you can see Hontoon Island—a hundred yards across the river, but a world away.

You can get there only by boat or the little park ferry. No vehicles are allowed, so, once on the island you have to walk to get anywhere. You even have to hike an easy quarter-mile to the campsites and rental cabins. Most people who stay overnight sleep in their boats at the river dock. It is an ideal park for boaters.

Like several other state parks, Hontoon Island has a small, intensely developed recreation area on the edge of a large natural preserve. The developed area contains a marina, store, two boat docks, picnic tables, overlook tower, six rustic rental cabins, a tent-camping area, and various places for easy bank fishing.

But inland from this developed corner, you will find almost 1600 acres of Florida the way the earliest pioneers found it. A long nature trail takes you on a 90-minute round-trip walk to a very large Indian mound at the southwest corner of the island, now inhabited by one of those ancient live oaks whose gigantic spreading limbs take your breath away.

Hiking around the island, you will discover many pristine plant communities. A large marsh borders much of the island, teeming with birds, insects, crustaceans and fish. Pine flatwoods spread around seasonal ponds in the

C

interior of the island. There is a fine hardwood hammock, as well as a river swamp marked by tall, moss-draped cypresses and red maple. Around the visitor area you will find the live oak and cabbage palm hammocks so characteristic of this region. These diverse plant communities support many kinds of wildlife—from tiny nocturnal shrews to secretive black bear.

The free ferry operates from 9 A.M. till one hour before sundown. You can leave your car in the parking area on the mainland at the ferry slip.

Hontoon Island is one of the few places that still look much the way John Bartram described them in the mid-1700s. Parks like this may soon be the only places in America where the undisturbed rhythms of nature may be re-perceived the way our ancestors saw them hundreds of years ago.

Address: Hontoon Island State Park, c/o Blue Spring State Park, Star Route 3, Orange City, FL 32763.

JETTY PARK (Brevard County)

On Cape Canaveral, 400 E. Jetty Road.

A small county park, about 35 acres, developed for camping, swimming, and fishing. It is primarily a beachfront park, with 108 RV sites and 50 tent sites (average fees), snack bar, laundry facilities, and fishing supplies. The main attraction is a 2000-foot stretch of sandy beach. As of this writing, there is no time-limit on your stay, but reservations are advised.

Rates are slightly above average.

Address above. Telephone 305/783-7222.

JONATHAN DICKINSON State Park

Thirteen miles south of Stuart on US 1.

Jonathan Dickinson is a very popular park and can fill up, especially on winter weekends, when the gates may close by 10 A.M. You can see why. The unspoiled natural river with all its changing magic and lushness, thousands of acres of native woodlands and outdoor space, fine campgrounds, picnicking areas, and outdoor recreational opportunities make this park an irresistible attraction for all of us who live in an urbanized environment where natural areas have been so sadly degraded, or paved over altogether.

Animals love the park too. Its size, diversity and natural condition create habitat for over 700 known species—including deer, rabbits, over a hundred species of birds, abundant fish, otter, a variety of snakes, and the steady background of crickets, grasshoppers, katydids, cicadas, and other insects that keep the night air singing. The park is a refuge for several species that are barely able to remain this side of extinction: Florida scrub jays, southern bald eagles, manatee, and red cockaded woodpeckers, for a start.

You can meet some of the wildlife on the three nature trails. The river trail takes you along the Loxahatchee River through tall pines, the dense tangle of mangroves and lush, cypress-dominated river swamp. A second nature trail takes you through unusual sand pine scrub—a world away from the swamp—to an observation tower on a rise known optimistically as "Hobe Mountain." The Kitching Creek trail, about a mile and a half in length, takes you through the rich wildflowers of the pine flatwoods and wet prairie to an overlook at the cypress swamp on Kitching Creek, then back along the mangroves of the river. On this trail you can see signs of the ecological fires that keep the pine woods healthy.

These trails give you the rare opportunity to be silent amid the sounds of birds, smell the pine-clean air, immerse yourself in the shapes and textures of nature, and guide your senses home.

A family of campers walks through the rich woods along the Loxahatchee River in Jonathan Dickinson State Park.

Rangers have recently completed a hiking trail to a primitive campsite. Ask about it if you are interested.

Inside the park you find five miles of one of the last unspoiled rivers in south Florida, the Loxahatchee. Its mangrove-lined lower reaches and narrow, cypress-walled upreaches are an unending musical modulation of beauties, especially seen from the slow, silent slicing of a single canoe. The Loxahatchee is being studied for possible National Wild and Scenic Rivers designation.

Some distance upriver you come upon the Trapper Nelson Interpretive Site—former home of a rugged and picturesque individual known once as the "wild man of the Loxahatchee."

Jonathan Dickinson State Park has two campgrounds, both with water and electrical hookups. The River camp area is located in a fine pine flatwoods, with partial shade and high palmettoes that separate the sites. The inland Pine Grove area sits beneath a solid stand of Australian pines, with sites tunnelled into them like caves. Pretty as it is, this is a good place to see how Australian pines totally crowd out native vegetation and do long-term ecological damage. On the edges of the campground you can find some fine examples of sand pines, growing on what are obviously former sea dunes.

A concession in the park rents horses for group tours (only) on the long riding trails of the park. At certain times of the year, they offer a moonlight ride on weekends.

The concession store carries snacks and limited groceries, rents canoes, rowboats and bicycles, and runs a boat tour upstream to Trapper Nelson's. There is a lovely swimming area near this store.

Jonathan Dickinson State Park gives you a first-hand look at one of Florida's major environmental problems: salt-water intrusion. Probably because of upstream irrigation, wells, and drainage projects, the flow of the river has diminished, allowing sea-water to intrude more and more upstream. You can see where the salt-tolerant mangroves are moving upstream, leaving the bleached skeletons of big cypresses along the river, where the increased salinity killed them. In many parts of the state, salt water is intruding into the underground water supply as freshwater is drawn out through wells.

This rich, diverse, huge (10,000-acre) park offers fishing (salt and freshwater), boating, camping rental cabins, horseback riding, swimming, bicycling, hiking, nature study, and invaluable natural areas to help you turn your recreation into re-creation.

Address: Jonathan Dickinson State Park, 14800 SE Federal Highway, Hobe Sound, FL 33455. Telephone 305/546-2771.

 ## KELLY PARK (Orange County)

From Apopka, go north on Fla. 435 about 5 miles, turn right on Kelly Park Road.

A fast, cold stream suddenly pours out of a rock face, flowing full-grown—a beautiful hint of the complex geology under your feet. Downstream there are swimming areas, picnicking facilities, grills, and restrooms. The camping area sits in the shade of medium live oaks and a few pines. Heavy leaf-fall keeps the ground clear of undergrowth, so the sites are quite open to one another. Between the campsites and the ranger residence, you can find an excellent example of a small dry sinkhole in the woods—like a bowl sunk into the earth.

Cold, clear Rock Springs, in Kelly Park, is the start of one of the state's most popular canoe trails.

After getting quite run-down from neglect, overuse and abuse, 200-acre Kelly Park has been beautifully restored, and the parks department has established a carrying-capacity of 1000 people to protect its fragile hilly terrain. Hiking through it, you will see some of the diversity found in adjoining Wekiwa Springs State Park: pine flatwoods, sandhills, hardwood hammocks, and marshy areas along the spring run.

Rock Springs Run is one of the state's most popular canoe trails.

Rates: average.

For information: contact Orange County Parks at the address under Magnolia Park. Kelly Park telephone: 305/889-4147.

157

LAKE ARBUCKLE PARK (Polk County)

On the northwest corner of the lake. Take 630 east from Frostproof, go right on Lake Reedy Blvd, wind around about four miles, and watch for sign to left.

This is a tiny county park on rural Lake Arbuckle—a big fishing lake surrounded with cypresses, oaks and marsh. There are eleven developed sites with water and electricity, with room for perhaps 30 primitive sites on the nine-acre park. The park is pleasant, rustic, and minimally developed. Two-week limit. Average fees. Pets permitted on leash.
Write: County Commissioners, Polk County, Bartow, FL. Telephone 813/533-1161. No telephone at park.

LAKE GRIFFIN State Recreation Area

A few miles north of Leesburg, entrance on US 27-441.

A 47-site camping area, with water and electric hookups, sits in an oak hammock close to US 27-441. Though the road is out of sight, you can still hear the trucks at night. The remaining uplands of the park spread out into spacious longleaf pine sandhills, but these soon trail out into the large marsh that separates the park from Lake Griffin proper. A canal cuts from the boat docking area to the mile-long channel known as Dead River, and out into the big lake, passing all the time through expansive freshwater marsh.

Lake Griffin is locally famous for its occasional "floating islands," composed of peat from the marshes that has broken loose and carries its load of grasses and small trees out into the lake. Fishing is said to be excellent.

There is a nice picnic area near the boat dock, and a nature trail passes through the oak hammock down to the edge of the marsh. There is no place here suitable for swimming.
Address: Lake Griffin State Recreation Area, P.O. Box 608, Fruitland Park, FL 32731. Telephone 904/787-7402.

LAKE KISSIMMEE State Park

Fifteen miles east of Lake Wales. Take Fla. 60, go north on Camp Mack Road.

The 5,000 acres of Lake Kissimmee State Park contain a rich variety of Florida habitats, plus some unusual history. Lakes Kissimmee, Rosalie, and Tiger border the park and provide good places for boating and fishing (no swimming). There are lakeside hardwood swamps, broad, open pine flatwoods, dense scrub, shady hardwood hammocks, flowering marshes, and open vistas of wet prairie along the edge of Lake Kissimmee.

The park has a wonderful variety of wildlife—supported by the diverse habitats. Bald eagles regularly nest here and fish the surrounding lakes. Bird life thrives on the open prairies. (The bird list contains over 150 species.) Alligator, deer, turkey, quail, gray squirrels, long-tailed showy fox-squirrels, and even

On weekends, rangers at Lake Kissimmee State Park re-enact the life of the Florida cowboys who rode these prairies a hundred years ago.

bobcat are still common here, as they were in early Florida. Sandhill cranes regularly stalk the open grasslands. Silent among the deep woods and twilight shadows, a few elusive Florida panthers walk the tightrope of their extinction.

A new campground has just been constructed in a stunningly beautiful hammock of spreading live oaks, with lots of sheltering vegetation separating the 60 sites. There are no hookups; water and a bathroom are located centrally. There is a dump station for RVs. It is the kind of place where you want to have as little as possible separating you from the freshness of the setting, so the limited facilities seem more like a blessing than a lack.

By all means, visit the observation tower at the edge of the picnic area and look out over the wide floodplain prairie that stretches to Lake Kissimmee. It is an exceptional place to observe birds (a marsh hawk skimmed and circled below me when I was there), and a rare place for gathering in some of the spaciousness of the native Florida prairies.

There are miles and miles of pinewoods, prairie, hammocks, and little dirt roads you can hike along, to immerse yourself in the high-quality natural setting of this park. Nature thrives here, and can be visited; but nothing is exaggerated, prettified or hyped-up for human entertainment. It's just *there*. Today, that is a small miracle in itself.

On weekends, the park gives an entertaining and informative "living history" program in which a ranger re-enacts what it was like to be a "Florida cow hunter" on the Kissimmee prairie back in 1876, when this was cow country like the Old West. Along with authentic equipment and tales, you can see one of the few remaining herds of original long-horned scrub cows.

In case you are planning to hike around in the park, remember that the flatwoods are likely to be wet in the summer, and progressively drier through winter and spring. Flood, drought, and fire are familiar and natural conditions for these woods.

Address: Lake Kissimmee State Park, Route 4, Box 243, Lake Wales, FL 33853. Telephone 813/696-1112.

 ## LAKE LOUISA State Park

Go south of Clermont on Fla. 561. Take Lake Nellie Road east to the park.

In the heart of central Florida lies the vast Green Swamp, a large, wild area that supplies water to all regions south and west of it. Here, the underground aquifer receives its valuable recharge of fresh water from lakes, ponds, streams, and rainfall. Lake Louisa State Park lies in the heart of this region and epitomizes its terrain, with fine examples of the cypress swamps, hardwood hammocks, pine flatwoods, sandhills, lakes, and streams found in the Green Swamp area.

This 1790-acre state park lies on the southern shore of Lake Louisa, including two and a half miles of the shoreline of that lake. Beautiful, clear 80-acre Bear Lake lies entirely within the park.

Day-use only. No camping at present. Swimming, picnicking, fishing, canoeing, and nature study are encouraged here.
Address: Lake Louisa State Park, Route 1, Box 107-AA, Clermont, FL 32711. Telephone 904/394-2280.

LAKE MONROE PARK (Volusia County)

South of DeBary on US 17-92, at the junction of I-4, immediately north of the bridge over the St. Johns River.

The entrance to this park comes up pretty fast, so watch for it carefully.

Lake Monroe Park is actually on a lake-sized part of the St. Johns River, where it has a boat launching ramp and fishing dock. It is primarily a park for water-access. There are 50 campsites, mostly well-shaded and well-separated by vegetation. Live oaks and tall old slash pines form most of the tree cover, with the familiar palmetto as the dominant ground cover. The area looks like pine flatwoods in succession to oak hammock. Some of the better sites tunnel like caves beneath the larger oaks.

An average camping fee is charged, and there is a resident manager. The only discordant note in this lovely little park is the yellowish smoke you can see from the tall power-plant smokestacks right across the road.
Address: Lake Monroe Park, DeBary, FL. Telephone 904/668-6522.

LAKE ROSALIE PARK (Polk County)

On the south side of the lake. Take 60 east from Lake Wales, go two miles north on Tiger Lake Road, bearing left.

Similar to Lake Arbuckle Park, but smaller: Twenty sites on about four acres. Water and electricity, boat docking, and picnic tables. Two-week limit. Average fees. Same mailing address as Lake Arbuckle.

LAKE WOODRUFF (National Wildlife Refuge)

Northwest of DeLand, entrance near DeLeon Springs.

Mostly shallow freshwater marshes bordered by swamps, this terrain is not very hospitable to humans, but it is a paradise for birds and other wildlife. Only the pine uplands feel like home to us, though with some effort we can navigate the rivers and lakes. But an enormous list of birds and animals make this marsh their thriving home, including some 200 species of birds, 21 species of ducks alone. The winter migratory season, from November through February, is the best time to see birds here, though many nest and stay year round.

The refuge is open to fishing all year, except in restricted areas. Limited hunting is restricted to bow and arrow and primitive guns. As in other national wildlife refuges in Florida, there are no camping facilities, and at this refuge there are no picnicking facilities. Drinking water and restrooms, though, may be found at headquarters.

Wood storks, Florida sandhill cranes, limpkins, ospreys, bald eagles, manatee, indigo snakes, alligators, and the round-tail muskrat may be seen on the refuge during the right season, if they are willing. But you can always count on the marshes to be there.

During the winter you might see marshes and pine flatwoods on fire during a controlled burn. Such fires are natural to these plant communities, and create better conditions for wildlife.

Address: Refuge Manager, Lake Woodruff NWR, P.O. Box 488, DeLeon Springs, FL 32028. Telephone 904/985-4673.

▲ LONG POINT PARK (Brevard County)

On A-1-A, a mile and a half north of Sebastian Inlet, 14 miles south of Melbourne.

A camping park on an island in the Indian River, with easy access for boating and fishing. The hundred-acre island has been cleared of virtually all growth and replanted in grassy lawns with a series of exotic shade-trees, including eucalyptus and the destructive melaluca. There are 114 developed campsites, with water and electricity (a few with sewer hookups), and the overflow area will hold another 50. Many of the developed sites are on the water, and you can launch a boat from your camp. In addition to two little

Long Point is a popular, well-kept county park, though almost all of the native vegetation has been cleared and replaced with lawns.

man-made lakes for swimming, there are playgrounds, a ballfield, picnic pavilions, a boat ramp, hot showers, laundry facilities, grills, and dump station. Boats can be rented at the concession store. Resident rangers provide 24-hour security. Pets permitted on leash. There is a 21-day limit. Average fees.

Long Point is an immensely popular camping park. It is generally full from Thanksgiving through Easter, and reservations are needed months in advance. Aside from the camping and climate, its main attraction is the nearby fresh and saltwater fishing.

Long Point is such a highly developed and maintained park that visitors to it should make certain they also have the opportunity to experience some of Florida's natural woods and swamps.

Address: Long Point Park, 9200 South A-1-A Highway, Melbourne Beach, FL 32951. Telephone 305/723-3839.

MAGNOLIA PARK (Orange County)

On Lake Apopka on Fla. 437, north of Ocoee.

This well-developed 56-acre park is little used now, because Lake Apopka, once one of the finest bass-fishing lakes in the south, has been reduced to an ecological disaster by decades of sewage, agricultural runoff, and citrus-processing pulp—aggravated by a couple of hurricanes that proved the final blow. The lake is now inhabited mostly by gar and other rough fish, covered with a death-green mat of thick algae, and sometimes gives off an odor you wish you hadn't smelled.

Lake Apopka has become an object-lesson in how to destroy a natural resource by using it as a dump.

Average fees.

For information, write Orange County Parks and Recreation, 118 W. Kaley Ave., Orlando, FL 32806. Park telephone: 305/886-4231.

MERRITT ISLAND National Wildlife Refuge

To Refuge Headquarters, take Fla. 406 east from Titusville, then go east on 402.

This 139,000-acre refuge came about because NASA needed an extensive buffer zone between its space station on Cape Canaveral and populated areas. As a result, one of the richest wildlife areas in Florida has been preserved— home of more endangered and threatened species than any other refuge outside Hawaii. Bald eagles nest here, along with wood storks and green turtles—all of them species that have been ground almost into extinction by the passage of human progress.

It is a superb area for birding—one of the best waterfowl sites in Florida—when clouds of ducks and coots descend for the winter. Almost two-thirds of the refuge consists of lagoons and marshes, with much of the rest in expanses of cabbage palm, palmetto, wax myrtle, and the kind of impenetrable thicket that people cannot stand, but which provides home and safety for many marvelous species, such as the indigo snake.

Two loop trails stretch almost 15 miles through the marshes, mangroves, and lagoons.

On the open beaches of Canaveral National Seashore (an affiliated park), refuge personnel carry out an extensive sea-turtle rescue program. They save the eggs from predators, incubate them, and release the young turtles on the remote beach.

Pelican Island, fifty miles south and the first national wildlife refuge, is also administered from this office.

As in all Florida's national wildlife refuges, camping is not permitted here, but it remains an outstanding place for nature study, birding, photography, waterfowl hunting in season, fishing, and the kind of deep breathing that you re-learn from a place that itself seems to breathe with life.

Address: Merritt Island National Wildlife Refuge, P.O. Box 6504, Titusville, FL 32780.

MOSS PARK (Orange County)

25 miles southeast of Orlando. Take Fla. 15, go left on 15-A, and left on Moss Park Road.

The original 50-acre park has been expanded recently by another 1500 acres, making it one of the largest county parks in the state. Located on a long spit of land between Lake Hart and Lake Mary Jane, Moss Park is a fine, large place for camping, boating, fishing, and swimming. With good fishing available on both sides, there are, of course, excellent boat docks. Recreation facilities developed in the park include tennis courts, a ballfield, playground equipment, a horseshoe area, and white sand beaches on the lakes. Covered picnic tables are scattered through the wooded area.

The 50 campsites (18 with water and electricity on-site) are well spaced and offer some privacy, and are a short walk from the boat launch. Boardwalks are planned across the large savannah, and should provide access to a superb nature-study area, especially for birding. Much of the new acreage is being left in its native state—an unusual and commendable decision for a county park.

The county is building cabins with kitchen facilities and a meeting hall, to rent to organized groups. There is a resident manager, and fees are average.

If Orange County can resist the temptation to overdevelop this park, its large unspoiled acreage promises to make it one of the outstanding county parks in Florida.

For information, contact Orange County Parks, address under Magnolia Park. Moss Park telephone: 305/273-2327.

OKEE-TANTEE RECREATION AREA (South Florida Water Management District)

On the northwestern edge of Lake Okeechobee, where Fla. 78 crosses the Kissimmee River. Take 441 south of Okeechobee, go four miles on Fla. 78.

With facilities directed toward Lake Okeechobee, this RV park provides a good place for fishing, boating, camping, and picnicking. Presently, 215 sites have been developed with water and electric hookups, and there are small additional areas for tent campers and groups not requiring hookups. More sites are planned. The park has its own restaurant, as well as a small store where you can buy supplies and rent boats and motors. A fishing guide service is available. Pets permitted on leash.

The campground is fenced securely, with highway access only through a locked gate, and it has security lights that burn all night. The park has superb hot showers. Average fees are charged, and there is a 14-day limit. Out-of-state visitors pay a dollar more per night.

Like most south Florida parks, Okee-Tantee is usually full from Christmas through Easter, when reservations are a must.

At present the campground is virtually shadeless, consisting mainly of a grassy fill-area with small planted trees and RV sites. The lake provides the only natural area.

Reservations may be made up to 60 days in advance. Write Park Manager, Okee-Tantee Recreation Area, Rt. 4 Box 644, Okeechobee, FL 33472. Telephone 813/763-2622.

ORANGE CITY RECREATION AREA (Div. of Forestry)

A mile south of Orange City, on the west side of US 17-92.

This little park on the highway next to the fire lookout tower offers two acres with 14 campsites. It is in a stand of sandpine scrub that offers good shade. Hot water, showers, tables and grills, scattered water taps provide the facilities. There are no RV hookups. Sites are nicely separated by undergrowth. An average fee is charged.

PHIPPS PARK (Martin County)

Eight miles west of Stuart on Fla. 76, 3 miles north on Locks Road to park.

The original plant community here was probably pine flatwoods, like the surrounding area, but it was bulldozed and burned to make a clearing for this park. Now, grassy lawns create open space, and shade is provided by Australian pines and Brazilian peppers—exotics that can cause serious ecological damage when they spread to the surrounding woods. The park has 50 campsites at present, on 80 acres, with ample space to picnic and play. Places to swim can be found nearby, and the adjacent St. Lucie Canal offers both freshwater and saltwater fishing. Rates are below average. No reservations are accepted. A resident manager provides security, and the park closes daily at 7:30 P.M. *For information, call 305/287-6565.*

PIONEER PARK (Hardee County)

In Zolfo Springs, on the Peace River where 17 crosses 64 west.

    This 100-acre county park has 100 developed campsites with water and electricity, plus room for another 100 sites (somewhat crowded) along Rock Lake. Facilities are good: hot showers, clean restrooms, campsites well placed among the trees.

    Unlike many county parks, this one has a very nice natural area along the Peace River—kept that way, perhaps, by the periodic flooding of the river which prevents development. In the middle of the park, there is also a fine cypress stand which has been left in its natural state.

    Camp one is located in shady oaks and palms along Rock Lake. Camp two is an open grassy area under tall pines. There is a resident manager in the park; stay is limited to two weeks; pets allowed on leash; fees slightly below average.

    The Peace River is a popular canoeing and fishing spot. Canoeists frequently put in at the park, or stop overnight. They are allowed to camp close to their equipment in the launch area.

    Like most south Florida parks, Pioneer Park is very busy from December through Easter. "Pioneer Days" are celebrated the first weekend in March each year. This antique-oriented old-time festival can draw as many as 30,000 people, so don't expect to camp anywhere nearby at that time without reservations.

Address: Pioneer Park, Box 326, Zolfo Springs, FL 33890. Telephone 813/735-0330.

PRAIRIE LAKES State Preserve

Ten miles NW on Fla. 523 from Kenansville (which is on 441). On Lakes Marion and Jackson.

    Wet and dry prairie and extensive marshland occupy much of this 8,000-acre nature preserve. It is a place of grasses, palmetto, wildflowers, and abundant wildlife. Live oak hammocks and pine flatwoods scattered around the prairie hold many ferns and some orchids.

    Prairie Lakes is presently open only for hiking and primitive backpack camping in two designated areas. There are 12 miles of trails in two loops over flat terrain.

    Minimal facilities. No developed campgrounds. This is a recently acquired area still being restored to its natural condition.

    Write for a brochure from the Department of Natural Resources, or contact the ranger at *Prairie Lakes State Preserve, P.O. Box 220, Kenansville FL 32739. Telephone (305) 436-1626.*

SADDLE CREEK PARK (Polk County)

About halfway between Lakeland and Auburndale off US 92. Turn north at sign on Fish Hatchery Road.

This 700-acre park has 350 dry acres available for recreational use, the rest for boating, fishing, and swimming in a large developed area. Forty developed campsites have water and electricity. There is a rifle range. Two-week limit. Average fees.

Same address as Lake Arbuckle.

ST. LUCIE LOCKS CAMPING AREA (Corps of Engineers)

Two miles northeast of Fla. 76A, about 6 miles southwest of Stuart.

A small camping area on the Okeechobee Waterway. Pull-in sites for RVs. Free. Boat launch area, picnic area, playground, showers, dump station. Seven-day limit.

Address: P.O. Box 328, Stuart, FL 33494. Telephone 305/285-2665.

SANDSPRIT PARK (Martin County)

3443 SE St. Lucie Blvd., Stuart.

Obscurely marked, a few miles south of Stuart, off A-1-A. It's best to call from Stuart for directions.

Sandsprit Park offers camping, saltwater fishing, and boating. It is a small county camping area with boat docks, about 13 acres in extent (minus erosion from a recent storm), with some 150 closely packed campsites. Cold showers. Dump station. There is no electricity available to campers and no pets are allowed. Fees are below average. No reservations. The park closes each evening at 7:30 and has a resident manager for security. The area is densely shaded by Australian pines, which periodically drop their long graceful limbs onto trailers below.

Address above. Telephone 305/287-5521.

THE SAVANNAS (St. Lucie County)

East of US 1, 1.3 miles on Fla. 712, six miles south of Ft. Pierce.

The Savannas is a fine natural marsh spreading out for nearly 500 acres, with another 100 acres of dry land for camping and recreation. This is a park for boating, freshwater fishing, birding, and nature study. The rare everglades kite has been seen here, and the marsh supports a large number of wading birds and waterfowl.

Campsites are first-come first-served, and the park usually fills every day in the winter season, as well as many weekends year round. There are 134 campsites at present, with a group area that will hold 20 more. Only the group site is reservable. Rates are slightly below average.

Unguided nature trails take you across some small islands onto the edge of the water. The whole park offers excellent canoeing through fresh, clear water. Canoes and boats may be rented. (There is a seven-and-a-half horsepower limit on motors.) Picnic tables and playground equipment are located near the campground. Visitors can swim in a man-made lake. A little concession store operates in the park, and full supplies are available nearby.

Address: The Savannas, 200 Midway Road, Ft. Pierce, FL 33450. Telephone 305/464-7855.

SEBASTIAN INLET State Recreation Area

On A-1-A at Sebastian Inlet, between Ft. Pierce and Melbourne.

There are good reasons why this is one of the most popular parks in the state. Almost three miles of straight sandy beach stretch up and down the coast. The Gulf Stream comes close to the shore at this point, and the park's jetty is famous for the fish caught on it. The inlet and Indian River provide ample space for boating and boat fishing. The McLarty Museum offers the state's finest exhibit on the sunken treasure and Spanish gold found offshore near the park. To top it off, in the winter Sebastian Inlet has the finest surfing in Florida.

As usual with state recreation areas, there is more. A natural buffer zone of undeveloped mangroves, coastal hammock, and dunes provides shelter for the wildlife and birdlife you see in the park. There are no formal nature trails at present, but you can easily canoe along the Indian River and see a few hundred acres of wild land. These wild areas protect the recreational zones, give them depth and integrity, and enrich the quality of experience available in the park.

Birds especially like this park. In the winter they flock in by the thousands, and the wide tidal flats give them a highly visible feeding ground. In the summer, large sea-turtles regularly choose this still-dark and undeveloped stretch of beach to dig their precarious nests and lay the hope for their threatened future.

The campgrounds are heavily shaded, though mostly by Australian pines. A number of sites face directly onto the inlet and give a fine view of the water. Below the campground there is a picnic area and a large boat ramp. In the winter, the concession store in the campground offers the usual light groceries and fishing supplies. Campfire programs and other interpretive activities are given by rangers all year.

Address: Sebastian Inlet State Recreation Area, P.O. Box 728, Wabasso, FL 32970. Telephone 305/589-3754.

SOUTHPORT PARK (South Florida Water Management District)

About 13 miles south of Kissimmee. Go south on Fla. 531, east on Southport Road.

This compact, attractive recreation area is located on the south shore of

Sebastian Inlet, along with good fishing and a fine beach, has the best surfing in Florida.

Lake Tohopekaliga. It has 41 developed campsites with additional primitive sites, located in a nice live oak hammock planted with grass.

There are ample boating facilities, a basin, and access channel to the lake. It is a good site for boating, fishing, and picnicking. A park store sells the usual snacks and supplies, and rents boats and motors.

Average camping fees are charged. Fourteen-day limit. Reservations are accepted up to 60 days in advance.

Write or call: Park Manager, Southport Park, 2001 Southport Road, Kissim-mee, FL 32714. Telephone 305/348-5822.

C

TOMOKA State Park

Three miles north of Ormond Beach, on N. Beach Street.

The first things you see are the trees: magnificent oaks, palms, magnolias, dozens of shrubs and understory trees, moss draping over limbs, light and shadow endlessly playing among them. Then you begin to see details: a golden orb weaver's web catches the light and shines against the dark forest. A still patch rustles and becomes a foraging bird. A cloud covers the sun, and all the trees seem to close their shutters in response.

Tomoka State Park has one of the finest coastal hammocks in Florida—a lush, rich, endlessly varying forest of full shade and tunnelled walkways. This forest has been famous since the earliest written records, and John James Audubon chose to come here to paint his birds.

You can camp in this forest. The sites are edged right in among the canopy of trees. You sleep wrapped in the rustle of wind in the leaves. Look in the right

Visitors walking through Tomoka State Park emerge from one of the most beautiful coastal forests in Florida onto the open expanse of the river.

direction from your tent and you may see no one. Even though much of this was once cleared for planting indigo in an old plantation, the hardwoods have returned in the past two hundred years, and they thrive here, because this is soil they helped create, shape, season, and hold.

The park has several fine picnic areas along the Tomoka River. Canoes may be rented, and you can paddle upstream past marshes and hammocks.

Fishing is still good, but once you read the warning, you may not want to eat them. The surrounding waters have reportedly been contaminated by inadequate municipal and private sewage disposal systems. Unless the water has recently been cleaned up, you'd be foolish to swim in it. Yet the age-old beauty of the river still draws one out on a boat, to taste the changing light on the brackish estuary.

In the park, a concession store provides the usual limited snacks and groceries. The Tomoka State Museum offers displays on natural and local history, as well as spunky and often humorous works of art by the late Fred Dana Marsh. The ancient Timucuan Indian village of Nocoroco was located here, and Harvey Oswald, who played an important role in settling the American Revolutionary War, had a large plantation here.

Nearby, everything is urban—a busy coastal city spreads through more and more of the surrounding woods, erasing them as it grows. But here, 900 acres remain of extraordinary coastal hammock and tidal marsh. It's the story of much of natural Florida: how a diamond the size of a boulder was chipped away till you could mount it on a ring.

At this writing, the State of Florida is negotiating to buy some of the hammocks north of Tomoka, so these woods may be saved. But large areas of irreplaceable natural beauty, historical importance, and archaeological interest are being destroyed every month. If you look around, you will see that most of what's saved is saved by being made into some kind of park. The rest is gone, or going now.

Address: Tomoka State Park, P.O. Box 695, Ormond Beach, FL 32074. Telephone 904/677-3931.

TOSOHATCHEE State Preserve

Between Orlando and Titusville, crossed by highways 520, 50 and the Beeline Expressway. Visitor entrance near Christmas, off 50.

Within a short drive of two major cities, bald eagles soar over 300-year-old cypress and virgin slash pines. Thousands of acres of unspoiled marshland ripple like waves on water. Following their ancient natural rhythms as they have since before humans began counting time, the eagles plunge into the wide river for fish. Or they steal food from busy ospreys in mid-air, then, with slow, rolling thrusts of their powerful wings, rise back to the high nesting sites. There, they look out over their domain, an expansive portion of Florida outdoors—in Tosohatchee State Preserve.

Even if you never go to Tosohatchee, just thinking about it does you good. Imagine this: almost 30,000 acres of Florida terrain, much of which has the feel and quality of wilderness. There are several thousand acres of virgin cypress swamp—a thing so rare there are only three or four known places in America where one can still be seen.

Think of this: Even though miles and miles of Florida consist of regular forests of planted slash pines, grown and tended as row-crops of trees, the native slash pine in its virgin habitat is almost unknown. In fact, the only sizeable tract is a 40-acre stand in Tosohatchee, where a stand of pines grows as pines have always grown, unlogged and unplanted, in the conditions they evolved to meet.

Think of this: 10,000 acres of marshlands bordering the wide sweep of the St. Johns River, rolling with the flood, seining out nutrients and pollutants, producing the teeming profusion that only a healthy marsh can make—year after year, with no fertilizers or insecticides, no plow or subsidy. Think of the scenic vista expanding before your eyes as the wide marshes spread out under the open sky, meeting the equally expansive grassland savannah: a deep expression of the specific natural features of this corner of the world—as powerful in its way as a mountain, as striking as deep woods. Only subtler.

Think of this: Several thousand acres of rich hardwood hammock hum to the endless interplay of live oak and cabbage palm. In the mottled shade, imagine deer, bobcat, turkey, barred owls, gray fox, red-shouldered hawks. Listen for songbirds hidden in the shadows. Imagine the marshes alive with egrets, herons, shorebirds, and in winter, imagine the open water dotted by flocks of migrating waterfowl. In your mind, place a few black bear in the wide woods and swamps, and imagine an occasional elusive, very rare Florida panther still finding here a last habitat and home. Think of ospreys so numerous that they nest on the pylons of the high-voltage wires that pass through one corridor of the preserve.

Trails have been opened for day-hikes through Tosohatchee. A visitor center is being considered in the old Bee Head Ranch House (a fine example of early cracker architecture; the wood porch houses a seasoned patina of ambient light). The Florida Trail route has been completed, with spots for overnight primitive camping. Plans are not yet settled, but the preserve may be the site of various scientific studies. It may be on the way toward becoming a major center for environmental education. There may be scheduled field trips you can participate in. Regional colleges may offer nature-study courses using the preserve as a classroom. You may find exhibits, interpretive trails, publications, museum displays, ranger-guided hikes and tours, scenic overlooks, and simple amenities. There are presently no plans for family camping.

Like all preserves, Tosohatchee will mainly be a place for nature—and a place where humans can come to renew themselves by contact with the immense depths of the natural world. In the natural areas of parks and preserves, there are breezes that can blow the dust out of your mind and re-center you in the awareness of what really matters. That alone is reason for preserving wild places.

Looking up into one of the tall, old virgin pines in Tosohatchee State Preserve, a place of rare spaciousness.

Since its purchase, Tosohatchee has been the center of a heated controversy. At issue is whether it will be maintained as a preserve or managed as a state forest or wildlife area for hunting. Large public outdoor spaces in Florida are already so rare that different public agencies battle one another for them.

There are two love stories behind Tosohatchee.

It was owned by a private hunting club for over 50 years. The small membership of this club allowed themselves only limited hunting and followed good management techniques on the property—such as regular ecological burning of the flatwoods. Logging was minimal. Over half a century, they privately preserved this 30,000-acre tract. And they came to love Tosohatchee as a natural home.

In the 1970s, as this part of the state exploded in piecemeal developments and mushrooming tracts of houses, the owners of Tosohatchee secretly asked Florida Audubon Society to find out if the state would consider buying the entire tract. They could have made more money dividing it for development, but the soul of the place has a power over those who know it. They wanted this land to stay the way it was.

The second love story enters here. By an overwhelming majority (75%)

voters in Florida had approved the Environmentally Endangered Lands Bond that provided $200 million for the purchase of rare and vanishing segments of natural Florida. In 1977, Tosohatchee was purchased under that program, in order to preserve its diverse and unique plant communities, profusion of wildlife, vital habitat for endangered species, scientific value, and uplifting scenic vistas.

Address: Tosohatchee State Preserve, Route 4 Box 812, Orlando, FL 32807. Telephone 305/568-5893.

After a summer shower, a black-crowned night heron rests on the dock at Trimble Park, on lovely Lake Beauclair.

▲ TRIMBLE PARK (Orange County)

In the northwestern tip of Orange County. Take 441 west from Orlando, go west on Fla. 448, north (right) on Dora Drive, and west (left) on Earlwood Avenue to the park.

On a peninsula jutting into lovely Lake Beauclair, Trimble Park consists of 71 acres of heavily wooded hardwood hammock—mostly live oaks and cabbage palms, draped with moss and growing to the water's edge. Boating access is exceptionally good. From this launch, you can go north through the Chain of Lakes to the St. Johns, or south to Lake Apopka.

The park has picnic tables, restrooms, showers, playground equipment, a swimming area, and a small campground, where sites are informally arranged. Underbrush has been cleared and replaced with grass, which makes it pleasant but offers little privacy. A resident manager provides security. Fees are average. *For information, write Orange County Parks, address under Magnolia Park. Park telephone: 305/383-2402.*

TURKEY LAKE PARK (City of Orlando)

3401 Hiawassee Road, Orlando.

Though it was developed for heavy use, this 300-acre park retains some of its natural areas. It fronts Turkey Lake, where you can fish from a long pier, launch or rent boats, canoes and sailboats, or swim. There is a family camping area with 32 sites and a primitive camping area for groups. The surrounding woods offer seven miles of hiking and nature trails, and three miles of bicycle trails. (Bikes can be rented at the marina.) A reconstructed cracker farm acts as a junior museum and has a petting zoo. There is an ecology center where rooms may be reserved for meetings.

Turkey Lake has the distinction of being the "beginning of the Everglades." The water starting here keeps flowing south, through the Kissimmee Valley, through Lake Okeechobee, and into the huge grasslands of the Everglades. Manipulation of the water flow here—150 miles north—can affect wildlife in Everglades National Park!

Camping fees are average. Cabins may be rented for up to 10 people.
For information and reservations, write: Turkey Lake Park, 3401 Hiawassee Rd., Orlando, FL 32811. Telephone 305/299-5594.

WASHINGTON OAKS State Gardens

On Fla. A-1-A, just south of Marineland.

Even a little park can have an exceptional diversity. You can walk among the boulders of a unique, rock-strewn beach, watch shorebirds, look into the teeming tidal pools. You can stop in the dry coastal scrub—those low thickets shaped by sand and salt wind—and perhaps the threatened scrub-jay will come out to watch you. You can slip into the rich coastal hammock of large spreading live oaks, palms, hickories, magnolias, ferns, and perhaps come across raccoons, squirrels, and large pileated woodpeckers.

Along the Matanzas River, you can look out upon wide tidal marshes humming with the unseen life of an estuary. As visible portions of that rich chain of life, you will see numerous wading birds, ducks, and gulls in their season.

And in the heart of the park, there are the gardens—planned ornamental gardens under large oaks and palms. Walkways lined with colorful blooms in springtime. Seats in the shade. The hum and smell of blooming profusion.

Part of a plantation that dates back to Spanish Florida, this land was donated as a park by Mrs. Owen D. Young in 1964. There are no camping facilities here. Swimming is not permitted because the rocks are slippery, sharp and dangerous (no joke). You can picnic in the shade of the hammock, or on a shelter on the open beach. Fishing is good in the Atlantic. But it is the gardens that make this park. And it is the integrity of the surrounding area—the rocky shore, the barrier island setting, the vanishing coastal scrub, the dense hammock and spreading western marshes—that give the garden a setting of great natural depth and integrity.

The park opens at 8 A.M. and closes at sunset year round. A small entrance fee is charged.

Address: Washington Oaks State Gardens, Route 1 Box 128A, St. Augustine, FL 32084. Telephone 904/445-3161.

WEKIWA SPRINGS State Park
Northwest of Orlando. Go east of Apopka on Fla. 436, follow signs north on Fla. 490.

Wekiwa Springs State Park is a miracle of diversity. Except for the beach zone, every plant community of central Florida is found here, compactly captured in one preserve. The park has such a fine array of natural features that it is used to train naturalists in the state park system.

Most visitors go only into the southeast corner, where there is a beautiful, large spring, surrounded by shade trees and grassy slopes. It has the magic and coolness of Florida's big springs, especially on a summer Sunday (when the park usually fills up and has to close its gates).

But there is 20 times as much park as the spring area—miles of trails, fire roads, rolling countryside, dense woods, continuously changing natural terrain. This is a portion of very genuine Florida—much as it was when the Indians lived in it.

In between the river and the high ridge, you will find an almost endless gradation of natural habitats. River swamp lines the streams, then grades into the large hydric hammock that covers much of the park—a lush, green area of ferny undergrowth and big hardwoods. Higher up the slope, pine flatwoods emerge on ground that is seasonally wet, but subject to periodic fires. Wet pockets hold bayheads and grassy ponds. Higher still, the flatwoods blend into longleaf pine sandhills, a dry community blessed with a wealth of spring and summer wildflowers. And along the ridge, interspersed in the sandhills, you will find dense thickets of tiltingly tall and irregular sand pines, home of the Florida scrub jay and other unique animals.

With all this space and diversity, the park hosts an abundance of wildlife—from silvery otters to burrowing tortoises. A number of rare and endangered species make their home here.

Wekiwa Springs State Park is an excellent place to see sinkholes and

Wekiwa Springs—shown here in a quiet moment—is a highly popular swimming area surrounded by several thousand acres of unusually diverse and interesting forest.

understand the geology underlying them. This park is essentially a 6,000-acre nature preserve with a recreation area in one corner around the spring.

There is no individual or family camping here, but during the winter season, rangers offer guided backpacking trips (by reservation) into some of the remoter reaches of the park. Cabins, with kitchen and accommodations for up to 140 people, may be rented by organized groups.

The self-guiding nature trail that starts from the swimming area and winds uphill offers the easiest way to sample the richness of nature here. Early in the morning, you may see deer and quick, bushy fox-squirrels.

Some of the finest canoeing in Florida is available here on the Rock Springs Run and the Wekiva River. On the latter, you will pass through the 3500-acre *Lower Wekiva River State Preserve,* a recent Environmentally Endangered Lands purchase not yet developed for public access. This new preserve will probably be open for primitive camping by those in canoes, perhaps with hiking trails, boardwalks and ranger-led activities. Most of the preserve consists of that dense, beautiful swamp that lines Florida's little rivers.

Activities in Wekiwa Springs State Park include fishing (you need a boat), canoeing, picnicking, swimming in the spring, and lots of room for hiking and nature study.

A concession stand near the spring head provides the usual snacks and refreshments.

Address: Wekiwa Springs State Park, 1800 Wekiwa Circle, Apopka, FL 32703. Telephone 305/889-3140.

▲ **WICKHAM PARK (Brevard County)**

In Melbourne on Parkway Drive. From I-95 going south, take Wickham Road exit, go left (south) 8.4 miles to Parkway, turn left at park sign. From I-95 going north, take second Melbourne exit (Fla. 511) to first light; go left (north) on Wickham Road 2.5 miles, right at Parkway. From US 1, turn west on Parkway. Drive one mile inside northern city limits of Melbourne.

Wickham Park is an excellent example of a large county park. It has 500 acres, and almost all of them are developed. The park contains a high concentration of facilities: 54 developed campsites with water and electricity, 32 primitive sites being developed; playgrounds, athletic fields and ball fields; a gun range and archery range; stables, rental horses and riding trails; jogging paths; two man-made swimming lakes; parking lots; ranger residences and park offices. Also, there are camp areas for boy and girl scouts.

Most of the original woods in this site have been cleared off or cleaned up. Palmettoes were bulldozed out to make room for wide grassy lawns, though a fair number of the larger longleaf pines still stand. In the 80 or so acres that are not yet developed, the pine flatwoods have gone unburned long enough to become almost impenetrable with undergrowth, and when a fire does happen, it kills the mature trees—a thing rare in nature.

The park has a fine nature trail with an excellent guidebooklet for use by teachers leading groups.

The camping area is highly lighted at night with bright security lights— something I find a disadvantage when sleeping in a tent, but which seems to make most people feel safer.

Besides well-kept restrooms and hot showers, plenty of bathhouse changing space, the park has pay phones, laundry facilities, a snack bar, an outdoor amphitheatre, and offers 24-hour security, with a resident manager and locked gate.

Although as many as 3,000 people may come here on a hot summer Sunday, Wickham Park does not yet have a limit on the number of visitors allowed at one time. This may change due to strain on the facilities.

You can also see the fate of many county parks here: Over 100 acres of the original park have been taken away by a community college, a high school, and water tower. Every large county park needs a natural buffer zone around it, to shield it from surrounding development. Indeed such "undeveloped" areas are often immensely valuable for protection, for wildlife, and for enhancing the recreational areas of the park. Yet this "undeveloped" land is often taken over, developed, and lost for park use.

Activities at Wickham: swimming, picnicking, family camping, youth camping, playing fields for outdoor sports, jogging, archery, target-shooting, and horseback riding.

Rates are average. Below average for county residents. Pets permitted on leash.

Address: Wickham Park, 2500 Parkway Drive, Melbourne, FL 32935. 305/ 254-1764.

Updates to Central (C) Section

New Listing: **Avon Park Bombing Range** (Fla. 64 on Lake Arbuckle and the Kissimmee River) permits general camping on certain weekends from approximately April through October. Sites have drinking water and restrooms. About a dozen RV sites are available for use by retired military only. For a recording giving current information, call 813/452-4223. For more detailed information, call 813/452-4119.

New Listing: **DeLeon Springs State Recreation Area** has opened, north of Deland, on US 17, adjacent to Lake Woodruff National Wildlife Refuge. Swimming, picknicking, fishing, canoeing, scuba diving; no camping yet. You can rent canoes. Phone 904/985-4212.

New Listing: **Bulow Creek State Preserve**, a large area of coastal hammock, pineland, and coastal marshes, links Tomoka State Park with Bulow Plantation State Historic Site. Though there are no facilities, the preserve is open for activities like fishing, crabbing, and canoeing.

Canaveral National Seashore. Main entrance is Apollo Beach on A1A south of New Smyrna Beach. Good trails nearby. There are a few places for backcountry camping, mainly by boat in Mosquito Lagoon; get a permit. The Playalinda station may be closed in Winter. Parts of the area may also be closed during launches from Kennedy Space Center. Main number: 904/428-3384.

Eustis RV Park is now Southern Palms RV Resort, a private facility whose more than 1200 spaces cater to people living there for extended periods. 1 Avocado Lane, Eustis 32726. Phone 1-800-828-6992.

Fort Christmas Museum is now open every day but Monday. Free. New Phone: 407/568-4149.

Fort Pierce Inlet State Recreation Area. New Phone: 407/468-3985.

New Listing: The 50,000-acre **Green Swamp Flood Detention Area**, between Clermont and Lakeland, has been opened to hiking, with 2 primitive campsites along the trail. Get the latest information from Florida Trail (see Addresses) or SW Florida Water Management District at 904/796-7211.

Hobe Sound National Wildlife Refuge has a new phone, 407/546-6141, and a strip of beach off Fla. 708, on the north end of Jupiter Island.

Jetty Park. More information: Jetty is a fully developed, well supervised, well maintained, busy county park just a few miles from the Kennedy Space Center. Camping fees are average. Full facilities. Store. Good beaches, good fishing places. Resident rangers, quiet hours after 10 p.m. No telephone reservations, no pets. 21 day limit. Write for information sheet: 400 E. Jetty Road, Cape Canaveral, FL 32920-2499. New phone: 407/783-7222.

Jonathan Dickenson State Park is adding a swimming area. Swimming in the river has been stopped due to pollution. New phone: 407/546-2771.

Kelly Park. New phone number: 407/889-4179.

Lake Arbuckle: Phone is 813/534-6075.

Lake Mills Park, 5 miles south of Oviedo off Fla. 419, has a dozen tent sites in a county park with a swimming area and a boardwalk.

Long Point Park permits you to bring only one pet. Reservations by mail and in person only (not by phone). No more rental boats. 14 sites have sewer hookups. New phone: 407/723-3839.

Lower Wekiva River State Preserve. New phone: 407/322-7587.

Magnolia Park has a new phone: 407/886-4231.

Merritt Island National Wildlife Refuge has added a visitor center (about 4 miles E. of Titusville on Fla. 402), which is open every day from November through March; closed Sundays the rest of the year. In winter months, the self-guiding wildlife drive is well worth a trip. Look at the "Calendar of Wildlife Events." The refuge also has a variety of trails up to 5 miles long. Drinking water is available only at the visitor center, so take your own.
Phone 305/867-0667.

Moss Park has a new phone: 407/273-2327 and charges a small entry fee.

New Listing: **Rock Springs Run State Reserve**, just north of Wekiwa Springs State Park has nearly 9,000 acres open to hiking, primitive camping from backpack or canoe, nature study, horseback riding, and seasonal hunting. Park entrance is at the end of Lake County Road 433, off Fla. 46, 8.3 miles west of Interstate Highway 4. For more information, call 904/383-3311.

Saddle Creek Park phone is now 813/665-2283.

The Savannas. 14 day limit, reservations taken up to 60 days in advance. No swimming. New address: 1400 Midway Rd., Ft. Pierce, FL 34982. New Phone: 407/464-7855.

Sebastian Inlet. Address : 9700 South A1A, Melbourne, FL 32951. 407/984-4852.

New Listing: **St. Lucie Inlet State Recreation Area** recently opened on the north end of Jupiter Island, adjacent to Hobe Sound National Wildlife Refuge. Access is by boat only. This 800-acre park provides a beach, boat docks, a boardwalk, toilets , but no electricity and *no drinking water*. There is a "worm reef" offshore popular with divers. 407/744-7603

Southport Park: phone changed to 305/933-5822.

New Listing: **Tenoroc State Reserve** is open, near Lakeland. This 6,000-acre donated park centers around lakes created by the reclamation of land that was strip-mined. Day-use only: good picnic spots, boat ramps, and wild stories about big bass in the lakes. Fishing reservations are recommended (up to 60 days in advance; call weekends only, during the day). Take US 92 from Lakeland east to Combee Road. Go north to Tenoroc Mine Road. Turn east. 813/665-8270.

Tosohatchee is now called a "State Reserve" and has supervised hunting in the fall. It also offers camping for youth groups, primitive backpack camping along the Florida Trail, and horse trails (no horses for rent). New address: 365 Taylor Creek Road, Christmas, FL 32709. 407/568-5893.

Trimble Park. The cabins are rented only to scouting groups. Ample picnic areas. Special facilities for the handicapped, including a five-senses garden and braille signs. New phone: 904/383-1993.

Wekiwa Springs State Park has added a shady 60-unit campground. The park also has good hiking trails through varied terrain and a horse trail (no horses for rent). New Phone: 407/889-3140.

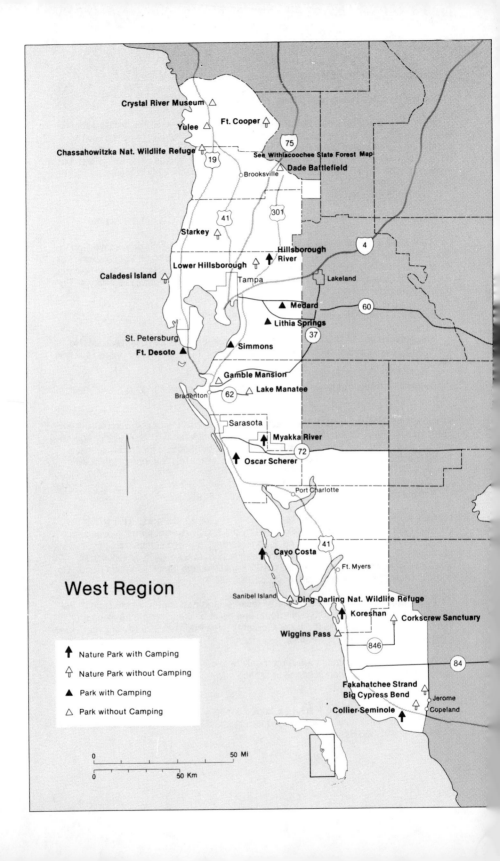

Crystal River Museum △

Yulee △   Ft. Cooper ⇧

Chassahowitzka Nat. Wildlife Refuge ⇧

⃝75

Sea Withlacoochee State Forest Map

⃝19

Dade Battlefield ⇧

○ Brooksville

⃝41   ⃝301

Starkey ⇧

Hillsborough ↑
River

Lower Hillsborough ⇧

Caladesi Island ⇧

Tampa

Lakeland

⃝4

Medard ▲

St. Petersburg

Lithia Springs ▲

⃝60

⃝37

Simmons ▲

Ft. Desoto ▲

Gamble Mansion △

Bradenton

⃝62   Lake Manatee △

Sarasota

Myakka River ↑

⃝72

Oscar Scherer ↑

○ Port Charlotte

⃝41

Cayo Costa ↑

Ft. Myers ○

West Region

Sanibel Island

Ding Darling Nat. Wildlife Refuge ⇧

Koreshan ↑   Corkscrew Sanctuary ⇧

Wiggins Pass △

⃝846

⃝84

Fakahatchee Strand
Big Cypress Bend ⇧   ○ Jerome

Collier-Seminole ↑   ⇧ Copeland

↑ Nature Park with Camping

⇧ Nature Park without Camping

▲ Park with Camping

△ Park without Camping

0   50 Mi

0   50 Km

West

CALADESI ISLAND State Park

Two miles west of Alt. US 19 in Dunedin, offshore. Access by boat or ferry only.

Caladesi is one of the few, rare, marvelous, undisturbed barrier islands in Florida. Much of coastal Florida used to look this way—a long strip of white sandy beach, rolling dunes fringed with tenacious grasses and tough low scrub, inland forests of wind-swept pines and palms, with dense palmetto undergrowth. Stately live oaks hold their moss-draped branches around an old water hole. And, on the eastern shore, a wide, dense thicket of mangrove swamp protects the shoreline and provides food and safety for waters teeming with birdlife and fish.

Almost everywhere else in Florida the barrier islands with their open air, sun, and sand have been built up with roads, homes, condominiums, hotels and, in some places, the carnival atmosphere of tourist beaches. Hardy native vegetation has been bulldozed and replaced with dainty—or dangerous—exotics.

Miraculously, Caladesi Island was spared, and now it is one of the most loved parks on the west coast of Florida—a little remote, a lot remarkable.

Caladesi has a history of being loved. In 1888, a Swiss citizen named Henry Scharrer bought a small sailboat in Tampa and set out to test it before leaving for South America. On that trial run, he took refuge on Caladesi Island during a storm. Hiking over the unknown island, Scharrer fell in love with it. He soon became a citizen, homesteaded there, married by moonlight one lovely evening, and raised a daughter in his "paradise."

On Caladesi Island today you can fish, picnic, go boating, stretch out on the long strip of beach, and wander at will through the pine and oak uplands till the sun goes down. Or you can nose your canoe in and out of the mangrove shallows on the east side, in company with colonies of birds. With any luck at all, an osprey will soar overhead, and you will see a winged piece of earth performing miracles against that large, open sky—miracles that nearly vanished a few years ago due to pesticide residues.

There are no overnight facilities on Caladesi Island. Camping is not permitted.

Concessionaires operate a ferry service and provide minimal snacks and supplies.

A new park, nearby *Honeymoon Island State Recreation Area,* should be open for day-use by the time this book is out.

Address: Caladesi Island State Park, P.O. Box B, Dunedin, FL 33528. Telephone 813/443-5903.

CAYO COSTA State Preserve

On Pine Island Sound, near Charlotte Harbor.

Cayo Costa (pronounced KAYuh COASTuh) and North Captiva Islands together form one of the state's newest preserves—both of them exceptional examples of the unspoiled barrier islands that once lined much of Florida's coastline. Cayo Costa, one of the largest undeveloped barrier islands remaining in the state, looks much as it did almost five hundred years ago when the Spaniards arrived looking for gold. Mounds in the area reveal thousands of years of Indian habitation.

The islands have miles and miles of beaches and dunes facing the open gulf. The interior of the islands is forested by pine flatwoods and oak-palm hammocks that are intermixed with tropical species. Salt marsh and mangrove swamps fringe the bay side and house one of the largest rookeries of brown pelicans in the state.

These beautiful, unspoiled islands are especially noted for their spectacular bird life. Loggerhead sea turtles nest on the beaches on dark summer nights.

Nature study, birding, fishing, shelling, and other beach activities attract most visitors here. There are no facilities, and camping is not permitted. *Address: Cayo Costa State Preserve, % Koreshan State Historic Site, P.O. Box 7, Estero, FL 33928. Telephone 813/992-0311.*

CAYO COSTA Reservation (Lee County Park)

Accessible by boat only, on an island between Captiva and Boca, in Charlotte Harbor.

This 640-acre island park contains a long strip of beach on the Gulf, mangroves on the bay, and walking trails through a wooded area with many Australian pines. Nearby waters are well known for good fishing. There is no electricity on the island, and you are advised to bring your own drinking water.

A hundred tent spaces may be found in the southwestern corner of the park, but you need to register with the caretaker before setting up. Fees are below average.

Twelve rental cabins may be reserved through the county office. For reservation form, write *Lee County Recreation Department, P.O. Box 398, Ft. Myers, FL 33902. Telephone 813/332-0808.*

CHASSAHOWITZKA National Wildlife Refuge

Off US 19-98 near Homosassa.

This 30,000-acre estuarine habitat is one of the finest waterfowl areas in Florida. Many kinds of ducks, numbering in the tens of thousands, winter here. The shallow bays, brackish marshes, creeks and ponds, swamps and island hammocks provide innumerable niches for a wide variety of other birds and animals as well. Herons, egrets, ibises, cormorants, eagles, pelicans, ospreys, mergansers, wood ducks—over 250 species of birds have been recorded here. The refuge also supports an abundant though less visible animal life. Mink, otter, raccoon, alligator, deer, turkey, bobcat and others make this wide, wild area their home. Manatee occasionally come up the rivers.

The main body of the refuge is accessible only by boat, and the few islands are either too fragile or too dangerous to permit hiking. There is one picnic area on the river. Camping is not allowed. Winter and late spring are the best seasons for observing wildlife. Fishing is excellent. One area on the refuge is open for duck hunting during season.

Headquarters are on US 19, 4 miles south of Homosassa Springs. *Address: Route 2 Box 44, Homosassa, FL 32646. Telephone 904/628-2201.*

COLLIER–SEMINOLE State Park

Seventeen miles south of Naples, on US 41.

Here, lush tropical hardwoods meet the swamps of the Big Cypress region at a coast of impenetrable mangroves. This is one of only three places in America where you can see the slender curve of the royal palm—that tree of shopping centers and branch banks—rise above the green backdrop of its natural setting.

Here, tropical and temperate zones mix together—with every kind of wildlife found in south Florida. Dry, sandy soil butts against deep, organic muck. Fresh and salt water mingle. River and ocean blend into one another at the fringe of mangroves and salt marshes. Land and sea meet the huge expanse of open sky. While even a slight change in temperature, salinity or waterflow could wipe out an entire habitat, everything lives, thrives, and flourishes by the most precarious of balances: a balance nature created over many thousands of years, and which man has recently taken upon himself to drain, fill, regulate, and alter. Yet, this is still Florida as man found it—wild, natural, savage, and delicate as an eyelid.

Collier-Seminole State Park is best thought of as a large preserve of impenetrable mangroves and marshes, with a small area developed for human use. Of its 6,500 acres, almost 4,800 are wilderness preserve for the tropical hammock, mangrove swamp, salt marshes and estuary. Once you get out of the campground area, you can begin to taste a sample of Florida's natural heritage in an area virtually undisturbed by modern man, and seek some of the mental spaciousness that wilderness has to offer. These remote areas are home to such rare and endangered species as Florida black bear, mangrove fox squirrel, red-cockaded woodpecker, and manatee, who still find the space here to live as they have for millennia.

Human activities include camping, boating, saltwater fishing, picnicking, and nature study. There is a fine nature trail through a tropical hammock and mangrove area. A replica of an 1830s blockhouse holds a small museum.

WILDERNESS PRESERVE. A 13-mile canoe trail spans the wilderness preserve, taking you through a section of one of the largest mangrove swamps in the world. There is a spot for primitive overnight camping. Because bugs are so

Most of Collier-Seminole State Park is an impenetrable tangle of mangrove swamp and marshes. From the popular campground in the vistor area, you can see lush native palms rising above the tropical hardwoods, near this little museum.

fierce in summer, only winter use is advised. You *must* register before and after this trip; there are dangerous currents to be forewarned of, and areas where even the most experienced wilderness traveller may be baffled by dozens of almost identical mangrove islands.

NOTE: In the summertime, shady areas without breeze are almost uninhabitable due to clouds of mosquitoes. Be advised.

NOTE: The 130-site campground is very popular in winter and is usually full from Thanksgiving to Easter. The surrounding county does not always have enough campgrounds or motels to handle the increased demand. If you are travelling at that time, plan ahead.

NOTE: The water here has such a strong iron taste that you may want to filter it.

Address: Collier-Seminole State Park, Marco, FL 33937. Telephone 813/394-3397.

COPELAND TOWER CAMPSITE

Although still appearing on most road maps, this site was closed to camping early in 1979.

The boardwalk at Corkscrew Swamp Sanctuary takes you through the only virgin cypress swamp remaining in South Florida. Forests of this magnificence once lined most Florida rivers and strands.

CORKSCREW SWAMP SANCTUARY (Audubon Society)

Entrance off C-846, 21 miles from US 41 at Naples Park, and 14 miles from Immokalee.

Corkscrew Swamp Sanctuary is unique. There is nothing like it: the last remaining example of an undisturbed south Florida cypress strand. It is magnificent beyond description. Immense, 500-year-old trees tower above you like gray giants, their trunks and limbs jeweled with orchids and air-plants. The ground is alive with fern-forests, big-eared fire flags rise from the standing water, wild hibiscus unfold a translucent grace, fallen logs host a world of mosses, tiny duckweed floats on the water, and dense crops of native water-lettuce turn the open ponds into thick carpets of green. There is a stunning, sleek, graceful little royal palm growing in the shelter of one of the giant cypresses. Everything *fits:* there is a sense of rightness here that you can find only in true wilderness—every leaf, twig, feather, bubble or glint rises to your perception directly from the deepest laws of nature, and you can feel the presence of the forces that shape the world. No human environment can give this. It is a magical place.

High in the moss-draped, spreading cypresses the wood storks come back each winter to breed. Corkscrew Swamp has the largest colony in the country, and this is one of their last refuges from human developments that have almost obliterated these strange, graceful birds whose biological clocks demand the kind of conditions people seek to remove.

Winter is the peak season for storks and other birds, which sometimes concentrate in breath-taking numbers. But you can never quite count on it. The animals are not fed here. They are not kept for show. Instead, they follow their ancient natural rhythms and come and go without consulting anyone. Nature keeps only its own appointments.

Summers at Corkscrew are times of lushness. The orchids bloom. The waters are alive with reproducing fish and aquatic animals. The rich vegetation is at its peak. Lichens flame into crimson following a rain. Oddly, mosquitoes are rarely bad—probably because there is so much life in the swamp to feed on them.

There is a fine little visitor center and a boardwalk trail almost two miles long, looping through a world unlike any other you will ever have the chance to visit. The guidebook is first-rate, and the staff occasionally offer excellent interpretive programs. Groups may request in advance a naturalist-guided tour. But more than most parks, what happens here is largely up to nature and you.

Take everything you need, because there are no nearby supplies except for light snacks in vending machines. Take binoculars and a camera with high-speed film (the light in the swamp is low).

In the mid-1950s, when Corkscrew Swamp was threatened with logging, drainage, and development, numerous individuals and conservation groups banded together to raise funds to purchase it. The Ford Foundation helped. Thousands of people, moved by the tragedy of our vanishing wilderness, gave money and time. Even the owners of the "timber"—in a move of great corporate generosity—donated a section as a memorial. These combined efforts resulted in the preservation and development of a place where you can easily enter and experience one of the great primeval forests of the world.

The Visitor's Center and boardwalk trail are open daily from 9 to 5.

Admission is in the $4 range for adults, less for students.

There are no camping facilities here, and overnight camping is not allowed within sanctuary boundaries or parking area. Because of their high impact on delicate areas, pets are not admitted. The boardwalk is accessible by wheelchairs, which are available.

Address: Corkscrew Swamp Sanctuary, Route 6 Box 1875-A, Naples, FL 33942. Telephone 813/657-3771.

CRYSTAL RIVER State Archaeological Site

West of US 19-98, just north of Crystal River.

These Indian mounds—some of the highest in Florida—mark the site of 1600 years of human habitation, and stand as the graveyard for a vanished civilization. For centuries, there was a flourishing city here, fed by the steady supply of shellfish in the river. Artifacts reveal that it had links with the ancient temple-builders of the Yucatan. Now, it is a place to walk quietly and listen to the sound of the rise and fall of civilizations lapping at the shore.

A fine museum houses somewhat technical exhibits of artifacts found here—a large spread of arrowheads, pottery pieces, and interesting historical exhibits that deepen your experience of Florida.

When you climb the steep steps of the largest temple mound and look through the limbs of leaning live oaks at the wide river spreading out before you, you may be shocked to find yourself almost on the roofs of a trailer park that jams up against the site—actually cutting into the mound itself. Now another boundary of the park is scheduled for development. The bustle of a modern suburb could make it almost impossible to find the quiet and the solitude necessary to send your imagination back through the centuries to those mysterious mounds. That would be a loss. So few things in our world reward reflection. It would be a shame to degrade one that does.

Address: Crystal River State Archaeological Site, Route 3 Box 457-E, Crystal River, FL 32629. Telephone 904/795-3817.

DADE BATTLEFIELD State Historic Site

One mile SW of Bushnell on US 301.

The bloodiest and most costly of America's Indian Wars started here in 1835, when Osceola's associates, Micanopy and Alligator, devastated a detachment led by Major Dade. The war is history, but the pine woods and palmettoes still stand, looking as they did during the battle. A museum at the site contains artifacts and exhibits about the battle, and the surrounding area functions as a large county park: open woods, grassy lawns, a ball field, good picnicking grounds, tennis courts, shuffleboard, horseshoes. A nature trail follows the Dade detachment through the fatal pines.

The park has a large rental hall and kitchen for day and night use, but no camping is allowed here.

One of the oldest roads in the state, the Old Fort King Military Road, goes through the park.

Address: Dade Battlefield State Historic Site, P.O. Box 938, Bushnell, FL 33513. Telephone 904/793-4781.

DING DARLING National Wildlife Refuge

On Sanibel Island, west of Ft. Myers on Fla. 867, across a toll bridge.

This fine natural area contains dry upland forests, dense mangrove swamps, and rich estuarine waters, to provide a varied habitat for a wide range of wildlife, especially migratory birds that winter here. There is excellent visitor access, with walking trails, a nature drive, an observation tower, a boardwalk, and a short canoe trail. No camping; access is limited to daytime hours.

The larger dunes are host to a dry habitat of cabbage palm, seagrape, gumbo limbo, strangler fig, and palmetto, as well as raccoons, rabbits, gopher tortoises, indigo snakes, and woodland birds.

The mangroves form the largest part of the refuge. Their tangled shade provides sanctuary for numerous birds and fish, including the ibis that nest there and bald eagles that come to feed.

Mudflats and roadside canals hold many wading birds, such as the roseate spoonbills, herons, egrets, and sanderlings.

The estuary of Pine Island Sound, with its prolific aquatic vegetation, provides a breeding ground and nursery for many kinds of fish. An estuary like this produces more life-giving energy per acre than any human agriculture.

The Sanibel Island Conservation Center, near the wildlife drive, offers a fine nature center with exhibits on the wildlife and ecology of the island. You can find information here on solar energy and see a model solar project. You might also find someone who will talk to you about ways residents of this island tried to develop *with* nature instead of against it. The Sanibel group has pioneered extensive use of native vegetation in landscaping, and can show you how this saves energy, time, effort, and environment.

Outside the center a network of nature trails leads through a predominantly mangrove area to an overlook. There is an excellent guidebook on sale at the center.

For additional information on the refuge, write *Refuge Manager, Ding Darling National Wildlife Refuge, P.O. Drawer B, Sanibel, FL 33957.*

FAKAHATCHEE STRAND State Preserve

Boardwalk on US 41 at Big Cypress Bend; Scenic Drive out of Copeland.

The state is still acquiring land in what will someday be a 60,000-acre preserve encompassing some of the most beautiful natural areas in Florida. There is no place in the state this size that has so much to offer. The largest stand of wild native royal palms in the world grows here, along with the world's only forest of royal palm and cypress. There are more orchids in this park than anywhere else in North America. Many rare and endangered species still live here, and the Florida panther prowls the strand as one of his last strongholds. It is a place of extraordinary wildness, variety, and natural wealth. Even though logging, drainage and fires have taken their toll, Fakahatchee Strand still remains one of the state's finest natural features.

In the remote areas of Fakahatchee Strand, Big Cypress, and a very few other Florida Parks, the remaining dozen or two Florida panthers walk the tightrope of extinction.

The natural setting of the preserve includes grassy prairies, pinelands, marshes, and coastal estuarine creeks packed with mangroves. But the central attraction is the large cypress strand—a remote, interior haven for wild creatures and wild orchids, logged over, but miraculously alive and well.

The easiest way to get a look at this territory is on the boardwalk at Big Cypress Bend, behind Indian Village, on US 41 about seven miles west of Fla. 29. Here, you can walk a dry path among virgin cypress, draped with orchids and jeweled with bursts of bromeliads—with the ancient cathedral trees towering above you. Like Corkscrew Swamp Sanctuary, this is a thrilling remnant of Florida's original wilderness. (Mosquitoes can be fierce in summer.)

The other access is through Copeland to the Janes Memorial Scenic Drive, a twenty-mile round trip. A few miles along this drive will show you all you can expect to see from a car of this exceptionally dense and lush swampland. About seven miles up, there is a nice picnic area. It's a slow, pot-holed road, so don't plan to zip through.

To really see the preserve, you would have to join one of the rangers on a "wade", or travel (carefully) on your own off the road, down the tram roads, into some of the sloughs. Needless to say, be informed and be prepared before you try this; it's as demanding as hiking in the desert.

If you travel to the end of the Scenic Drive, you will see what has been called one of Florida's most immense and disastrous real estate developments. Years ago, an unthinkably vast region (260,000 acres) of cypress swamp was drained and a huge grid of roads put in. Many lots were sold, but when I last visited it, almost nobody was living there. This has been cited as a classic example of a development that caused severe ecological damage, yet was in the end defeated by the environment it tried to subdue.

All plant and animal life in the preserve is protected. Collecting of plants is strictly prohibited and enforced. No camping; minimal facilities; minimal programs.

Address: Fakahatchee Strand State Preserve, P.O. Box 548, Copeland, FL 33962. Telephone 813/695-4593.

FORT COOPER State Park

A few miles south of Inverness, off Fla. 39.

A difficult moment in Florida's history is captured in this 700-acre park, which now serves to provide open space for visitors and access to lovely, clear Lake Holathlikaha. The park is primarily used for swimming, fishing, picnicking and nature study. There are no camping facilities. Hours are from 8 AM till sunset.

Near the lake's edge on the Old Military Trail, a fort was hastily erected to provide a place for General Winfield Scott's sick and wounded soldiers to recuperate for a couple of weeks in 1836, during the darkest days of the Second Seminole War.

Now you will find a hardwood forest of oaks, hickories, magnolias, and sweetgums, and, farther from the lake, the open, dry grassy sandhills of longleaf pines. As in all state parks, a large portion of the area is left undeveloped and in its natural state, in order to maintain a high-quality environment and enhance the recreational areas in the park.

Address: Fort Cooper State Park, P.O. Box 1541, Inverness, FL 32656. Telephone 904/726-0315.

FORT DESOTO PARK (Pinellas County)

In St. Petersburg, at the southern tip of the city. Go south on US 19, west on 54th Avenue, and take the Bayway (toll road) into the park.

Fort DeSoto Park is a major urban recreation area and an excellent example of a large county park. Spread over five islands, this 900-acre park offers camping, fishing, bicycling, boat ramps, piers, more than seven miles of waterfront, almost three miles of swimming beaches, large picnic areas, the remains of a historic fort, and shellfishing in nearby waters. There are lots of water-birds and shorebirds who consider the park home, and the rangers maintain an excellent nature trail. It is a park of well-mowed lawns, many Australian pines, and groves of native palm trees from the park's own nursery. Features of the park range from crowded fishing piers to deserted mangrove coastline.

The park is staffed with resident rangers, and though it is traversed by a county road open 24 hours a day, the camping area is locked at night for security. There are public phones and laundry facilities located in the camping area, as well as a concession with fishing supplies and a restaurant near the pier.

Campsites are choice—well-designed, separated from one another by a wall of native vegetation, equipped with water and electric hookups, and close to the modern restrooms. Fees are about average, but the unusual reservation system is designed to favor local residents and their guests over tourists. Reservations must be made in person and paid in advance; you should write or call for details.

If you are in the area, you may want to visit some of the other Pinellas County parks. At Heritage Park the county has reconstructed ten acres of historical buildings—including a log cabin, an old railroad station, a cane mill, an old barn and an 85-year-old house with its original furnishings.

Brooker Creek Park, on Lake Tarpon, preserves the last natural creek in heavily urban Pinellas County. It is an area where eagles still are said to nest, along with great blue herons, numerous ospreys, and a large rookery of wading birds. The park has an observation tower and boardwalk near the lake, a swimming area, picnic shelters, and boat dock. No camping.

Like some of the other major counties in Florida, Pinellas wisely chose to spend its park money to buy large tracts of land for regional parks. Local townships have been given the responsibility for providing most recreational facilities, such as pools and ballfields, while the county concentrated on large projects out of the reach of individual towns. Without some policy like this, few of Florida's urban counties would have much open space, given the state's rate of development.

Address: Pinellas County Parks, 407 South Garden Avenue, Clearwater, FL 33516. Park telephone 813/866-2662.

GAMBLE PLANTATION State Historic Site
Also known as "J.P. Benjamin Memorial."

On US 301 in Ellenton, north of Bradenton.

Here is history on a busy road, a memorial to a way of life long gone. Inside the thick "tabby" walls—made of a sort of oyster-shell concrete—you may get out of earshot of busy 301, even though the trucks are roaring past a hundred yards away. And when you do, you are wrapped in the silence and coolness of an older world. Beautifully crafted antiques present themselves to you at every turn. And each is in its proper setting—where it was made to be used.

A superb tour portrays the way of life lived by the wealthy planters of the late 1840s in this remote, swampy part of Florida. The rooms are resonant with that history.

The United Daughters of the Confederacy deserve credit for rescuing the Gamble Mansion in 1925, when it was being used as a warehouse, and donating it to the state.

Tours are given on the hour from 9 to 4.

Address: Gamble Plantation State Historic Site, Ellenton, FL 33532. Telephone 813/722-1017.

The Gamble mansion—dating from the 1840s—has been beautifully restored and furnished with antiques from that period. The park service gives excellent tours several times a day.

HILLSBOROUGH RIVER State Park

Six miles south of Zephyrhills, entrance off US 301. NOTE: Some maps show this park on the wrong road, and there are few signs. Watch carefully.

The Hillsborough River makes this park. Clear, dark water flows through a rich profusion of trees. You feel at once that you are in a "primal place"—one that has looked this way for centuries. The river and surrounding hammock are stunning. Given half a chance, they will take your breath away. It is the kind of place that seems to be moving at immense speed, racing with life, though everything is still. It has the magic of an undisturbed natural area: every sense drinks deeply, and you know there is always more beyond what you can perceive.

The river is spanned by two footbridges, one of which was built by the Civilian Conservation Corps in the 1930s—works of art in themselves. You can just stand and look at them with pleasure, and the view of the river from these bridges seems inexhaustible. Trails line the river, and there is a fine nature trail through the nearby hammock.

Walking the nature trail, you may be startled to come to the edge of the park and see how these rich woods vanish instantly at the fence line. Without parks to preserve them, most great natural areas in the state might be cleared for pasture or development.

The river is surrounded by interior pine flatwoods; a fine hardwood hammock flourishes along the bank; the lowlands are punctuated by cypress domes and freshwater marshes; and the river supports a thriving community of plant life and aquatic animals.

There are areas in the park for camping, picnicking under large spreading shade-trees, swimming, fishing, hiking, canoeing, and bicycling. Rangers give slide shows and nature talks at the campfire circle.

Highly unusual for Florida, limestone rocks jut out in a stretch of the river, forming one of the few "rapids" in this region of the state. Many of the rocks support lovely microhabitats of ferns, grasses, and insects.

Two large camping areas offer fine sites amid longleaf pines, oaks, and palmettos. Buffer vegetation is good in some sites; others are more exposed. At night you may find swamp rabbits nibbling the grass in your campsite.

The river was closed to swimming when I was last there, due to contamination from cattle ranches upstream. But a man-made lake provides a curious swimming area in the park. This pool, though, is very heavily used on warm weekends, and local swimmers often fill up the park at that time because of an apparent lack of local facilities. This is a shame. There are plenty of places to put swimming pools, but few fine natural areas like this one that reward silence and contemplation.

Additional wild areas downriver can be traversed only by canoe. There is some talk of allowing primitive camping there.

Across the highway from the entrance, the park system has done a

When it is not overrun with swimmers, the Hillsborough River is a place of deep, peaceful beauty. A few miles upstream from this footbridge, interesting historical programs are offered at reconstructed Fort Foster.

stunning job of reconstructing a pioneer Florida fort—Fort Foster—and has an interesting interpretive program at that site. Ask about it when you arrive. This portion of the river, though only a few hundred yards from busy 301, is a charmed world of moving water and mottled shade.

Address: Hillsborough River State Park, Route 4 Box 250-L, Zephyrhills, FL 33599. Telephone 813/986-1020.

KORESHAN State Historic Site

In Estero, south of Ft. Myers, on US 41.

This park reflects that freedom of religion which is one of America's most basic values. In the middle of the nineteenth century's utopian revelations, Cyrus Reed Teed established the unusual religion of Koreshanity. With his powerful personality and vision, he attracted numerous professional people down to a remote Florida wilderness river where they spent days digging with their hands and nights in communal celibacy, to create an exquisitely beautiful settlement. Today, the structures and grounds convey a strong, subtle presence, and you

197

know at once that you are in a place shaped by human beings under the influence of something deeper than their daily selves.

The park has a fine camping area with plenty of native vegetation separating the 60 sites. Average fees. Harmless native woodrats climb the stubby palms like squirrels. Fish are plentiful in calm little Estero River. A nature trail takes you through the beautiful natural woods along the riverside. The river makes a memorable canoe trip (canoes can be rented nearby). There are good picnicking places and a playground for children.

Ranger-led tours of the settlement buildings are offered several times a day. A small fee is charged.

Address: Koreshan State Historic Site, P.O. Box 7, Estero, FL 33928. Telephone 813/992-0311.

One of the exquisite original buildings at Koreshan State Historic Site, built over a hundred years ago by a utopian religious community that moved to what was at that time a remote Florida wilderness.

 LAKE MANATEE State Recreation Area

About 15 miles east of Bradenton on Fla. 64.

This park serves to provide day-access to Lake Manatee, a long, narrow reservoir. Here you can fish, swim in a guarded area, launch your boat, or picnic. The park is open from 8 AM till sunset. No camping is allowed.

The 500 acres upland of the lake's edge hold some of the typical watershed for this region: pine flatwoods, hardwood hammock, pine sandhills, and some acreage of sand pine scrub. Visitors may hike the fire trails into the natural area. *Address: Lake Manatee State Recreation Area, Myakka Star Route, Parrish, FL 33564. Telephone 813/746-8042.*

LITHIA SPRINGS PARK (Hillsborough County)

Take Fla. 640 southeast of Brandon to park road.

This 300-acre county park on the Alafia River (pronounced AL-uh-FYE) offers fishing, canoeing, swimming and playground activities, along with 60 developed campsites with water and electricity. There is a concession stand, bathhouse and picnic area. Average fees.
For information contact Hillsborough County Parks at the address under Medard Park. Park telephone: 813/689-2139.

Lower Hillsborough River, preserved to aid in flood control, will someday be a major regional recreation area.

199

LOWER HILLSBOROUGH RIVER WILDERNESS PARK (County)

Fla. 579 at the Hillsborough River.

In conjunction with the Southwest Florida Water Management District, Hillsborough County is developing a major recreational facility in the 17,000-acre flood detention area downriver from Hillsborough River State Park. Mostly a huge cypress swamp, with some flatwoods and sandhills, the park will eventually feature picnic areas, trails, tent camping, bike trails, canoeing, and a magnificent nature preserve. Present activities are limited mainly to fishing and canoeing.

Wildlife is very abundant now and includes a number of endangered species. It remains to be seen how much wildlife can survive development in and around the park.

This will one day be a major regional park, with more than 1.5 million people living within an hour's drive of it.

For information, contact Hillsborough County Parks at the address under Medard Park.

MEDARD PARK (Hillsborough County)
Also called "Pleasant Grove Reservoir."

Southeast Hillsborough County. Go 6 miles east of Brandon on Fla. 60; take Turkey Creek Road two miles south to park.

An area of abandoned mine-pits was converted into a reservoir in the early '70s, and the surrounding woods have been developed into a park totalling 1200 acres.

The 800-acre reservoir forms the central attraction in this park. It is said to have some of the best fishing in the county. There are developed camping facilities, as well as opportunities for swimming, hiking, boating, and picnicking. Horseback trails have been planned through the surrounding stands of pine and oaks. Camping fees are average.

For information, write Hillsborough County Parks, P.O. Box 1110, Courthouse, Tampa, FL 33601. Telephone 813/272-5840.

MYAKKA RIVER State Park

Seventeen miles east of Sarasota, on Fla. 72. NOTE: the north entrance, shown on maps as Fla. 780, is open only on busy weekends and holidays; it is CLOSED all other times.

A pair of sandhill cranes standing in the layered twilight waters, asleep, bills tucked under their closed wings.

Choruses of frogs tuning up for the night, each entering on some unpredictable but impeccable rhythm.

Alligators emerging at dusk to wait motionless in the millennia of reptilian patience.

A few spoonbills mixed in the flock of ibis: pink reflections among the white.

Everywhere you turn, you are surprised by wildlife.

Yet there is something more that is not these living things—not the hundreds of wading birds wheeling on some unseen pivot in the sky; not the moving shadows of raccoons, opossums, bobcats; not the barred owls breaking up the deep cricket silence of the evening; something not the sleek silent deer on the marsh's edge; not the rattlesnake disappearing into pinestraw; not the heavy black heads of wood storks at the shallow shoreline; not the fish breaking the immense flat surface of the starlit lake. There is something that is not the great

One of Florida's finest nature areas, Myakka River State Park alternates between spacious vistas and dense forests.

blue heron frozen in concentration in the disguising grasses, not the green chameleon flaring its red throat. Not the buzzing, the humming, the singing, the chirping, the drumbeat rhythms and small crying songs that fill every night-space, till a random silence startles like a broken window.

Life teems here in this rich river-valley. Yet you feel something that is not that life. You feel the place: the river, the valley, the lake, marshes, pinewoods, the deep hammock shade and the impenetrable palmetto prairies. You feel the *space,* the ecosystem—thirty thousand acres of lush, productive, wild, natural land.

We usually notice plants and animals. We can focus on them—they stand out, they are colorful, they fly, dart, clash, struggle, bloom. Their time scale is something we can comprehend. So we watch birds. We fish. We look at flowers. We wait for deer to emerge at dusk. We listen to the katydids.

But behind them all looms the landscape, and it is the landscape that gives life and meaning to all the wildlife and birdlife, all the fish and buzzing profusion. In a place like this you can not only have your breath taken away by the sudden soaring of a hundred egrets against the cloud-flecked sky—but you can feel nature like a deep, breathing presence behind those dazzling figures.

No matter how long we live in climate-controlled houses, well-lit cities, amid the blare of our manufactured images, nature is still where we were born. Our deepest rhythms are its rhythms. Behind the ducks and deer, the bass and ibis, the baby alligators and immense oaks, there is something that we still recognize as home: that meeting of land, sky, and water that supports so rich a setting; that spacious vista underneath an open sky where every sense finds an endless variety of forms to fulfill it; where the city-tightened body loosens and expands, and discovers that wild nature is the world it was born to learn from, set to respond in; and that these long sunsets and moonrises re-tune something deeper than our knowing, to make us more human and more whole.

Here you can clearly see how a spacious and healthy natural environment produces profusions of wildlife. Here are marvellous dense hammocks of oak and palm, extensive marshes, wide expanses of palmetto-prairies, tall pine flatwoods, river-bottom and lake-life, floodplain forests along the river—and all the throbbing life that lives and feeds on such diversity. No one feeds the animals but nature, and they are here because they are living manifestations of the forces that shape this landscape. Everything belongs.

The campgrounds are not the best (76 sites spread among 2 camps, water and electric hookups in most). They are somewhat crowded and some are too close to the noise of the sewage lift station. The bathrooms are old and frayed. But that doesn't matter. It is such a rare privilege to visit a spacious piece of original Florida that inconveniences seem trivial. Even the ravenous summertime mosquitoes are forgiveable.

The park has a fine little museum and an excellent series of ranger-led programs. There are fine picnicking areas along the river and lake. A few log cabins can be reserved (well in advance). Fish are plentiful if the exotic waterweed, hydrilla, is not choking them out. The Myakka is being studied for designation as a National Wild and Scenic River. There is a concession with the usual picnicking and fishing supplies; it also runs a tram tour and boat tour of the park, and rents boats, bicycles, and canoes for poking around the long shoreline

A red-shouldered hawk—part of the abundant wildlife visible at Myakka River State Park.

of the Myakka Lakes. Groceries are readily available a few miles outside the park.

The southern part of the park is a wonderful 7500-acre **Wilderness Preserve**, limited to day-use by foot and canoe. Here you can seek an even deeper experience of the Florida wilderness, enriched by the voices of your own solitude. Those who want to camp with greater privacy can backpack to a primitive site in the main park.

Like several important Florida parks, Myakka owes its start to a few generous people. In 1934 the sons of Mrs. Potter Palmer donated a large tract of this land to Florida in memory of their mother, for use as a park. The state acquired additional lands, and in 1935 the out-of-work men of the Civilian Conservation Corps put their hard labor and fine craftsmanship into developing this park for public use. From the beginning, people have mattered to parks.

And in time to come, as we become even more insulated from our tough, fragile roots in nature, parks like this will matter more and more to people.

In the winter season, reservations are essential. Migratory birds reach spectacular concentrations during that time, though the park is beautiful and can be enjoyed (with a good tent and repellant) all year.

Address: Myakka River State Park, Route 1, Box 72, Sarasota, FL 33577. Telephone 813/924-1027.

W

OSCAR SCHERER State Recreation Area

Two miles south of Osprey on US 41.

Most people come here to swim in the little lake, or picnic along the river. But there is a dimension to this park that goes beyond recreation, for it is important in the lives of the noblest and the fussiest of our rare birds. Bald eagles may occasionally soar overhead from their nearby nesting site, and, if you look at them long enough, a cocky, curious, threatened scrub jay may slip in and steal your picnic.

The very features that make this an attractive natural park—the hundreds of acres of pine woods, the lovely tidal creek with its marshes, mangroves, and estuary—also make it a vital habitat for these and other rare species.

Besides swimming and picnicking on the lovely lake, the park offers both fresh and saltwater fishing. South Creek is a popular place to canoe. The large campground (104 sites with water and electricity) is especially well-developed, with sites that seem tunnelled into the shady woods. An excellent, self-guiding nature trail takes you along the creek.

A concession in the picnic area sells the usual snacks and supplies, and rents canoes and bicycles.

Address: Oscar Scherer State Recreation Area, P.O. Box 398, Osprey, FL 33559. Telephone 813/966-3154.

On the South Creek canoe trail, at Oscar Scherer State Park.

204

SIMMONS PARK (Hillsborough County)

On Tampa Bay, northwest of Ruskin. Go two miles west of US 41 on 19th avenue.

This bayside, mangrove-dominated, 500-acre park offers a place for water-sports—swimming, boating, fishing and canoeing. The camping area features 60 sites with water and electricity. Fees are average.

For information, contact Hillsborough County Parks at the address under Medard Park.

STARKEY WILDERNESS AREA (Pasco County)

In Western Pasco County in the Pinellas-Anaclote River Basin.

This 5400-acre park may not be open yet, but when it is, it will probably continue to remain in as natural a state as possible. It will serve primarily as a well-field for the regional water supply, with recreation activities probably limited to nature trails, hiking paths, and limited camping.

For information, contact the Southwest Florida Water Management District, 5060 US 41 South, Brooksville, FL 33512.

WIGGINS PASS State Recreation Area

About 30 miles south of Ft. Myers. Turn off US 41 onto County Road 901 at the sign.

Dear little Wiggins Pass! This small area (166 acres) leaves you torn between rejoicing and weeping. You rejoice because it provides access to a truly fine piece of beach on a beautiful barrier spit—where the ocean and sky open out on the wide Gulf. Yet you weep because, when you turn around and face inland, all you see are the tall walls of condominiums, like giants from outer space stalking across the little landscape.

All over Florida, parks are losing their sense of spaciousness as developments crowd upon their boundaries, bulldoze away buffer zones and fill up the wild horizons. Without losing a square inch of public land, a park can lose half its sense of space when buildings pant at its perimeter. And the wildlife—which knows no boundaries—will become less frequent inside parks, because they have lost the surrounding habitat that is crucial for many of them.

Wiggins Pass is a day-use beach. You can swim in fine surf, and brown under that lovely sun. Fishing in the bay is popular, and there is a picnic area shaded with exotic Australian pines. Fine hardy sea-grapes give life to the bathhouse area, and boardwalks protect you from the sandspurs while they protect the slight dunes from the wear of many feet.

In early summer, Wiggins Pass rangers take visitors along with them on the nighttime "turtle walks." Depending on the weather, beach, season, tide, luck, and the turtles, you might see a giant sea-reptile haul herself onto the shore, and in a primeval scraping of flippered feet, dig out a small cave to contain all her

At Wiggins Pass—as at more & more of Florida's beaches and parks—human developments such as these condominiums crowd up against the recreation area, walling out much of the spaciousness that parks try to preserve.

hopes for the future. But remember, the turtles don't work for the state. You might go out and get mosquito-bit and aggravated to death by sandflies, and see nothing but the stars that presided over the birth of the world.

Because there are so few public beaches in this area, Wiggins Pass is very busy, especially when the human migrants arrive in the wintertime. It can be filled to capacity and closed by 10 or 11 AM on a winter weekend. Plan for this.

North of Wiggins Pass, accessible by boat only, lies the long, thin stretch of **Barefoot Beach State Preserve,** a Florida beach captured in its natural condition—a rare thing for this corner of the state.

Address: Wiggins Pass State Recreation Area, 11100 Gulf Shore Blvd., North Naples, FL 33940. Telephone 813/597-6196.

WITHLACOOCHEE State Forest

Off I-75 south of Leesburg, near Brooksville.

The Withlacoochee State Forest consists of three separated areas: Croom, Citrus, and Richloam.

The **Croom District,** the main visitor area, is a varied region of longleaf

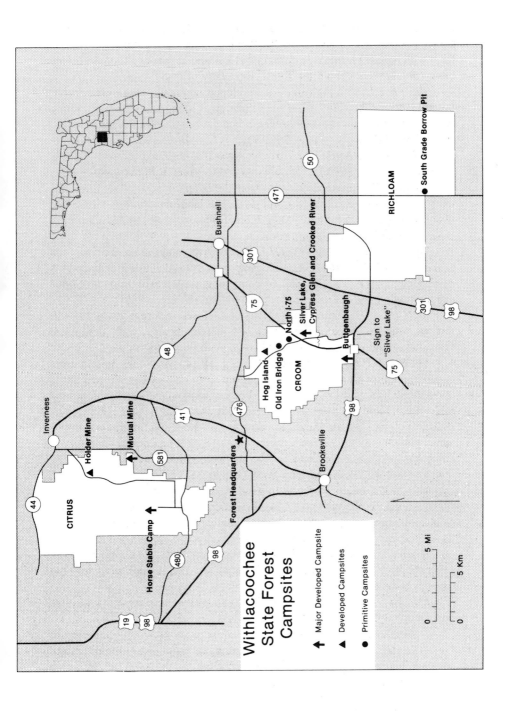

pines and turkey oak hills, live oak thickets, hardwood hammocks, cypress ponds, prairies, and ravines, with the Withlacoochee River running through it, lined with typical Florida river swamp and lowland hammock. There are many beautiful areas throughout the forest, especially near the river.

SILVER LAKE is the principal developed recreation area in the forest. Some 120 campsites are spread over three areas along a lovely lake, with a swimming beach, rustic bathhouses, and boat launch area for fishing, boating, and skiing. The easiest route to Silver Lake is from Brooksville: go east on 98, cross I-75, turn left (north) on a little access road leading into the forest. There is a sign at that turn. Average fees are charged to camp at Silver Lake.

Interstate 75 runs about 50 yards from the campground at Silver Lake, and the trucks boom past all night. But down the lake, the Cypress Glenn and Crooked River campgrounds offer more isolation in developed campsites among a beautiful shaded hammock.

Upstream there is the *NORTH I-75* primitive campsite on the river, and farther still the *OLD IRON BRIDGE* campground, located in a high hammock ridge along the river. This site is being upgraded into a fully developed campground.

HOG ISLAND, farther upriver, has been closed in recent years, but will also be reopened as a major developed recreation area, with designated campsites, running water, and a bathhouse with flush toilets.

The *BUTTGENBAUGH MOTORCYCLE AREA* is one of the most unusual features in a Florida park. Old mine pits have been converted into one of the finest motorcycle parks in the country. There is a large developed campground and miles of varied cycle trails. The required permit may be obtained from the resident ranger. Cyclists should familiarize themselves with the rules for this area, because they are enforced, and violators lose their permits. Entrance is alongside the Holiday Inn on Fla. 50, just west of I-75.

The **Citrus District** of the Withlacoochee State Forest, located to the northeast of Croom, adjacent to Inverness, consists mainly of longleaf pine sandhills, oak scrub, sand pine, and some rocky hammocks, with lakes made from a few abandoned mines. It is a dry region, with no running streams. Three developed areas permit camping.

HOLDER MINE Recreation Area offers camping around the sloping sides of an old mine pit with a lake in the bottom of it. The 20 sites are grassy and open, in pinelands.

MUTUAL MINE, similar to Holder, is a prettier site and has a resident attendant.

HORSE STABLE CAMP (also known as Tillis Hill) is developed for horseback riding and dog field-trials. Campsites are primarily for those engaged in horse and dog activities, or other legitimate group activities. Advance reservations are required for this area.

The **Richloam District** of the forest, located southeast of the Croom

District, across US 301, is primarily used for hunting and fishing. Several primitive campsites are made available during hunting season, but only one is currently open year-round: *South Grade Borrow Pit,* on Fla. 471. Richloam is the wettest district in the forest, covered mainly by pine flatwoods, gallberry, palmetto, hardwood hammock, and cypress swamps. Like most flatwood areas, it can get soggy during rainy weather.

All three districts of the Withlacoochee State Forest have miles of developed hiking trails, with good brochures available from forest headquarters.

Forest Headquarters is located on US 41 at Fla. 476. Nearby, there is a good nature trail into a longleaf and sand-pine forest that is succeeding to hardwoods due to the exclusion of natural fire. Another nature trail around nearby McKethan Lake takes you from bottomland hardwoods into high pine forest. Informative brochures are available for both trails.

Camping in the forest is permitted *only* in designated areas, and note that all camping facilities may be filled on a busy holiday weekend. An average fee is charged in all developed campgrounds; primitive sites are free. Pets are not permitted in the developed campgrounds or swimming areas.

Address: Withlacoochee State Forest, 7255 US 41 North, Brooksville, FL 33512. Telephone 904/796-4958.

The big wheels at Yulee Sugar Mill State Historic Site. Historic and archaeological sites in Florida are being bulldozed & built over at a staggering rate.

YULEE SUGAR MILL State Historic Site

Take Fla. 490 a few miles west from Homosassa Springs.

This site shows what happens to much of Florida's history. In spite of efforts by several groups, this fine old piece of history is overrun with the bustle of the present. As you walk from the parking lot and lovely, shaded picnic area toward the old ruins, you have to cross a fast, busy highway that cuts right through this little site. In the roar of trucks, within sight of the great stan-dardized convenience store, within earshot of a mobile home park, you can ponder not only the ruins of a pioneer sugar plantation (what brave souls carved a living out of these deep swamps), but you can also ponder how rapidly Florida's history is being cut away, bulldozed, filled in, built over, and sealed under concrete. It takes a formidable leap of imagination to put yourself in the boots of these pioneers, as you stand amid the roar of traffic and look at the big, geared sugar-mill wheels rusting in the shade. Yet sites like this are invaluable. Only through them can we begin to preserve a sense of the time and place of early Florida. Only through them can we reconstruct another kind of life. Without history, we are at the mercy of our own images of ourselves.

Address: Yulee Sugar Mill State Historic Site, P.O. Box 166, Homosassa, FL 32646. Telephone 904/797-2590.

Updates to West (W) Section

Boyd Hill Nature Trail. Located on Lake Maggiore, right in St. Petersburg. Trails and boardwalks through more than 200 acres of hardwoods, sand pine scrub, pine flatwoods, lakeshores, and other natural habitats rare in a big city. Nature Center with aquariums and other exhibits. Guided tours available. 1101 Country Club Way South, off 9th Street South. Small admission charge. Phone 813/893-7317.

Caloosahatchee River State Park, shown on some maps east of Fort Myers, is not yet open to the public.

New Listing: **Cayo Costa State Park** was recently created by combining the two old Cayo Costa parks. Access by boat only. Primitive camping. There are some primitive cabins on the water (reservations necessary). Drinking water and restrooms, but no electricity. There is supposed to be a tram to take you (for a fee) from your boat to the cabins. You can also reach the island by tour boat. Phone 813/964-0375.

Chassahowitzka National Wildlife Refuge. New phone: 904/382-2201. (They pronounce it chaz-*wits*-ka.) The best times to see wildlife are winter and late spring. Part of the refuge is closed in fall and winter as a wildlife sanctuary.

Corkscrew Swamp Sanctuary is 15 miles east of I-75, exit 17. ZIP changed to 33964. No food sold.

New Listing: **Crystal River National Wildlife Refuge**, in Kings Bay, has recently become one of the most popular places for divers to see endangered manatees. During winter weekends, as many as a thousand divers visit the springs and the nearby dive shops. A major visitor center is planned. If you dive here, check the rules carefully; some areas are closed. Address: through Chassahowitzka NWR, 904/382-2201.

New Listing: **Don Pedro Island** is owned by the state parks system. It is in Charlotte County, north of Gasparilla Pass. A little, undeveloped stretch of beach accessible only by your own boat. Some restrooms, but no drinking water.

New Listing: **Egmont Key National Wildlife Refuge**, in Tampa Bay, though established because of its wildlife and archaeological sites, swarms with visitors to its beaches during the summer.

Fort DeSoto Park. New address: Tierra Verde, FL 33715. New phone numbers—campground office: 813/866-2662; park office: 813/462-3347. Brooker Creek Park has been renamed to John Chestnut Park.

New Listing: At **Franklin Lock** the Army Corps of Engineers operates a small campground primarily for those using the Okeechobee Waterway. It's on the north side of the waterway, approximately 10 miles east of Fort Myers, on county Road 78. Average fees for developed sites; some less developed sites are free.

New Listing: **Homosassa Springs**, formerly a tourist attraction, has become a part of the state park system. Because of the animal rehabilitation program, it has many birds of prey, and it has manatee year-round, along with an underwater observatory where you can see them. This new park came with a zoo that included a hippopotamus and features alligator feeding shows and native snakes. Phone 904/628-2311.

Honeymoon Island State Recreation Area, just north of Caladesi Island and accessible by car, is fully open. The superb beach was eroded down to rock by a hurricane, but it is supposed to be replenished by the time you read this. Lots of people, day-use only. Phone 813/734-4255.

Updates to the West Section (cont'd)

Lake Manatee State Recreation Area has added a campground.

New Listing: **Little Manatee River State Recreation Area** has just opened, with a 60-site campground. It's located in southern Hillsborough County, off US 301, near Sun City Center. Phone 813/634-4781.

Lower Hillsborough River Wilderness Park. *Trout Creek Recreation Area* is a good spot for fishing and canoeing. It is northeast of Tampa near I-75 and Morris Bridge Road. A group camp (for scouts and similar organizations) has been added at Dead River. For canoeing and hiking, enter at *Morris Bridge* or *Flint Creek*. Information: 813/986-2172.

Medard Park has a new phone number: 813/681-8862. Nearby *Alderman Ford* has a backpacking trail with primitive camping (phone 813/681-7990).

Myakka River State Park. ZIP is 33583. Recently renovated and in fine shape. There is no camping in the wilderness part of the park, but there is a very good 37-mile *backpacking trail* with four overnight camping areas in the main part of the park.

Oscar Scherer State Park no longer has a store to sell supplies or rent canoes.

Passage Key National Wildlife Refuge, in Tampa Bay, now has a restricted zone around it during nesting season: you cannot approach the island at all from April to August.

New Listing: **Rookery Bay National Estuarine Sanctuary**, south of Naples on Fla. 951, preserves 6,000 acres of bays, creeks, mangrove forests, and islands for wildlife, research, and education. Check in at the Collier County Conservancy's nature center on Shell Island Road. Bring repellant. Phone: 813/775-8845.

Simmons Park has been renovated. New phone: 813/645-3836.

Starkey Wilderness Area is open for hiking. Get information from the SW Florida Water Management District, Brooksville, FL 33512-9712. Phone 904/796-7211.

Suncoast Seabird Sanctuary, Inc. This famous center for the rescue and rehabilitation of wild birds is open for visiting every day from 9 a.m. till dark. Located on the coast just north of St. Petersburg: 18328 Gulf Blvd., Indian Shores, FL 33535. 813/391-6211.

Wiggins Pass may be extended in the next few years up to Johnson Park to form a major new beach park south of Fort Myers.

Withlacoochee State Forest. *River Junction*, just across the river, is a now a fully-developed companion campground to Silver Lake. *Hog Island* has reopened as a major recreation area with campsites and amenities. *North I-75* and *Old Iron Bridge* campsites are closed. *Buttgenbaugh* is now called *Croom Motorcycle Area*.

All developed camping areas in the forest now charge fees. The undeveloped camping areas are still free.

New Listing: **The Ybor City State Museum** has fine exhibits on the colorful ferment of Tampa's past—in a neighborhood strong in coffee, cigars, and history. Address: 1818 9th Ave., Tampa. Phone 813/247-6323.

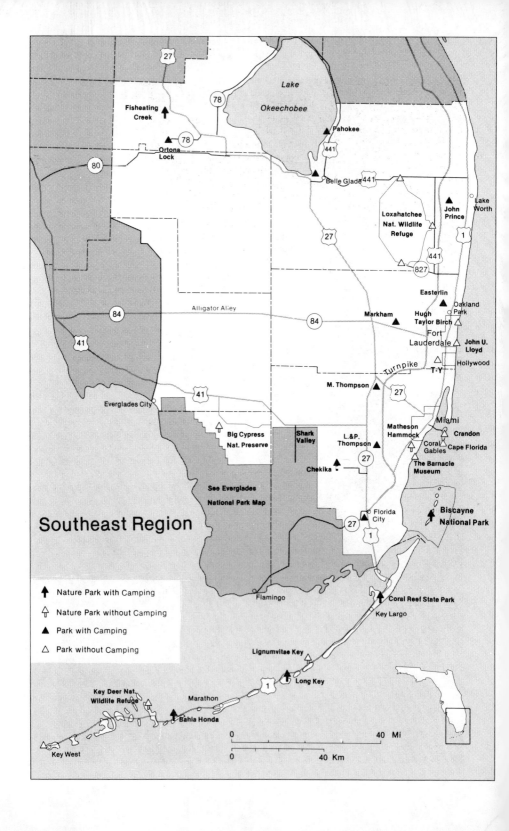

Lake
Okeechobee

Fisheating
Creek

Ortona
Lock

Pahokee

Belle Glade

Loxahatchee
Nat. Wildlife
Refuge

John
Prince

Lake
Worth

Easterlin

Oakland
Park

Markham

Hugh
Taylor Birch

Fort
Lauderdale

John U.
Lloyd

Hollywood

Alligator Alley

Turnpike

T-Y

M. Thompson

Everglades City

Miami

Matheson
Hammock

Crandon

Coral
Gables

Cape Florida

Big Cypress
Nat. Preserve

Shark
Valley

L.&P.
Thompson

The Barnacle
Museum

Chekika

See Everglades
National Park Map

Florida
City

Biscayne
National Park

Southeast Region

Flamingo

Coral Reef State Park

Key Largo

♠ Nature Park with Camping

⇧ Nature Park without Camping

▲ Park with Camping

△ Park without Camping

Lignumvitae Key

Long Key

Key Deer Nat.
Wildlife Refuge

Marathon

Bahia Honda

Key West

0   40 Mi

0   40 Km

Southeast

BAHIA HONDA State Recreation Area

About two-thirds of the way down the keys, on US 1.

It's pronounced Bay-uh, and it has the finest beach in the Keys; a natural wide sandy beach sloping out into waters deep enough to show the astonishing blue-green clarity of liquid crystal. These waters tell you that you are in the tropics. As in all the keys, when slow waves come in early or late in the day, reflections of the twilit sky multiply into moving slices of deep rose and deeper blue. The salmon colors of the sky migrate across reflecting waves, break on the beach, and dissolve into glistening sand.

These little islands are like another world. This is the tropical paradise of many dreams: little lush, jungle-like forests, dense with a dream of trees; dark borders where thick mangrove swamps stalk around the island and try to march out to sea; tall sand-dunes sloping down to a long strip of beach. Beyond that, there is the forever-mysterious boundary where land—naked—slips off into the unfathomable ocean; where the tropical light comes up like a new sun and goes down like a symphony. An air of excitement clings to every living thing that clings to these little, improbable islands, which seem that they might vanish if you blink.

There are two camping areas on Bahia Honda. The main one is very open,

Bahia Honda State Recreation Area, the finest beach in the Keys.

216

with bare ground and no shade to speak of. But it is located near the marina, the west swimming area, and the old bridge. It is especially convenient for RVs. The new camping area, carved out of the hammock on Sandspur Beach, offers shade and sites separated by dense growth. These sites are near the superb beach and nature trail, and further from busy US 1. Camping fees are about a dollar above average.

Activities include swimming and beach activities year round, good saltwater fishing (the area is famous for tarpon), boating and sailing, picnicking, snorkeling, and nature study. There is a concession with the usual snacks and fishing supplies. A separate dive shop, with gas for boats, is located next to the marina. There is a public telephone.

Fuller groceries and supplies are available in Marathon, about 15 miles away. In the summer, mosquitoes arrive unpredictably and extract their ounce of blood.

A nature trail takes you through a subtropical beach and hammock to the fringe of mangroves, giving you a glimpse of what the Keys looked like when the Spanish found them hundreds of years ago. You can see rare silver palms in their native habitat. A high-quality interpretive booklet guides you through this rich area.

Address: Bahia Honda State Recreation Area, Route 1 Box 782, Big Pine Key, FL 33043. Telephone 305/872-2353.

THE BARNACLE State Historic Site

In Coconut Grove, south of Miami.

When you leave the bustle of Miami to visit the tiny 5-acre site containing an old house called "The Barnacle," you suddenly move back a hundred years. Another era reigns: a vast uninhabited region of tropical forests, mangrove swamps, deserted beaches, waving marshlands, and pristine bay. Here a few hardy souls came in the late 1880's to establish the remarkable village of Coconut Grove. Its history has been captured in the photographs of Commodore Ralph Munroe, who built The Barnacle.

No matter where they are found—the stacked adobe dwellings of the Taos Indians, cottages of the English countryside, cracker homesteads, Seminole chickees—wherever you find buildings that arise out of a sensitive interaction with the setting, the weather, local materials, and the landscape, they always have a power and beauty beyond description. Such places are like natural organisms: They look like they grew there. You can see and feel how the features of the house grew in response to the site and the climate, to the needs of the people and the exigencies of the setting.

The Barnacle has this special quality. Everywhere you turn, there is some feature that shows a sensitive and intelligent use of materials, a perceptive and frugal solution to some problem, a flourish like tendrils on a vine.

217

And for good reason. The Barnacle is the house of a shipbuilder—the craft that most exactingly trains people to attune their needs to the demands of the environment and the qualities of the materials at hand.

The Barnacle State Historic Site: In the middle of busy Coconut Grove, a breath of fresh air from a former age.

The Barnacle (with many of its original furnishings) and the sleek sailing ketch "Micco", both built in 1891, give you some long, rich moments' respite to forget about the overhanging condominiums, the concrete jungle full of ravenous cars, and the endless hamburger alleys nearby that clatter at your attention. Here you can enter imaginatively into another period of history, when the works of humans lay more lightly on the land, and feel the fresh breeze of that perspective.

Tours are provided at 9, 10:30, 1:00 and 2:30, Wednesday through Sunday. A small fee is charged to everyone over six.

Address: The Barnacle State Historic Site, P.O. Box 330995, Coconut Grove, FL 33133. Telephone 305/448-9445.

BELLE GLADE MARINA CAMPGROUND (City)

At Lake Okeechobee, west of Belle Glade on Fla. 717.

When the lake level was recently raised, much of the old campground flooded, and a new campground is under construction (it may be finished by now). When completed, it will be large (300 sites), well laid out (especially for RV's), somewhat crowded, with full hookups, good security, and easy access to the big lake. In the past, this campground has primarily been used by those who come to fish during their vacations.

Current rules include an average camping fee, a four-week limit (with possible extension), and pets permitted on leash. No reservations are currently accepted, though it would be wise to call. Fees in the new camping area will be slightly above average. There are weekly rates.

The new camping area will have a central boat marina and launching area, though it may still be possible to use some of the older campsites—which permitted launching from your site.

A marina and concession are found in the park. Nearby Belle Glade is convenient for supplies.

Address: Belle Glade Marina Campground, 110 SW Avenue E, Belle Glade, FL 33430. Telephone 305/996-6322.

Some sites at Belle Glade Marina allow you to dock your boat right next to your camp.

BIG CYPRESS National Preserve

Crossed by US 41 and Fla. 94, around Monroe Station.

This 500,000 acre preserve is one of the last large natural areas left in the East. Big Cypress consists of vast areas of little, stunted, picturesque dwarf cypress scattered across the prairies and marshes, grading into somewhat larger trees in the cypress domes and strands, and interspersed with pine islands. The area is wet in summer and dry most winters, with frequent fires in the pinelands and marshes in the dry season. In spite of the name, you won't see any giant trees in Big Cypress.

Public access to Big Cypress is minimal at present. A segment of the Florida Trail crosses this area, and other trails may be developed in the future. A visitor center is planned at Oasis (east of Monroe Station, not shown on most maps).

Big Cypress Preserve was acquired to help protect the water-flow to Everglades National Park, and may never be an appropriate location for much recreational development. Hunting is permitted in season.

Florida 94 (the "loop road") is at present a narrow, one-lane severely pot-holed road, washed out in places. In recent years, it has been passable by truck, but very slowly and carefully. Perhaps this will be restored some day as a scenic drive. In the mid-winter season, it is lined with hunters and crowded with vehicles.

No camping. No facilities. Few towns. Scarce supplies.

For information, contact the Naples office of Big Cypress National Preserve, at 813/261-1066.

The loop road through Big Cypress Preserve, one of the last large wilderness areas on the East Coast.

BISCAYNE NATIONAL PARK
(Formerly Biscayne National Monument)

In the southern part of Biscayne Bay. Headquarters and boat launch are 9 miles east of Homestead on North Canal Drive, at Convoy Point.

NOTE 1: *Access by boat only.*

NOTE 2: There is **NO FRESH WATER** available in this park.

You must have your own or a rented boat to explore this park, where you can find some of the finest examples of undeveloped Florida Keys in existence, and dive to a living coral reef that is the northern extension of Coral Reef State Park.

Be sure to get information from park headquarters before going out. Reef waters are unpredictable, and certain keys are protected nesting sites.

Dense mangroves fringe these islands, and inland you can find the tropical hardwoods of south Florida, including some wonderful remnants of large mahogany. The only development is on Elliot Key, where there is a primitive campground and ranger station. You can hike the length of this island on a bulldozed road whose story is worth asking about.

Activities include boating and fishing, camping, picnicking, hiking, swimming, snorkeling, and scuba diving. On weekends a snack bar is open on Elliot Key and emergency gasoline can be bought (at very high prices).

Remember to carry water.

Address: Biscayne National Park, P.O. Box 1369, Homestead, FL 33030. Telephone 305/247-2044.

CAPE FLORIDA (Bill Baggs Cape Florida) State Recreation Area

On Key Biscayne, south of Crandon Park.

Cape Florida not only has a mile of fine, wide, sandy beach, but the park occupies a point of land that has been at the intersection of Florida history since Ponce de Leon sailed these waters in 1513. The fine old lighthouse and keeper's house have been restored and offer an interesting look at life when south Florida was Indian territory and impenetrable swamp.

Those dense trees all over the peninsula are Australian pines—which in most places are a curse disguised as a shade-tree. The park service is slowly attempting to replace them with native trees.

A bicycle trail winds through the park. Saltwater fishing is popular on the seawall in the bay. Swimming is good year-round. There is shade for picnicking and a concession with the usual refreshments.

Mainly, Cape Florida offers the leisurely glory of a Florida beach and is one of the most heavily used recreation spots in the Miami area. No camping. On weekends, watch for traffic jams.

Address: Bill Baggs Cape Florida State Recreation Area, 1200 S. Crandon Blvd., Key Biscayne, FL 33149. Telephone 305/361-5811.

CHEKIKA State Recreation Area
(Formerly Grossman Hammock)

Eleven miles NW of Homestead. Follow signs off Fla. 27, and remember the way back.

At 640-acre Chekika, a slightly sulphurous, cool, pleasant lake spills out of an artesian fountain created during an unsuccessful drilling for oil in the 1940's. Buses of children come here to cool off, families arrive to picnic, lovers seek out the shady hammock, and kids from the city discover native Florida at the edge of the marsh. The 20 unreservable campsites (no electricity) get lots of use. Chekika has the bustle of a high-use outdoor recreation area. It is a sort of inland beach.

Yet there is more. Chekika is a microcosm of the Everglades region. It contains sawgrass glades, isolated tree islands, and a marvellous subtropical hardwood hammock. The manmade lake has given rise to willow-thickets and marshlands. Wildlife flock here, especially in the dry winter season, when it is an oasis in a land of drought.

The nature trail through the hammock forest has one of the best guidebooks I have seen. Be sure to pick up a copy and spend some quiet, thoughtful time on the trail. Cycles of flood, drought and fire come to life as shaping forces of this vast land. Changes in elevation of only inches come to seem like mountains, for, on those inches of rise, whole different worlds of trees and animals stake their existence. A little museum houses exhibits on the Everglades, and rangers offer special programs in the winter season. Hot and buggy in the summer. Average fees.

Address: Chekika State Recreation Area, P.O. Box 1313, Homestead, FL 33030. Telephone 305/253-0950.

CORAL REEF STATE PARK (John Pennekamp)

In Key Largo, off US 1.

There is nothing else in the continental US to compare with a living coral reef. In other Florida parks, you can see wild areas of deep woods, dense swamps, semi-tropical jungle, wide sweeping marshes, snarled mangrove islands and long bare strips of sandy coast. But here the wilderness is underwater: a whole magnificent habitat of plants and animals unlike anything above. It is truly another world. Forests of living coral animals grow like branching trees, like antlers, like huge convoluted stone brains, like living boulders, like delicate embroidered fans. Clusters of differing corals inter-weave to form multi-pocketed, chambered refuges for a myriad of brilliantly colored swimming rainbows. The shapes, forms, colors, and movements are more like dreams than perceptions. This is surely science-fiction.

But no, it is real. The reef represents 12,000 years of slow building by the tiny polyps that lay down the solid coral beds and intricate skeletons. These

At Coral Reef State Park—the country's first underwater park—you can immerse yourself in the vivid colors of the living reef.

corals provide foundation, shelter, food, and safety for the greatest collection of living things to gather in any one place on the earth.

You need to know this: The reef is about five miles offshore. You cannot swim to it, and the waters are tricky with shoals, shallows, and coral outcroppings. Unless you are an expert boater skilled in these waters, you will have to take a charter boat to the reef. That's expensive, but very worthwhile. The park concession also offers glassbottom boat tours of the reef twice a day.

But the best way to see the reef is by snorkeling or scuba diving. Snorkeling trips, requiring no diving experience, leave daily from the park and from nearby dive shops. These are not cheap. Recent prices range from $15 to $25 and up, depending on the length of the trip. Nothing else can compare with the experience of swimming face to face with the exquisite and alien elements of this undersea world.

If you do nothing else, spend an hour or two in the new *Visitor Center.* It is without doubt one of the finest nature museums in Florida. Beautiful exhibits show the coral, fish, mangroves, and tropical hammock, and tell about the Florida Keys. You can walk around a huge indoor aquarium with an underwater reef in it. Small aquarium tanks along the walls, accompanied by excellent color transparencies and written explanations, capture the ecology of the reef in a vivid and unforgettable way. Slide shows can be viewed in a special room. This museum is a masterpiece; don't miss it.

Other features and activities of the park include: camping amid tropical vegetation and sea-grapes (47 sites with water and electricity), picnicking, swimming, saltwater fishing, boating (large launch), snorkeling, scuba diving. Motor, sail, paddle boats, and canoes can be rented. A concession store provides the usual snacks and limited supplies, as well as diving equipment.

Park rangers offer a number of interesting activities, including an introduction to snorkeling, slide shows, and guided canoe trips along the quiet, remote mangrove coastline. Check for the latest schedule.

Make reservations well in advance. Parks in the Keys are popular all year and are likely to be filled every day of the winter season. Mosquitoes and sand flies can be fierce intermittently all summer, but anyone well-prepared for this can be reasonably comfortable.

Address: John Pennekamp Coral Reef State Park, P.O. Box 487, Key Largo, FL 33037. Telephone 305/451-1202.

CRANDON PARK (Dade County)

On Key Biscayne, off US 1. Take Rickenbacker toll bridge.

A beautiful, large county park, with sandy beaches on the Atlantic. Almost 700 acres in extent, the park includes picnic areas, a skating rink, a zoo, amusement rides, a ballfield, marina, concession with refreshments, bath-houses, playground, nature trails, and some ranger-led naturalist activities.

Although for most people this is primarily a beach park, it still contains about 200 acres of undeveloped area for walking, bicycling, and escape.

No camping.

For information, contact Dade County Parks and Recreation, 50 S.W. 32nd Road, Miami, FL 33129. Telephone 305/638-6414.

EASTERLIN PARK (Broward County)

In downtown Oakland Park.

Fifty-six acres of drained, remnant cypress swamp provide a pleasant setting for a small camping area with 45 improved sites, picnic area, playground, bicycle trail and nature trail. The park is entirely surrounded by city. It has an excellent nature program. Fees are average.

Address: 1000 NW 38th Street, Oakland Park. Telephone 305/776-4466.

EVERGLADES NATIONAL PARK

Main entrance west of Florida City on Fla. 27. Watch for signs.

Most of Everglades National Park is a huge expanse of sawgrass marsh—as flat as the ocean—cut by sluggish sloughs and punctuated by scattered "islands" of dense trees. There is no Tarzan-like jungle here, with wild animals waiting to spring upon the unwary visitor. Instead, the park is a place so subtle that you may have to re-tune your preceptions and quieten your usual activity in order to let the deep, quiet richness of this unique area enter and grow in your awareness. This is not likely to happen to you in your car. You will need to get

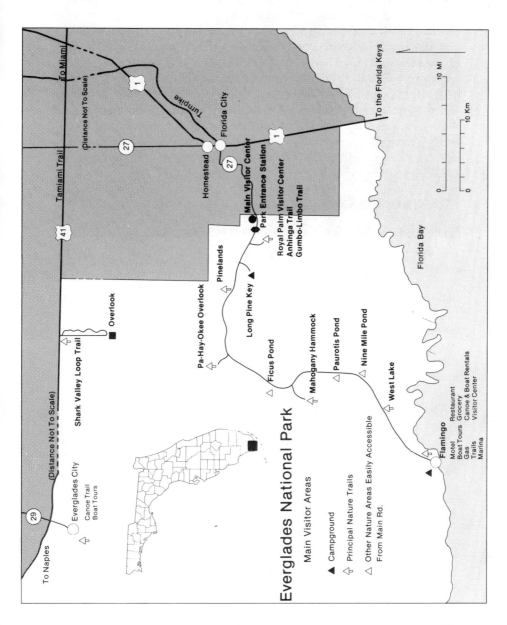

CYPRESS HEAD

During the Ice Ages, cypress forests
disappeared over all of Europe and most of
North America. Remnants remain in the
South. Like most northern trees, they
lose their leaves in winter. Under best
conditions, they become huge trees. Here
they are small because of unfavorable
local environment.

Many Florida parks have boardwalks, nature trails, exhibits, brochures, and ranger-guided tours that give you an excellent introduction to Florida ecology.

out, walk some short trails, watch, wait, listen, and for a while take the rhythm of your breathing from the deep breathing of the place.

Temperate and tropical zones mingle here. In the mysterious "hammocks," familiar northern species, such as moss-draped live oaks, crowd in dense forests with unusual tropical species such as mahogany, gumbo-limbo, and poisonwood. These live oaks may be studded with orchids and star-like drooping bursts of bromeliad airplants, above the fern-carpeted ground. White-tail deer browse near tropical butterflies. A mockingbird may sit in a lysiloma tree that has colorful tree-snails ornamenting its bark. Unmistakable mark of the tropical forest, the strangler fig's writhing trunks slowly choke out fully grown trees. One glance may include the familiar bald-cypress and the tropical mastic and wild coffee. A cardinal may sing in the same woods that hold the nests of the roseate spoonbill.

And, just outside the close tropical growth of these tree-islands, the glades open up and spread out in a seemingly endless expanse of spaciousness and sky. The wind moves across them in waves, and you can see the transit of the clouds' shadows on this rich flat land.

From huge spaces to tiny details; from immense open sunsets on Florida Bay, to the lattice-work on a dragonfly's wing; from the horizon-reaching spread of wide glades, to dew-drop pearls on a tiny spider's web: Your attention

226

shuttles from one extreme to the other as you visit this park. Many visitors extend this shift by taking binoculars and a hand-lens, which open up still other spaces in this world of unending detail and unending modulations of a profound and unhuman harmony.

The park has two seasons. Summers are hot, muggy, humid, and swarming with mosquitoes. It is difficult to stand still in any shady, windless place; the only relief is out in the sun and breeze. Summer is also the wet season, with big gray thunderstorms conquering the horizon. With all this water, the park's wildlife spread out over the whole million-and-a-half acres, and, though they are very much present, you see few animals or birds.

By contrast, winters are mild, cool enough to discourage most of the bugs, and very dry. Some years there are days of frost. The yearly drought that begins in the fall and grows through late spring and early summer forces all the park's scattered wildlife to concentrate desperately around the remaining waterholes, lakes, and sloughs, where they appear in spectacular numbers. Winter is *the* season for this park.

Winter is the time to see amazing numbers of alligators, deer, turtles, fish, otter, and other animals of south Florida. But most spectacular are the birds. Herons, egrets, roseate spoonbills, wood storks, white ibis, gulls, limpkins, gallinules, anhingas, cormorants, bald eagles, hawks of many kinds, clouds of

Rangers patrol remote areas of Everglades National Park by airboat. Private airboats are prohibited but you can buy rides outside the park in nearby glades marshes.

227

swallows—these and more give the Everglades a noisy, busy, colorful vitality that no one can be indifferent to.

Indeed, Everglades National Park has only continued to exist because people care. Everglades taught us that it is not enough to set aside land for a park. Unexpectedly, nearby developments almost devastated the park. The huge water-manipulation projects upstream—the canals, reservoirs, impoundments, dikes, floodgates, and dike-like roadbeds—seriously interfered with the water supply to the park. It was almost too late when people realized how finely the life of the Everglades was tuned to the irregular but precise fluctuations of water, to the exact amount and timing of its arrival. When people changed the water cycles upstream, the park nearly died. And still, after some uneasy compromises assured the park at least a supply of water, the world's largest jetport was almost built on the park's neck, pressing down on the vital artery of its fragile water supply. Thanks to national outcry, the park survived.

Yet Everglades National Park is still at the mercy of almost everything that happens for up to 150 miles upstream—where its watershed begins. Unlike most national parks, which are set in remote mountain wildernesses, Everglades is at the end of a watershed, receiving everything that flows into it—pesticides, fertilizers, chemical wastes, agricultural effluents, exudations from road surfaces, asbestos from the worn linings of many brakes, and all the other industrial byproducts of our world. Huge as it is, Everglades is still fragile; small changes in its water cycle may cause large, long-term, irreversible alterations in the park. Small changes in its delicate and delicately timed chemistry could wipe out whole species—especially those that cling to south Florida for their last hold on existence.

Yet it is here now. Go, enjoy, enrich yourself with its expanse and density. And, from your enjoyment, learn to care for the Everglades and for other Florida parks, so that—with all our care—they will still be here in decades to come, when we will need them even more.

BE PREPARED

Although there is a wealth of information on the ecology of Everglades National Park, you may have trouble finding a simple, accurate guide. The following practical information should be especially helpful for first-time visitors.

First of all, *plan ahead*. There are no provisions in the park except in Flamingo, at the end of the 40-mile road (60 km). Take with you everything you will need, including a water bottle. Write ahead for official park information, and read it carefully. You will receive a beautiful, informative, but confusing color brochure.

Stop at the Main Visitor Center and ask for all the literature you might need for your visit—trail guides, canoe trails, bird lists, tour information, ranger-led activities, etc. Once past the Visitor Center, you will not be able to get park publications till you reach Flamingo.

Keep these in mind:

1. Take comfortable clothes and good walking shoes. Long pants and a lightweight, long-sleeved shirt are a must. Mosquitoes are likely to devour anyone in shorts.

On this ''swamp stomp'' a ranger at Everglades National Park introduces visitors to the periphyton whose growth forms the basis for the rich animal life in the park.

2. Winter is *the* season for this park. Summer has its beauties (orchids blooming, wildflowers in the pines) but the mosquitoes can be truly overwhelming then. Cool autumn days are the park's undiscovered season. But in the winter—from Christmas to Easter—mosquitoes abate and wildlife abound. People abound too; winter is the park's crowded season.

3. If you want to feed alligators, go to one of the tourist attractions in the state where this is allowed. Don't feed alligators in any Florida park. Alligators fed by humans lose their natural fear of man and may become dangerous and have to be removed. Rangers will arrest and prosecute anyone feeding alligators.

4. This is a wonderful wildlife park. Take binoculars, a bird book, a hand lens. Pick up one of the superb books on the park at the Main Visitor Center. I recommend *EVERGLADES: The Story Behind the Scenery*.

5. The park charges a daily vehicle entrance fee of two or three dollars. But note: if you leave the gate and come back in, you may have to pay the entrance fee again—even if you only go to the Main Visitor Center. Watch out for this policy.

6. Please don't collect anything here. The wonderful plants, animals, insects, butterflies, and tree-snails are all protected for future park visitors to enjoy.

7. You can buy airboat rides *outside* the park, in nearby private glades lands, such as those along the Tamiami Trail. Private airboats have long been forbidden in the park, and official airboats are used only by rangers and scientists working in remote areas.

8. This is a semi-tropical climate. Take it easy. Be informed about sunburn, sunstroke, and heat prostration.

9. There is no public transportation inside the park. Tour buses operate out of Miami.

10. The road inside the park is 40 miles long (60 km). The only gas, food, lodging, or supplies are at the end, in Flamingo. The long stretch from Long Pine Key to West Lake has no drinking water or restrooms. Plan for this.

11. Take insect repellant. In warm months you cannot do without it, and even in the winter there can be occasional outbreaks of biting bugs. Any good commercial repellant will help. Near the coast in warm weather, the tiny biting sand-flies ("no-seeums") can make life miserable when they come out to feed (usually late afternoon). One commonly used repellant for them seems, oddly, to be a bath oil made by Avon, called "Skin So Soft." Some rangers recommend mixing this with commercial repellant, to keep away both mosquitoes and sand-flies.

These simple preparations can help you avoid almost certain misery, and free you to enjoy this great park.

WHAT TO DO

Nature is the single and enduring attraction here. Reach out to understand and appreciate the park's tremendous beauty, depth, variety, and subtle power. For a start, try to experience each of the major natural habitats of the park. These are:
1. Everglades marshlands and sloughs
2. tropical hardwood hammocks ("tree islands")
3. south Florida pinewoods
4. scrub cypress
5. mangrove swamps
6. semi-desert coastal prairie
7. estaurine waters of Florida Bay.

The interpretive activities here are unusually good. The trails are first-rate, and the ranger-led tours excellent. You will find an abundance of good literature on the ecology of the park—and it's well worth learning about. This is a magical place, but it's subtle. You may have to learn what to look for before you can really see it.

Here are some suggestions on how to plan your visit.

A. If you have **only a few hours**, don't just drive to Flamingo and back. You'll miss everything that way. Instead, start with the slide show at the Main Visitor Center and go straight to the Royal Palm area. There, divide your time equally between the *Anhinga* and *Gumbo-Limbo Trails*. Spend all of your few hours there only. These wonderful trails will take you through sweeping Everglades marshes into Taylor Slough (one of the richest wildlife areas in the park) and through a fine example of a tropical hardwood hammock. The trails are each less than one-half mile long, but they are deep windows into the mysteries of the park.

B. If you have **half a day**, start with *Anhinga* and *Gumbo-Limbo Trails*, seek out some ranger-led activity (perhaps a slog across the glades to a tree island), then go to as many of the other major trails as you can, spending a leisurely, contemplative period at each one. Don't be afraid to linger in a place you like. Seeing two or three aspects of the park in depth is far more valuable than skimming over the whole thing lightly.

The other major trails are:

Pinelands: where you see fire ecology at work in a flower-rich pine and palmetto flatwoods and cross the edge of a hardwood hammock. About half a mile long.

Pa-Hay-Okee: A short (100 yard) boardwalk takes you from the parking lot to an overlook above the sweeping expanse of glades, the "river of grass,"

The boat trail tunnels through the mangroves at places on the Wilderness Waterway, a ten-day canoe trip through Florida's remotest swamps.

unique in all the world, that forms the heartline of this park. You also pass through a fine portion of a "scrub cypress" forest of old but diminutive trees. This is a wonderful place to watch the sunset and moonrise.

Mahogany Hammock: A boardwalk of less than half a mile takes you through a short section of glades marsh to a dense, shady tropical hardwood hammock that contains bigger trees than the Gumbo-Limbo Trail. Huge mahoganies dominate. A *very* slow, thoughtful, appreciative walk, reading all the labels and stopping frequently to contemplate, takes about 40 minutes. Don't rush through.

The *Mangrove Trail* at West Lake gives you the first opportunity in the park to enter the mangrove habitat on a short boardwalk, and see first-hand this extraordinary and extraordinarily valuable plant community. Bird-life around the lake can be very impressive. Mosquitoes can be rough in warm weather.

Just north of West Lake, the main road crosses a broad swath of coastal prairie—where you find desert plants like cactus, yucca, and thick succulents.

C. If you have **all day**, do the above more slowly, and add a late-afternoon visit to Flamingo. There, check into ranger-led activities, then take the tram or boat tour—which will be a beautiful, safe, and educational trip into another region of the park.

D. For a visit of **more than a day**, you have two options on where to camp in the park (described below), as well as a motel, cabins, and houseboats that may be rented through the concessionaire in Flamingo. Reservations are suggested all year for the rentals, and are necessary in winter.

With more than a day to spend, take more time on the walks. Make every possible effort to be out at dawn on the Anhinga Trail or on one of the lakes facing east. Spend the long sunsets on an open place like Pa-Hay-Okee. No time of day is better for wildlife, for the park experience, or for your spirit than the arriving and departing twilight. Don't let the routines of the day steal these times from you.

Revisit the places you liked most. Go back to the edges of Mahogany Hammock or Anhinga Trail after dark; walk silently and immerse yourself in the sounds of night. (Take a flashlight.)

Go on a ranger-led hike across the glades to a hammock. Or on a ranger-led canoe trip. Or car caravan. Or bird hike. Or rent a canoe and strike out on your own for half a day's trip on one of the trails near Flamingo. Hike or bike one of several trails through the mangroves to lakes, bays, and estauries. Hike the pinelands around Royal Palm, and explore some of the hidden hammocks on your own.

Everglades National Park offers many opportunities for a profound and rejuvenating experience with nature, but you must take the initiative yourself. It is not an amusement park; the activities are not scheduled like a tour. If you are uncertain what to do, ask any ranger for a suggestion.

Pinelands camping area in Everglades National Park—a comfortable, shady site near some of the best nature trails.

E. During a **longer stay**, you will want to visit *Shark Valley* and either take the tram tour, or, better yet, rent a bicycle and bike the 15-mile loop through a rich and varied wildlife area. Shark Valley is an exceptional place to see birds and alligators, and, seven miles out, there is an overlook onto the wide glades. (Water and restrooms there.) This makes a fine one-day side-trip. Many people come back year after year. The ranger-led interpretive tours are first-rate, and are specifically tailored to the interests of each group.

Note: the tram closes during high water. In 1979, for example, it was closed from Sept. 9 through Dec. 21, and service may be further reduced due to fuel restrictions. Inquire at the Main Visitor Center about the schedule at Shark Valley. (By the way, there are no sharks at this end of the valley.)

F. For the ultimate experience of the park, you may want to consider canoeing the *Wilderness Waterway* from Flamingo to Everglades City, a trip that takes about 10 days and removes you totally from civilization during most of that time. It is a strenuous trip, demanding careful planning. You must register with the park before undertaking it. See the published Guide to the Wilderness Waterway before planning this trip.

Shorter canoe trips and boat tours are available from the ***Everglades City*** entrance, south of Naples. These are your best brief introduction to the Ten Thousand Islands labyrinth of mangrove swamp.

Those seeking an easier visit can lodge at Flamingo, eat in the restaurant or cafeteria, rent boats, or charter fishing expeditions.

No hunting is allowed in the park, but there are many opportunities for excellent fishing—in lakes, the Florida bay, in the Ten Thousand Islands, and on back-country boat trails.

The park is increasing its interpretive activities in the Key Largo Ranger Station (off US1 in Key Largo). Ask at the Main Visitor Center for the latest information.

CAMPING

Everglades National Park has two camping areas, one near each end of the park road.

Long Pine Key Campground has 108 sites amid the pine and palmetto flatwoods, fairly well shaded but sometimes rather open to one another. There are no water or electrical hookups at the sites. Water and restrooms are centrally located. There are no showers, and only cold water is found in the restrooms. Nearest supplies are in Flamingo (34 mi/57 km) or Homestead (15 mi/24 km).

Flamingo Campground has 235 drive-in sites plus 60 walk-in tent sites. There are no water or electrical hookups, but there are cold-water showers near the centrally located restrooms. The sites are sunny, with scattered medium-sized trees—oaks, sea-grapes, and palms. The campground is near the Flamingo cafeteria, store, and gift shop.

The Flamingo Campground is buggier than the one at Long Pine Key, and only a small number of very well-equipped and stoical souls ever dare to camp there during the summertime, mainly because of the sand-flies. In winter months, they are rarely a problem.

The park does not accept reservations for campsites. They are strictly on a first-come-first-served basis. If you want a site during the busy winter season, you must arrive *early* in the morning, take a number, and wait to see if there is an opening that day.

Fees are slightly below average (cheaper for the walk-in sites), and are charged only from November 1 through April 30. Camping is free the rest of the year, because of the hot, humid weather and mosquitoes—even though that's when the orchids bloom and fireflies bless the pinewoods. Rates are half-price for holders of Golden Age cards (available at the gate.) There is a 14-day limit during the busy season; 30 days the rest of the year. Pets are allowed on leash in the campground, but are forbidden on the trails. Both campgrounds have sewage dump stations.

Note: you need a good, bug-proof tent or camper to camp in the park. You can't just roll out a sleeping bag, because, if the bugs are out, you'll get eaten alive. As late as November, I've seen seasoned backpackers pick up and leave in the middle of the night, due to the mosquitoes. But that's because they were not prepared. Don't be frightened away; just be ready.

Those same mosquitoes are one of the most vital links in the park's complex food-chain. For that reason, the park is not sprayed. Mosquitoes, too, are wildlife. They belong.

The extraordinary natural depth and beauty of this park make it worth every inconvenience.

Address: Everglades National Park, Homestead, FL 33030. Telephone 305/247-6211.

FISHEATING CREEK Campgrounds and Wilderness Area

On US 27 at Palmdale, one-half mile north of Fla. 29.

The listings in this book are restricted to publicly operated campgrounds and nature parks, but an exception must be made for this unique private park. Operated by Lykes Brothers Inc., Fisheating Creek is comparable to a large, well-run county park, with the addition of some of the finest wilderness in south central Florida.

There are three campgrounds. The main campground has fully developed facilities and 160 sites, most with sewer, electric and water hookups. There are security lights, a resident manager, a locked gate, a public telephone, playground—all the amenities of an RV-oriented camping park, plus an exceptional natural setting of dense cypresses and beautiful old oaks. Fees are average to above average, but monthly rates are available. Reservations are necessary during the busy winter season.

Campground two consists of a 400-acre are set aside for use by motorcycle campers.

Number three is the Wilderness Campground, located in 2,000 acres of orchid-studded cypresses along Fisheating Creek—one of the most scenically beautiful spots in the state. There are minimal facilities, and some areas are accessible only by four-wheel drive. Fishing is said to be good, but no guns are allowed. In the summer this area is very wet and boggy.

Camping in the Wilderness Area is inexpensive, with group rates to scout and church groups. Free to local county residents.

Pets are permitted on leash in all three areas.

One- and two-day canoe trips can be taken on Fisheating Creek west of the main campground. Reservations are required. Canoes may be rented, and there is a brochure describing the trail.

The owners of this outstanding private park deserve special credit for taking care to preserve this wonderful portion of original Florida wilderness.

For information and reservations, write Lykes Fisheating Creek Campgrounds, P.O. Box 100, Palmdale FL 33944. Telephone 813/675-1852 (8 a.m. to 10 p.m.).

FLORIDA CITY RV PARK (City)

Davis Parkway and Krome Ave. (Fla 27), in Florida City.

Strictly for RV's, this urban camping park occupies a whole city block on the edge of town, near the farmers' market. Some 250 developed sites (with water and electric hookups and central dump station) have been placed on a few acres. Some of the sites are in an open grassy field, and others are tucked beneath the shade of medium-sized oaks and pines.

Fees are slightly above average, cheaper by the week. Pets are permitted on leash only. There is a laundramat, a central dump station, and the restrooms have hot showers. Supplies are plentiful nearby.

The Florida City RV park is heavily used in the winter season (December through Easter) and is usually filled in December and January. Most users are retired persons, many of whom regularly winter here. The park offers some regular recreational activities for campers, such as crafts classes.

No reservations are taken, but you can call to see whether or not there is space. Tents are not usually allowed.
Address above. Telephone 305/248-7889.

HUGH TAYLOR BIRCH State Recreation Area (Birch Park)

In Ft. Lauderdale, off A-1-A.

In 1893, Hugh Taylor Birch was driven ashore on his sailboat. A young man in search of wilderness, he found it here: miles and miles of almost uninhabitable mangrove swamp and dense tropical hammock, one of the most remote portions of the American frontier. He lived here and loved this area till his death in 1942, when he bequeathed this park so future generations might see a remnant of the Florida he had first found and loved so long.

And it is only a remnant. Seen from the air, 180-acre Birch Park is the only island of green in the solid sea of concrete and asphalt that makes up the jumble of Ft. Lauderdale. The mangroves and the tropical forests are gone—bulldozed over, burned, cut out. And in place of their shade, now there is the glare of concrete. This park is a small, sad miracle in south Florida.

Yet it is still something of a miracle. A fine stretch of beach runs along the Atlantic. The Australian-pine dominated interior serves as a lovely city park—heavily used for picnicking, play, fishing, weddings, walks, and contemplative afternoons watching the sun set behind the condominiums.

The nature trail takes you through a little remnant of the original tropical forest that once made this area a botanist's paradise. An anomalous miniature train offers a 3-mile ride through the trees and along the Waterway. There are picnic areas, wayside stops, paddleboats for rent on the small freshwater lagoon, fish to be caught in the Waterway, and camping facilities reservable by large organized groups (only). No family camping.

236

The busy urban beach at Hugh Taylor Birch State Recreation Area.

The LosAngelization of Florida is nowhere more complete than in the urban megalopolis that includes Ft. Lauderdale and Miami. The few little remaining green areas—jewel-like parks—are flooded with visitors, whose recurring presence reminds us how much urban dwellers need the breath of nature to help keep them sane.

Address: Hugh Taylor Birch State Recreation Area, 3109 Sunrise Blvd., Ft. Lauderdale, FL 33304. Telephone 305/564-4521.

JOHN PRINCE PARK (Palm Beach County)

Lake Worth: Congress Ave. and Lake Worth Rd. Take exit 36 east from the Turnpike.

This large lakeside county park (over 600 acres) provides numerous recreational opportunities. There are 266 developed campsites on a lovely shaded arm of the lake, with an overflow area for 100 more. The developed sites have water and electric hookups, and hot showers can be found in the restrooms. Pets are permitted, but only on leash.

Large picnic areas, three softball fields, three boat ramps, six bathhouses on the lake, a golf range, bicycle path, playground, short nature trails, concession, good fishing, and rental boats make this highly developed park a center for intensive outdoor recreation.

Park developers have clearly made two crucial choices here: to develop the area to its fullest (rather than leaving large natural areas), and to landscape the park with beautiful foreign trees and plants and large grassy lawns. It is a "developed" and "landscaped" park, in contrast to a "nature park." Visitors here should make a point of visiting a nature park as well, to experience the wonderful, original south Florida habitat.

As in most south Florida parks, the campground here is regularly full from

Christmas through Easter, when reservations are essential. Fees are average, and reservations can only be made by mail, with payment in advance.
Call or write: Campground Reservations, Palm Beach County Parks and Recreation Department, 2700-6th Ave., Lake Worth, FL 33461. Campground telephone 305/582-7992.

JOHN U. LLOYD BEACH State Recreation Area
(Lloyd Beach)

Off A-1-A in Dania, south of Ft. Lauderdale.

Lloyd Beach is one of the most popular beaches on the lower east coast of Florida. It has over two miles of beach, a little estuarine creek lined with mangroves, and a scrappy remnant of the tropical forest that once occurred throughout this area, but now remains only in a few isolated parks. The facilities are modern, the atmosphere pleasant, the access easy.

For these reasons, little Lloyd Beach (only 244 acres) is one of the most heavily used parks in the state. From March through September, the park fills and closes every weekend, sometimes as early as 9:30 AM when all the parking places are taken. Easter weekend sees the largest crowds. All these visitors take their toll; this new park already shows some wear and tear. But it is not a large enough park that sections can be closed off to recover.

It is not numbers of people that hurt—it's the high impact made by thoughtless visitors who litter, strew garbage, damage vegetation with their cars, cut down trees, vandalize the facilities, ignore regulations, disturb other visitors and hurt one another. This is the park story everywhere, amplified by numbers. It will take a profound change in people's attitudes to solve the problems created by people. How can that happen?

Lloyd Beach attracts manatees regularly in the winter, when they explore Whiskey Creek (New River Sound) inside the park. The park carries out a sea-turtle hatchery program as part of a nationwide effort to save these rare creatures from extinction. Birds flock here, because it is one of the last refuges of green space in the surrounding sea of concrete and steel. People flock here for the same reason.

Rangers give excellent interpretive programs—including guided walks and several fine slide shows (one on the manatee). You can rent boats at the concession and canoe a short way up Whiskey Creek to enjoy birds and the mangroves. It is one of the few creeks in south Florida where you can get away from motorboats for a while. Jetties at the north end of the park provide excellent saltwater fishing. The stretch of beach needs no instructions. An offshore reef near the north end is frequently used for scuba diving, and picnic tables give you a place to gather with friends under the shade of spreading trees.

Lloyd Beach even has a foot in local history (so to speak), because it was on the long coastal route taken during the 1880's by the "barefoot mailman" who regularly walked this lower coast to deliver mail to remote settlements.

Day-use only, except during special interpretive programs and peak fishing periods. No camping.

Address: John U. Lloyd Beach State Recreation Area, 6503 North Ocean Drive, Dania, FL 33304. Telephone 305/923-2833.

KEY DEER NATIONAL WILDLIFE REFUGE

On Big Pine Key. Take Fla. 940 off US 1.

A miniature white-tail deer found only in the Keys, the Key deer had diminished to only 50 animals by 1947, due to overhunting, poaching, and especially the widespread destruction of habitat. After 25 years of protection on the refuge, the herd has grown to more than 400 animals. These small attractive deer may be seen along the refuge drive and nature trail in the early morning, late afternoon, and evening. Unusual pockets of limestone on these Keys catch and hold rainwater, which the deer depend on as a source of fresh water.

Mangrove swamps fringe the refuge, while the higher ground supports a forest of slash pines and palmettos, along with tropical hardwoods draped with the bromeliads and orchids that are so characteristic of the Keys. The refuge is kept in as natural a condition as possible, and it attracts rare birds such as the roseate spoonbill, great white heron, reddish egret, and mangrove cuckoo. There is a local race of raccoons here, pale in color.

The other National Wildlife Refuges in the Keys are accessible only by boat and are not included in this book.

No camping. Day use only. Free.

For additional information, contact the Refuge Manager, P.O. Box 510, Big Pine Key, FL 33043. Telephone 305/872-2239.

KEY WEST

Key West is the end of the road and the beginning of the sea. Like many old seacoast towns, it is a special place. Exquisite old houses line entire streets. Much of the downtown has been restored, and it is an art center where the artists mostly paint (you guessed it) Key West. The city is a meeting ground of races and cultures, and has a bright Caribbean ferment to it.

There are a number of private and municipal attractions which you will not be able to miss, and two important state sites are currently under development. *A state museum* will soon be opened at Key West, depicting the style of life of the natives, the "Conchs." *Fort Zachary Taylor* State Historic Site, when it is ready, may house the finest collection of Civil War armaments in existence. Inquire when you arrive, to see how much is open for visitation.

About 70 miles west of Key West, over open ocean, *Fort Jefferson*

National Monument stands in the Dry Tortugas. This abandoned fortress has been settling and cracking almost since the first brick was laid in 1846, but it is still impressive. Each summer large numbers of sooty terns migrate to a nearby island to nest, as they have done at least since Ponce de Leon observed them in 1513. You can camp, picnic, and snorkel on the coral reefs, or visit the Fort during daylight hours. But there are no facilities, no housing, no water, no meals or supplies here. You have to provide your own transportation too. Fort Jefferson is the remotest park in Florida. For more information, contact Everglades National Park.

Address: Fort Zachary Taylor State Historic Site, P.O. Box 4100, Key West, FL 33040. Telephone 305/294-2354.

LARRY AND PENNY THOMPSON PARK (Dade County)

12451 SW 184th Street (at 125th Ave.), adjacent to the new zoo.

Note: There are *two* "Thompson Parks" in Dade County. Make sure you have the right one!

"Larry and Penny Park" is one of the few areas left in Dade County where any native plant community can still be found intact, particularly the wonderful native pinewoods that have mostly been replaced by cities and towns. The 275-acre strip of Caribbean slash pine and palmetto flatwoods provide habitat for over 250 species of plants, and give a glimpse of what the pinewoods of south Florida were like before development. Fire scars on the trunks tell you that this forest receives regular ecological burning to keep it healthy.

A 60-acre campground with 240 developed sites provides full water, electrical, and sewer hookups for campers. Like many city and county parks, the campground is RV-oriented. Sites are located in an old experimental grove, amid trees of mango, lychee-nut, avocado, and citrus. Some sites are shaded now, others will be when the newly planted oaks grow. Large expanses of mowed lawn cover the ground between sites. Four modern restroom buildings provide excellent facilities and hot showers. There is a small store and laundramat.

Larry and Penny Thompson Park has five miles of bike and walking paths, 2.5 miles of bridle paths, a 22-acre manmade lake for swimming, boating, and fishing, and some areas for nature study. There is a special play area for handicapped children.

The campground is regularly full from Christmas through Easter. When the lake is completed, the natural areas of the park will probably experience heavy day-use. This park is rapidly becoming a fully developed, heavily used, very busy recreation area close to downtown Miami.

Fees are on the high side, but you get a lot for the price. Pets are permitted on leash. The park has resident rangers, a 24-hour security patrol, and has recently added a water slide and rental boats.

For general information call 305/233-8231. For campground reservations call 305/232-1049.

LIGNUMVITAE KEY State Botanical Site

Off US 1 near Islamorada, in the Keys.

Lignumvitae Key is one mile and fifty years away from US 1. This is the

Now a State Botanical Site, Lignumvitae Key was almost cleared for a housing development. This beautiful park preserves what may be the only complete example of the exquisite tropical forest of the Keys. The rest has been crowded out by people.

only readily accessible Florida key that is still in its natural state—and it is a jewel. You have to get there by boat, and it's just far enough away that you have to want to be there. With luck, it will always remain a little inaccessible.

There need to be parks like this—out of the way, special, undeveloped, natural. Parks for people who want to experience original Florida, dense with history and nature. Where visitors must be willing to walk a mile, and where sometimes only mosquitoes can bear to be there.

Unlike the surrounding keys, Lignumvitae is not sprayed for bugs. As a result, the first thing you see is butterflies: There are 26 species of them here, flapping in colorful rhythm in the dense woods. Or you might arrive when thousands upon thousands of copper-winged dragonflies are crowding the one open lawn. Or when swallows again and again aim their long bombing swoops across the grass and ride the high sea-wind back to the starting point. The place is alive.

And life here has a deep, rich, authentic feel to it. The island has not been compromised with invasions of Australian pine; the tropical hammock has not been bulldozed or burned; the mangroves weren't cleared. It's just *there,* as it has been for centuries. And the forest that has been developing for centuries stuns, captivates, surrounds, and fills you. You walk through tunnels in the overhanging trees. Shapes and profusions press at you from all sides. This is the most tropical portion of the United States. No pine forest here; no New England maples. It's a small, rich, salt-pruned jungle (which keeps the trees from being giants). Tree-snails stand out against the dark bark like Christmas ornaments. Things blossom unexpectedly. Modest little trees turn out to be a thousand years old. Ancient coral skeletons dot the path—reminding you that all this was under water once.

Lignumvitae Key is a botanical treasure. It evolved over many centuries on those exposed corals, building up land and forest together, capturing species from the coast of Florida and from the Caribbean. Of a hundred species of trees here, seventy are found nowhere else in the country. As you walk through its shady paths, you can *feel* the integrity of the woods. This—something in you says—is nature undisturbed. And it is the only large piece of undisturbed nature left in the Florida keys.

Gumbo limbo, Jamaican dogwood, poisonwood, mahogany, mastic, stopper, lignumvitae—strange tropical forms surround you with beauty and mystery. Yet all of this was nearly lost forever. Lignumvitae Key was saved only because, at a point when it was scheduled to be cleared for a housing development, the Nature Conservancy secured the island until the state parks could take it over in 1971.

Because the area is so fragile, you need a ranger-guide before you can leave the small clearing around the old Matheson house. A two-hour guided tour is given at 9 AM and a one-hour tour at 1 and 3, Wednesday through

Sunday. There is a small fee. Charter boats leave for the island from nearby marinas.

This park is a nature preserve. There are no recreational facilities, and camping is not allowed.

For information, contact Lignumvitae Key State Botanical Site, c/o Long Key, State Recreation Area, P.O. Box 517, Long Key, FL 33001. Telephone 305/664-4815.

The end of a clear, sunny day at Long Key State Recreation Area.

LONG KEY State Recreation Area

On US 1 halfway down the Keys.

This park consists of a narrow strip of beach on the Atlantic side, with fine waters for swimming, snorkeling, fishing, boating and a spacious vista for the sunrise. Located right on the ocean, the 60 campsites (water and electricity) are well-shaded by a dense stand of exotic Australian pines.

A small but nice portion of the key has been kept in its natural state—partly because it is not well suited for recreational development, and partly because natural areas in the keys are rare and valuable. A new nature trail takes you through the mangroves, through the rich, low tropical hammocks that once covered all these islands (before they were bulldozed), and into the community of hardy plants that grow on the thin slice of beach. Boardwalks take you to a scenic overlook platform in the mangroves, and a footbridge crosses a lagoon much-loved by wintering birds.

As you sleep on this long thin island, you will be lulled into peaceful silence by the lapping waves. Then, when the trucks start bombing past a few yards away on US 1, you may feel how greatly we shut down our senses to survive the clatter of this busy world.

Long Key draws regular visitors back year after year, to the place where they can swim right in front of their campsites. Fees are about a dollar above average. Make reservations early. If you don't have reservations, plan to arrive early in the morning, be prepared for a long wait, and don't count on being able to get a place, especially in the winter.

Birding is excellent in winter, and even in the limp heat of summer when mosquitoes periodically go on rampage, the grey ghosts of pelicans glide past, and a great white heron might be mirrored in the shallows when you wake up.

Activities: swimming, snorkeling, beach activities (year round), saltwater fishing, camping, picnicking, nature study, silence, and sunrises.
Address: Long Key State Recreation Area, P.O. Box 776, Long Key, FL 33001. Telephone 305/664-4815.

LOXAHATCHEE National Wildlife Refuge

Inland west of Lake Worth.

There are three entrances: "Twenty Mile Bend" is 18 miles west of Lake Worth on US 98. "Hillsboro Recreation Area" is on Fla. 827, about 10 miles west of Deerfield Beach. "Refuge Headquarters" is on US 441 between Fla. 804 and 806.

This 220 square-mile segment of the Everglades is part of that system of levees and canals that has been man's main, controversial, and precarious attempt to manipulate large portions of the south Florida environment. Saw-grass marshes, wet prairies, sloughs, and tree islands make up most of the refuge—ill-suited for humans, but a paradise for wildlife.

Most people come to fish or go boating or observe the alligators, wood ibis, great white herons, roseate spoonbills, or other birds and animals. Or they just come for the sense of space, the presence of nature. Birding is good all year round, especially in the winter, and you can fish from the Hillsboro and Headquarters entrances. Regulated hunting of waterfowl is permitted in season. A concession at the south end provides supplies, guides, rental boats, and airboat tours. Boats may be launched in all three entrance areas.

Mosquitoes can be fierce in warm weather. Day-use only. No camping. Admission to the refuge is free.
Address: Refuge Manager, Route 1 Box 278, Delray Beach, FL 33444. Telephone 305/732-3684.

MARKHAM PARK (Broward County) ▲

16001 State Road 84, Ft. Lauderdale. Ten miles west of Turnpike exit 12.

This 600-acre county area is the northernmost camping park with an Everglades setting. A big glades area can be seen in adjacent Conservation Area 2B, which attracts a spectacular number of birds when it dries down (usually in January and February).

A strangler fig at work on a jungle plum. Southeast Florida once had numerous "hammocks" of fascinating tropical trees, but now only a few remain in parks like Matheson Hammock, Lignumvitae Key, and Everglades National Park.

Eighty nice, shady, well-separated campsites are now in operation, 60 with water and electricity. Average camping fees are charged to county residents all year, and to everyone in the summer. In the winter, above-average fees are charged to non-residents. There is a 2-week limit. Reservations may be made, and require a 2-day minimum. Campers have till 8 pm to check in. Nearest supplies are a mile and a half away, but a camp store has been planned.

The campground is usually full on weekends after Thanksgiving, and full all the time from Christmas through Easter.

You can rent boats and canoes in the park, launch them in the perimeter canals or lift them over the dike into the Conservation Area when it has water in it. Bass fishing is said to be excellent.

No off-road vehicles are permitted in the park.

Facilities and activities include picnicking, guided nature study, a jogging parcours, a habitat-zoo, laundry, hot showers, a model airplane field, and an astronomical observatory (open to the public on Saturday nights). There is a superb booklet to accompany your walk along the nature trail.

Ft. Lauderdale is rapidly expanding toward this park, and it will soon lose its remote character to become a highly developed, busy urban park. At night the city already lights up the eastern sky, and the crickets are periodically drowned out by the roar of trucks and landing jets.

With luck and good planning, this park could be developed to emphasize native plants and restore some of the vanishing habitat needed for wildlife in the county. Though the park now has deer, armadillo, raccoons, possums, many harmless snakes, occasional foxes, and even elusive bobcats, future development in and around the park will determine whether these survive. As in all disturbed glades land, militant exotic plants (like Brazilian pepper) are marching in and massacring native habitats.

Address above. Telephone 305/472-5882.

 MATHESON HAMMOCK PARK (Dade County)

In Coral Gables, 9610 Old Cutler Road.

In a region almost entirely stripped of its native vegetation, this park preserves an invaluable segment of the original mangroves and semi-tropical hardwood hammock that once covered the coastline. An active park has been developed around them, with places for fishing and boating, a marina, and a lovely, round, sand-rimmed atoll pool for swimming. And even though it's a lot tamer than the original, you can still enter a forest of mysterious tropical trees and get a glimpse of what the original hammocks of south Florida were like before they became Miami. No camping.

For information, contact the address under Crandon Park.

MILTON THOMPSON PARK (Dade County)

On Fla. 27, 12 miles north of US 41, 2 miles south of US 27.

Milton Thompson Park (not to be confused with Larry and Penny Thompson Park in this county) has a small camping area on the edge of the Everglades. Though 640 acres in extent, only 35 acres are really accessible. In a setting of natural Everglades marsh progressively overrun by melaleuca trees, the park offers 43 sites with water and electric hookups, along with 25 undeveloped sites. This is mainly a park for getting away from it all—into that corner of the Everglades nearest Miami. Three small lakes were created to dredge up fill for the camping areas. They have fish in them, but they're hard to catch. A small park store provides the only supplies for 13 miles along this presently-remote corner of Dade County.

The park has a public telephone, a 2-week limit, and a boat ramp on the canal adjacent to Conservation Area 3. Reservations are not taken. Fees are average. The park is normally full from Christmas through Easter and on holiday weekends. No picnicking; just camping.

From this park you can vividly see the extraordinary changes melaleuca trees are making in the south Florida landscape. Ten years ago, this was all native sawgrass marsh. Now it is everywhere sprinkled with trees and streaked with dense stands of foreign, indestructible, fast-growing melaleuca.

The park is extremely buggy in warm wet summer months.
For information call 305/821-5122.

MOORE HAVEN LOCK Recreation Area

At Moore Haven.

There is presently no camping at this location, even though some maps indicate otherwise.

ORTONA LOCK Recreation Area (Corps of Engineers)

15 miles west of Moore Haven, off Highway 78. Not accessible by car from 80.

A little camping area on the Okeechobee Waterway. Ten campsites, free of charge. Boat ramp, picnic tables, restrooms with showers. Seven day limit.

PAHOKEE State Recreation Area

On Lake Okeechobee at Pahokee, on US 441.

At first glance, there's not much here: a thin strip of park squeezed between the tall flood-dike and the water's edge. Forty campsites and a picnic area. A county marina in the middle. A place to swim. Some Australian pines for shade. That's about it.

Yet that does not say it all. Even such a tiny area (only 30 acres) can give access to that great mystery that draws people from hundreds of miles around to stand at the edge of land and listen to waves lapping on the shore. Or to launch their boats on the wide, featureless face of a giant inland lake, leaving the transient widening of a vanishing wake behind them. Or to drop their lines through the commonplace miracle of water, and ponder the unseen life living there. Or to wade a few yards over the comforting rocks into the watery world we find so irresistible and closed to us. Who could possibly put a value on what

A nest-building osprey comes to rest on a mangrove. All the natural life of South Florida hangs by the thread of water, and people—with their thirsty cities—hold the scissors. Can we learn to thrive in a thriving environment, or will we crowd out the beauty so many come to Florida to see?

happens to people's lives when the waves whisper all night to them? Or when they cannot avoid the expanse of sky? Or when stars shine down on them like searchlights, to wake up long-forgotten depths of being?

Aside from the surface activities of fishing, swimming, camping, picnicking, aside from recreation, parks like this are valuable because they provide a setting for re-creation.

Fees are average. Like most south Florida parks, this one is usually filled in the winter months.

Update: Now Pahokee Marina Campground, Pahokee, FL 33476. Telephone 407/ 924-7600. Big development planned on this site.

SECRET WOODS PARK

2701 W. State Road 84, Ft. Lauderdale 33312. Telephone 305/792-8528.

This is the Broward County nature center: 30 acres of oak hammock, cypress swamp, maple wetlands, pond apple swamp, and mangrove. Three thousand feet of boardwalk provide access to the nature study area and photographers' blind. This major nature study center offers displays, public programs, and ranger-led activities.

TOPEEKEEGNEE-YUGNEE (T-Y) Regional Park

In Hollywood, I-95 at Sheridan Avenue. Entrance on North 3rd.

T-Y is a 150-acre regional park built around a nice freshwater lake. It is fully developed for active recreation, with almost every kind of facility imaginable, and provides a much-needed park for local residents. An entrance fee is charged.

No camping. Day-use only.

Address: T-Y Park, 3300 N. Park Road, Hollywood, FL 33021. Telephone 305/961-4430.

Updates to Southeast (SE) Section

The Barnacle is at 3845 Main Hwy., Coconut Grove.

New Listing: **Barley Barber Swamp**. 400 acres of old cypress swamp, with a mile-long boardwalk. East of Lake Okeechobee. Entrance on U.S. 98 4.3 miles north of Port Mayaca. By appointment only. Call Florida Power & Light at 407/640-2089.

Belle Glade Marina. 350 developed sites, many with boat access. Washers and dryers. Small area for tent camping, another for scout groups. Phone: 407/996-6322.

Big Cypress National Preserve. Oasis Station: 813/695-4111. Headquarters: 813/695-2000. Primitive camping along some water bodies near Oasis. No drinking water. The Florida Trail goes through Oasis. Loop road: 4-wheel drive recommended, especially on the western half.

Biscayne National Park. Drinking water on Elliott Key only. Snack bar closed, no fuel available in park. Biscayne Aqua-Center operates boat tours and snorkeling trips in the park (reservations: 305/247-2400). Elliott Key has 64 slips, 35 primitive campsites, and a ranger station. Camping, picnicking, and docking at Boca Chita Key (bring your own water). Camping is free. Lobstering is restricted in much of the park; check the regulations. New ZIP: 33090-1369. For park information, call 305/247-PARK.

Coral Reef Park: The Coral Reef Park Company runs boat trips, diving tours, equipment rentals, and a dive shop. Phone 305/451-1621; from Miami call 305/248-4300. Elsewhere in Florida: 1-800-432-2871.

New Listing: **The Deering Estate** has become a county park. No camping, but worth a visit. SW 167th St. between Old Cutler Road and Biscayne Bay. 305/257-1631.

Everglades National Park. The road to the park has been renamed 9336. (Follow signs from Homestead.) Entrance fee now $5. The main visitor center has new exhibits and a film introducing the park. At Royal Palm, there are exhibits, restrooms, and a store. You can rent boats at Flamingo, but not houseboats. Get a permit before you go on the Wilderness Waterway. Shark Valley tours now run all year. The Key Largo station has no visitor programs.

Fisheating Creek, now the Palmdale Campground, no longer has the 2,000 acre wilderness area or sites on the creek. No horseback riding, no off-road-vehicle area, and no canoe trips (though you can rent canoes). P. O. Box 298, Palmdale, FL 33944.

Florida City RV Park has sewer hookups in 200 of its RV sites. Pets must be under 15 lbs. Tent campers can stay only one night. 601 NW Third Ave., 33034.

New Listing: **Fort Zachery Taylor** is open, with a swimming beach and a museum with an interesting collection of Civil War armaments. Phone 305/292-6713.

Lignumvitae Key. Tour boats go to the island more frequently. For reservations and times, call 305/664-4815. New Address: P. O. Box 776, Long Key, FL 33001.

Loxahatchee NWR. Visitor center at Headquarters has programs, boardwalk, nature trail, and calendar of events. For airboat tours and boat rentals: 407/426-2474. New address: Rt. 1, Box 278, Boynton Beach, FL 33437. Phone 407/734-8303.

Markham Park. Minor changes: Same fees now to everyone. Check in by 7 p.m. There won't be a camp store after all. You can launch boats but not rent them. The jogging parcours, habitat zoo, and laundry are gone. New phone: 305/389-2000.

New Listing: **John D. Macarthur Beach State Recreation Area** is open south of West Palm Beach. 225 acres, containing some of the finest hardwood hammock in Palm Beach County. No camping. Phone 407/627-6097.

New Listing: **Oleta River State Park**. About 900 acres on brackish water just across from Haulover Beach and Florida International University, on NE 151st St. No family camping here, though there is a camping area for registered youth groups. It has an interesting canoe route through lagoons and culverts. Phone 305/947-6357.

John Prince Park has a new phone: 407/582-7992.

New Listing: **Quiet Waters Park** in Deerfield Beach offers many highly-developed recreational activities, including cable-pulled water skiing, miniature golf, windsurfing, fishing; rental boats and bicycles, a big playground, and swimming. Tent camping only. You can rent tents (which are much cheaper Sunday through Thursday). 6601 N. Power Line Road, Deerfield Beach FL 33073. 305/421-3133.

Index

Photo Credits

Courtland Richards, page: 144

Department of Natural Resources, pages: 30, 100, 115, 125, 155, 170, 197, 199, 213, 226, 237, 245

Division of Forestry: pages 65, 68

Florida Game and Fresh Water Fish Commission, pages: 28, 32, 33, 51, 95, 97, 138, 140, 179, 181, 192, 212

Florida News Bureau, Department of Commerce, pages: 2, 3, 6, 7, 8, 10, 11, 12, 15, 19, 23, 24, 25, 36, 37, 40, 42, 44, 46, 47, 52, 53, 56, 63, 70, 71, 73, 76, 77, 80, 83, 84, 87, 90, 93, 94, 96, 102, 105, 106, 111, 114, 117, 124, 127, 136, 141, 146, 148, 152, 159, 169, 177, 180, 187, 188, 195, 198, 201, 204, 209, 211, 212, 216, 220, 227, 229, 231, 233, 241, 248, 250

Gerald Grow, pages: 17, 27, 108, 121, 122, 131, 133, 149, 157, 162, 173, 174, 203, 206, 219, 243

U.S. Forest Service, pages: 120, 130

About the Author

A native of south Georgia and north Florida, Gerald Grow lives in Tallahassee with his wife and two sons. He has taught at San Francisco State, St. Mary's College, and Florida State University. He directs the program in magazine writing and production at Florida A&M University's School of Journalism and writes about business, government, and the environment in Florida. He is a founder and member of the board of directors of the Coastal Plains Institute.

"Excellent. The author knew in great detail what he was talking about and was totally in love with his subject."—A.C., *naturalist*

"Our customers have been asking for a guide like this. It's long overdue."—*Southface Wilderness.*

"Up-to-date. Comprehensive. Describes many fascinating places to visit."—*Philadelphia Inquirer.*

"You can be sure this book will be with me when I go to Florida."—S.P., *outdoor writer and photographer.*

"All the information you need for a thorough Florida experience—beaches, forests, rivers, swamps, marches, wildlife, and other natural treasures."—B.M., *naturalist*

"I am the Family Camping and Canoeing Director of our church. The book is just great."—R.J., *Clearwater, FL.*

"I can't tell you how helpful the book has been. Every park we are going to is covered in the book. I had all the other publications I could get my hands on, but yours is far and away the best."—C.H., *Fort Lauderdale, FL.*

"We want to teach our children about the 'real' land, and this book really helps. Thank you."—the M's, *Vero Beach, FL.*

"Just what we have been looking for."—H.W., *New York.*

"Thank you for a great book."—J.D., *Margate, FL.*

"An extremely informative, accurate, and enjoyable book. Overview of natural habitats especially helpful, as were addresses for further information for each entry. Appreciate your concern for this, the 'real' Florida."—J.J., *Bradenton, FL.*

"An excellent guide with good organization which facilitates finding things quickly."—N.B., *Tampa, FL.*

"Find it very helpful as a newcomer to Florida."—R.G., *Longwood, FL.*

"Superb—It has really made our Florida trip a delightful experience."—B.P., *Maine.*

"Highly readable—not just informative. A valuable addition to any nature-loving visitor's library."—D.V., *Georgia*

(Continued on the next page.)

What readers are saying about **Florida Parks.**
Continued from the front...

"What could have been a very dry compendium is instead an excellent guide in an engaging style."—D.M., *Philadelphia*

"This book is excellent; one of the best of its kind I have ever used. Reading it makes it hard to wait for the next trip. I have completed 3 trips using the book and am planning many more."—N.H., *Gainesville, FL.*

"Delighted with the book. Thanks for such a good work and help to us all. Have given two as gifts."—M.W., *West Palm Beach, FL.*

"We love your book. We have already made several outings with the aid of *Florida Parks.* We are both thankful that someone took the time to visit these places and compile all that information. It really helps planning for a trip when you know what to expect when you get there."—G.W., *Mims, FL.*

"A complete, practical, and realistic guide. I'm 81 years old and still camp."—H.S., *FL.*

"We have visited 87 state parks and 26 national parks nationwide. I have been looking for a book like this for ten years and was delighted to find it."—T.B., *Indiana*